The
Proud Knowledge

By the same author

The Charted Mirror: Literary and Critical Essays (1960)
The Fugue and shorter pieces (1960)
The Story of the Night: Studies in Shakespeare's Major Tragedies (1961)
The Landfallers: a Poem in Twelve Parts (1962)
The Colours of Clarity (1964)
The Lion Hunt: a Pursuit of Poetry and Reality (1964)
Wood and Windfall (1965)
A London Childhood (1966)
Widening Horizons in English Verse (1966)
Later English Broadside Ballads (ed., with Joan Black) (1975)
Planet of Winds (1977)

The
Proud Knowledge
Poetry, Insight and the Self, 1620–1920

John Holloway

ROUTLEDGE & KEGAN PAUL
LONDON, HENLEY AND BOSTON

First published in 1977
by Routledge & Kegan Paul Ltd
39 Store Street,
London WC1E 7DD,
Broadway House,
Newtown Road,
Henley-on-Thames,
Oxon RG9 1EN and
9 Park Street,
Boston, Mass. 02108, USA
Printed in Great Britain by
Ebenezer Baylis & Son Ltd
The Trinity Press, Worcester, and London
© John Holloway, 1977

ISBN 0 7100 8541 9

Contents

. . . it was not the pure knowledge of nature and universality, a knowledge by the light whereof man did give names unto other creatures in Paradise, as they were brought before him, according unto their proprieties, which gave the occasion to the fall; but it was the proud knowledge of good and evil, with an intent in man to give law unto himself . . .

(Bacon, *The Advancement of Learning*, Book 1)

Preface and Acknowledgments

None of the discussions in this book is designed as exhaustive of its subject, and some are much briefer than it would be easy to make them. That is to help the reader to keep sight of the train of thought which connects them all; and because criticism calls for brevity.

Italics, throughout the book, are *the writer's* unless the text says otherwise. They are not infrequently used in quotations, to help the reader to identify what is being taken as support for the argument. The result is inelegant, and occasionally barbarous. But a critical book is not for reading as an anthology, and the arrangement adopted saves some vapid repetition.

References to passages quoted give the first line only of the quotation, and where several passages running almost consecutively are quoted a reference is usually given only to the first of them. The abbreviations 'l.' and 'll.' before line references are omitted (as is 'p.' before page references where possible) as superfluous. References to Wordsworth's *The Prelude*, unless noted otherwise, are to the 1805 text. Works and editions quoted, and an index of poems discussed, are at the end of the book.

The reader is asked to re-read (or still more, if necessary, to read) the poems discussed, before he reads the discussions.

Chapter II, in an earlier version, was the 1966 Andrew Lang Lecture at St Andrews and appeared in *Forum for Modern Language Studies*, January 1967. Chapter III originally appeared in *Le Romantisme Anglo-Américain: Mélanges offerts à Louis Bonnerot*, Paris, 1971. Both are reprinted here, in revised form, with grateful acknowledgment.

I should also like to acknowledge with gratitude the help given me by the staff of the University Library and the English Library, Cambridge, on many occasions; by my 1972 doctoral seminar students at the Johns Hopkins University, for their searching and stimulating discussion of many of the ideas in this book; and to Routledge's editorial staff for suggesting many improvements in the typescript.

I
The Proud Knowledge

The chapters which follow deal with the appearance in English verse of a number of new ways of constructing a poem. Chapter III is about poems which present to the reader an object intently contemplated and perceived by the poet. Chapter IV discusses several poems of a narrative kind in which characters are presented with a special depth and resonance. Chapter V is about poems which recount the pursuit of a certain kind of quest or pilgrimage; and chapter VI those which, written in the light of poems of the first kind, form a more or less overt repudiation of the idea of the quest and the quest-poem. Chapter VII deals with poems of what might be termed the decline and regeneration of the Self; chapter VIII, poems in which the characters' lives have a peculiar and meaningful kind of uneventfulness. The place of chapter II and of the final chapter, on some poems of Hardy, will transpire later.

I

The method adopted in this book has not been to do 'readings' of the poems, while ignoring the interests and preoccupations of the writers: whether that means Neo-Platonism, say, or simply the poets themselves and the problems of their own lives when they wrote. At the same time, however, the writer of a poem always has besides all those matters another interest as well: the completion of a successful poem. Doubtless he will not, at least readily, let this do violence to his Neo-Platonism or to the truth about the social realities of his time, or whatever it may be. But as a poem gets written it comes to have a momentum of its own. It makes demands of its own. In the end – if it is a success, or even if it is a significant failure – it comes to have a nature of its own. This unique, individualized nature is the most interesting thing about a successful poem, and it is what this book is about in the first place. The evidence that the poem goes beyond, and wins an independence from, the poet's intellectual or autobiographical or other interests when he began to write, lies in the first-hand experience of reading. I do not know what other evidence could take that evidence away.

The new ways of writing a poem discussed in this book begin to appear, on the whole, in the course of the eighteenth century. Some poems of earlier date may at first seem of the same kind; but on a closer look, this usually proves not to be so. The point is discussed in detail later, and here it is perhaps enough just to cite a poem like Vaughan's 'Cock-Crowing', which indeed seems to be an intent meditation upon the nature of the cock and his cry; or Vaughan's poem 'The Quest', which might be thought an example of the works considered in chapter V. Again, a poem like Donne's 'A nocturnall upon S. Lucies day', a poem which presents to the reader the deep grief and despair, and then the recovery from that of the poet, might be thought among the poems discussed in chapter VII. But it is not hard to see that these earlier poems are different from later ones. To summarize merely, at this stage: in the earlier poems, contemplation or quest or self-recovery are rhetorical structures before they are anything else. They are means of organizing and expressing ideas, attitudes, convictions, or experiences, which are themselves in some sense already established. One is reminded of Pope's lines in *An Essay on Criticism*:

Men must be taught as if you taught them not;
And things *unknown* propos'd as things *forgot* . . . (574)

For the young Pope, newness of truth is an embarrassment that is best disguised as the opposite of itself. The eighteenth- and nineteenth-century poems which are to be discussed later were inclined towards a fundamental, a polar difference. To say that is not to make a judgment of value.

One may ask how it was, and why it was, that new ways of constructing a poem appeared. There is no simple answer, and doubtless there is a measure of truth in many answers. At the simplest level one might say that a series of attempts were made to create new poetic forms that lacked any classical precedent, after a period (1660–1730, let us say) during which the poetic forms taken from the classical literatures were particularly dominant. One could refer also to the personal problems of certain of our important poets, and say that they worked out poetic forms such as would help them to express and resolve those problems. One could stress the effects of the recovery of our older literature (or other older literature) by some writers: Wordsworth's communion with Milton, Blake's concern with Sophocles, Byron's knowledge of Spenser, Keats's of Shakespeare or Chaucer. Again, preoccupation with individual physical objects in our world, with humble people or human failures, with moods of melancholy, or with travel and the exotic, may all be seen in terms of 'Romanticism'; and the poems considered in this book, or most of them, related in a miscellany of ways to the many and varying aspects of a literary period.

My first purpose is not to answer questions like these by writing history. This book is primarily intended to be about the inner, the inmost quality and nature of certain poems. But there is something of a general and historical kind, which deserves to be considered here, because it seems on reflection to draw all these poems together. It is not simply part of the miscellany of historical considerations which may be brought to bear on them, but a single running thread. The business of the rest of this Introduction is to consider it.

II

It is not obvious at first that the guiding ideas of each of these new ways of constructing a poem may be related to a single theme: the powers and potentialities of the individual and the self. Yet it seems to be true that each of these poetic forms (for that, in a certain somewhat distinctive sense, is what they are) is in fact one reflection of an idea about man's potentialities and about the ambitions which, in view of them, it is proper for him to form, or proper to form on his account.

Here is what Pico della Mirandola wrote in 1486, in his *Oration* on the dignity of man. It gives a new turn to the perennial idea that Man stands at the crown of creation, by the stress that it puts on the idea that he, alone among created nature, may exercise an independence for himself, and determine his own nature by it. The closing words of the passage are not a digression from the idea of Man's dignity, and it will transpire that the idea they express played a significant part in the developments this book reviews:

> [God] . . . took man as a creature of indeterminate nature and, assigning him a place in the middle of the world, addressed him thus: 'Neither a fixed abode nor a form that is thine alone nor any function peculiar to thyself have we given thee, Adam, to the end that according to thy longing and according to thy judgement thou mayest have and possess what abode, what form, and what functions thou thyself shalt desire. The nature of all other beings is limited and constrained within the bounds of laws prescribed by Us. Thou, constrained by no limits, in accordance with thine own free will, in whose hand We have placed thee, shalt ordain for thyself the limits of thy nature. We have set thee at the world's centre that thou mayest from thence more easily observe whatever is in the world. We have made thee neither of heaven nor of earth, neither mortal nor immortal, so that with freedom of choice and with honour, as though the maker and moulder of thyself, thou mayest fashion thyself into whatever shape thou shalt prefer. Thou shalt have the power to degenerate into the lower forms of life, which are brutish. Thou shalt have the power, out of thy soul's judgement, to be reborn into the higher forms, which are divine.   (Cassirer, 224–5)

Pico's chief emphasis is on the idea that Man can be what he chooses. Man can make his own nature and position in the world. One aspect of this is that he can *know* what to choose; and can know that, by knowing his own distinctive station in the cosmos ('that thou mayest from thence the more easily observe whatever is in the world'). It is this idea which assumes an especial importance in the present enquiry.

Perhaps it is necessary to make a preliminary distinction between the accumulation, more or less in Baconian fashion, of the detail of knowledge about the cosmos, and the acquiring of a kind of Faustian knowledge which lets man, in one decisive movement, into the inmost secrets of the world and his own situation, and makes him the master of both. Bacon also had a conception of mastery in material things as his ultimate, but the two approaches are very different. There is perhaps no need to recall Marlowe's treatment of the Faustian idea (save to note in passing that he could give it only a derisory content when it came to detail), but the famous lines from *Tamburlaine*, Part I, deserve to be quoted:

> Nature that fram'd us of foure Elements,   (II.vii.18)
> Warring within our breasts for regiment,
> Doth teach us all to have aspyring minds:
> Our soules, whose faculties can comprehend
> The wondrous Architecture of the world:
> And measure every wandring plannets course:
> Still climing after knowledge infinite,
> And alwaies mooving as the restles Spheares,
> Wils us to weare ourselves and never rest . . .

No passage in English better expresses the theme with which this chapter is concerned; even if Marlowe's conclusion in 'the sweet fruition of an earthly crown' is (to speak with restraint) deflationary.

Descartes is full of cautions and disclaimers, but one part of Pico's conception forms the generating idea of the *Discours de la Méthode*:

> Ainsi mon dessein n'est pas d'ensiegner ici la méthode
> que chacun doit suivre pour bien conduire sa raison, mais
> seulement de faire voir en quelle sorte j'ai tâché de conduire
> la mienne. (34)

Modestly, or perhaps diplomatically, Descartes does not insist upon the ultimate bearing of his remark. He may not be proposing to instruct others in how they should think about the problems of man's situation and knowledge, and may say that his account is a mere personal 'histoire, ou, si vous l'aimez mieux . . . une fable'; but save on one condition, the implication of his words would be that if so, what he wrote would have a merely idle interest for others. The one condition is, that it is part of the nature of things that a man may set about the enquiry into truth in his own way, along some quite individual personal line, doing it all by himself – *and succeed*. Descartes is discreet in revealing that this is his position, but he is also quite intransigent:

> . . . pour toutes les opinions que j'avais reçues jusques
> alors en ma créance, je ne pouvais mieux faire que
> d'entreprendre une bonne fois de les en ôter, afin d'y en
> remettre par après ou d'autres meilleures, ou bien les
> mêmes, lorsque je les aurais ajustées au niveau de la
> raison. Et je crus fermement que par ce moyen je
> réussirais à conduire ma vie beaucoup mieux que si je ne
> bâtissais que sur de vieux fondements, et que je ne
> m'appuyasse que sur les principes que je m'étais laissé
> persuader en ma jeunesse sans avoir jamais examiné
> s'ils étaient vrais.   (Part II, p. 44)

The individual thinker (at least when this is Descartes himself) can pursue enlightenment independently. By so doing he will equip himself better than society can equip him through what it traditionally passes on; and the enlightenment in question that he will derive by this means is nothing other than what Bacon called 'the proud knowledge of good and evil' (see the epigraph to the present work), which is the essence of the conduct of life.

After the time of Descartes, it becomes easier to find men thinking it right to enter on a personally chosen and individually pursued road towards knowledge of the basis and fundamentals of life: all as part of, and following from, Pico's conception of man as possessing the 'abode, form and functions' that he chooses for himself. Spinoza directs upon Descartes very much the same logic as Descartes, twenty-six years before, had directed upon those who had supplied him with the ready-made opinions he no longer found enough:

> . . . I prove many things in a way that is different from
> that in which they were proved by Descartes, not in order

to correct Descartes, but only the better to retain my own
order . . . and not to increase the number of axioms, and
. . . for the same reason I prove many things which
Descartes merely asserts without any proof, and . . . have
to add other things which Descartes omitted.   (134–5:
Letter to Meyer, 3 August 1663)

Two years later, Spinoza not only expresses more clearly still
how the personal route to truth is for him the superior route;
but adds something that, coming from him, is especially
striking and revealing:

. . . since I openly and unambiguously confess that I do
not understand Holy Scripture although I have spent some
years in the study of it, and since it has not escaped my
notice that when I have a strong proof no such thoughts
can occur to me that I can ever entertain any doubt about
it, I acquiesce wholly in that which my understanding
shows me, without any suspicion that I may be deceived,
or that Holy Scripture, although I do not search it, can
contradict it: for truth does not conflict with truth . . .
Even if I were once to find untrue the fruits of my natural
understanding, they would make me happy, since I enjoy
them, and I endeavour to pass my life not in sorrow and
sighing, but in peace, joy and cheerfulness.   (172–3:
Letter to van Blynenburgh, 28 January 1665)

In this memorable passage Spinoza goes on from the intrinsic
superiority of the self-directed path towards truth, to reveal
how he senses such pursuit of truth as an integral part of himself,
essential to his inner well-being and self-fulfilment. Truth
comes, or at least, it most memorably and most reliably comes,
in answer to a call from the deep and central part of our nature.
To pursue it is to become what we truly are.

III

Those words of Spinoza, with their obvious resonance for
literature and the study of literature, are especially to the
point if we recall that perhaps the nearest counterpart in French
writing to Descartes's personalized route of meditation was

not an author in his own right but an imaginary figure who was
the creation of a literary author: Rousseau's 'Vicaire Savoyard'.
The Vicaire's celebrated 'Profession de foi' in *Émile* in effect
opens with an admission that at a certain time in the past, the
speaker was in the same state as Descartes at the beginning of
his enquiry; and it adds something which reveals how near his
position is to that of Spinoza. This is so because for the Vicaire
also, the personalized and meditative pursuit of truth becomes a
necessity if the welfare of the Self is to be maintained. The
metaphor by means of which the Vicaire expresses the predica-
ment of the ignorant and unexploring self deserves to be
remembered. It is one variety of a metaphor which will recur:

> J'étais dans ces dispositions d'incertitude et de doute que
> Descartes exige pour la recherche de la verité. Cet état
> est peu fait pour durer, il est inquiétant et pénible . . . Je
> méditais donc sur le triste sort des mortels *flottant sur cette
> mer* des opinions humaines, sans gouvernail, sans boussole
> [compass], et livrés à leurs passions orageuses, sans autre
> guide qu'un pilote inexpérimenté qui méconnait sa route,
> et ne sait d'où il vient ni où il va.   (321)

Later he says:

> des mystères impénétrables nous environnent de toutes
> parts: ils sont au-dessus de la région sensible; pour les
> percer nous croyons avoir de l'intelligence, et nous n'avons
> que de l'imagination.   (323)

This sense of the predicament of the lost Self is immediately
followed by another significant metaphor:

> Chacun *se fraye*, à travers ce monde imaginaire, *une route*
> qu'il croit la bonne: nul ne peut savoir si la sienne mène
> au but.

The Vicaire soon finds, as Descartes did, a primary and in-
expugnable truth to launch him upon his way over the stormy
sea of human speculation. It is far from Descartes's *Cogito*:

> J'existe, et *j'ai des sens* par lesquels je suis *affecté*. Voilà la
> première vérité qui me frappe et à laquelle je suis forcé
> d'acquiescer.   (325)

Sentio ergo sum: for the Vicaire, that is the starting-point. It defines the nature and direction of the enquiry. It is pursued 'dans la sincerité de mon coeur', it draws upon the innate principles of activity and will of the Self, it is not an intellectual enquiry like Descartes's because 'les idées générales et abstraites sont la source des plus grandes erreurs des hommes' (331). The active principle of the Self is what unifies our sensations from the various senses into a single integrated experience, and it is in the unity of the cosmos that the 'homme simple et vrai' will see reflected the intelligence, activity and will of the Creator: 'toujours est-il certain que *le tout est un*, et annonce une intelligence unique' (335). The 'Profession de foi' professes a briefer concatenation of truths than Descartes, but one after another they issue forth; and unquestionably it is the 'proud knowledge of good and evil' with which they deal. Only, their provenance is wholly non-Cartesian:

> En suivant toujours ma méthode, je ne tire point ces règles des principes d'une haute philosophie, mais je les trouve au fond de mon cœur écrites par la nature en caractères inéffacables . . . tout ce que je sens être bien est bien, tout ce que je sens être mal est mal . . . (348)

> Exister pour nous, c'est sentir; notre sensibilité est incontestablement antérieure à notre intelligence . . . (353)

It is at this point that the place of the 'Profession' in *Émile* as a whole begins to assume significance; and its setting will prove to be significant also. The whole 'Profession de foi' is the culmination of Emile's growing up. It embodies the knowledge that will complete and indeed *perfect* him as a man and a human. From the last quotations one sees why. The sensibility is the core of man: therefore, what is spoken in the sincerity of the heart answers to the demands and needs of the core of the self. When the epiphany of Truth arrives, it constitutes an epiphany of the truth-knowing self. The meaningfulness of the occasion is marked by its setting:

> On était en été, nous nous levâmes à la pointe du jour.
> Il me mena hors de la ville, sur une haute colline,
> au-dessous de laquelle passait le Po, dont on voyait le

cours à travers les fertiles rives qu'il baigne; dans l'éloignement, l'immense chaîne des Alpes couronnait le paysage; les rayons du soleil levant rasaient déjà les plaines . . . On eut dit que la Nature étalait à nos yeux toute sa magnificence pour en offrir le texte à nos entretiens. (319–20)

Such a scene will recur in the present discussion.

IV

The 'route' that the Vicaire Savoyard was called upon to make out for himself across the wide *sea* of life (see p. 8 above) was a route in respect only of knowledge. One fictional character, the hero of *Robinson Crusoe*, was faced with a larger task: nothing less than to determine, in accordance with Pico's words, 'what abode, what form, and what functions' should be his over the whole extent of life. Crusoe's task was therefore a practical task. Because of this, it connects less directly with the various new poetic 'forms' which this chapter has ultimately in view: in a word, Wordsworth's *The Prelude* undertakes something very much like what the Vicaire Savoyard had undertaken, but Crusoe's essential work had to be different.

Crusoe, one might say, was the general case of which the other was the special, cognitive case. Crusoe had to solve the problems of life – all of them – for himself, deprived of guidance from society or tradition. At the beginning of his island epic he is 'sav'd, as I May say, out of the very Grave' (46). 'I walk'd about on the Shore . . . and my whole Being . . . [was] wrapt up in the Contemplation of my Deliverance' (46). He is at the nadir of human resource:

> . . . In a word, I had nothing about me but a Knife, a Tobacco-pipe, and a little Tobacco in a Box, this was all my Provision, and this threw me into terrible Agonies of Mind . . . (47)

Yet with this nothing as starting-point, and beginning at the very bottom of life, Crusoe rises by his unaided efforts to the summit of it.

> . . . It cost me much Labour, and many Days, before all these Things were *brought to Perfection*. (60)

That is what he says, early on in his narrative, about building up the cave and his house. The phrase comes again: later, his grindstone 'cost me a full Week's Work to bring it to Perfection' (83). *Perfection*: it is the other end of Crusoe's quest for the general conditions in which a man should live; the narrative is explicit as to the limits from which, and to which, it pursues its course.

Equally, it is explicit that this course is to be traversed successfully by the very means that Descartes and Spinoza relied on: the solitary effort of the enquiring mind:

> . . . and here I must needs observe, that as Reason is the Substance and Original of Mathematicks, so by *stating and squaring every thing by Reason*, and by making the most rational Judgment of things, *every* Man may be in time Master of *every* mechanick art. (68)

The impression given by the narrative is that in the end Crusoe has nothing left to wish for. He reaches what is in truth, as opposed to vain show, the summit of human felicity. 'Labour, application, and contrivance' bring him to a point where he can say:

> I had nothing to covet; for I had all that I was now capable of enjoying; I was Lord of the whole Mannor; or if I pleas'd, I might call my self *King, or Emperor* over the whole Country I had Possession of . . . (128)

The idea comes again:

> It would have made a Stoick smile to have seen, me and my little Family sit down to Dinner; there was *my Majesty* the Prince and Lord of the whole Island; I had the Lives of my Subjects at my absolute Command. (148)

Save for society (Crusoe says shortly after this), he wants for nothing; and this felicity he has achieved by his unaided efforts and reason.

This is not a context in which it is necessary to discuss what Defoe meant by reason; but it is to the point to notice how much emphasis, in one sense or another, Crusoe places upon the idea. His pursuit was in the first place not of truth but of the conditions in which it was possible for him to sustain life. But two things are clear. First, those conditions were to be achieved by the unremitting use of his mental powers: rational judgment was necessary, and enough, for the mastery of 'every mechanick art'. A process of *enquiry* was essential for the sustaining of life on the island's terms (and the implication is, that mankind collectively have had to follow the course that here, one of them is having to follow in isolation). Second, Crusoe's enquiry is no practical one alone. Indeed, one of the most impressive things about the narrative is the degree to which it seems to make Crusoe's achieving of the practical needs of continued existence one with, integral with, his achieving of moral and religious enlightenment. Crusoe's progress is from the state of thoughtless man living as the slave of chance and misfortune, to that of thoughtful man who is master of his condition.

This begins to show quite early on, when he is first beginning to establish himself:

> The growing up of the Corn . . . had at first [i.e., from the very first] some little Influence upon me, and began to affect me with *Seriousness* . . . (89)

This seriousness wears off as his condition improves: 'I had no more Sense of God or his Judgments . . . than if I had been in the most prosperous Condition of Life' (90). Later, when he begins to be ill,

> conscience, that had slept so long, began to awake . . . the good advice of my father came to my mind, and presently his prediction . . . That if I did take this foolish Step [viz., to go upon the voyage] God would not bless me, and I would have Leisure hereafter to reflect upon having neglected his Counsel. (91)

A prayer comes spontaneously to his lips; and when he eats the turtle's eggs that he roasts in the ashes, 'this was the first Bit of Meat I had ever ask'd God's blessing to . . . as I cou'd remember, in my whole Life' (91).

The process of moral reflection and enquiry, which is so much a part of the whole, now begins to take shape (italics in this passage are in the original throughout):

As I sat here, some such Thoughts as these occurred to
me.

What is this Earth and Sea of which I have seen so
much, whence it is produc'd and what am I, and all the
other Creatures . . . whence are we?

Sure we are all made by some secret Power, who form'd
the Earth and Sea, and Air and Sky; and who is that?

Then it follow'd most naturally, It is God that has
made it all: Well, but then it came on strangely, if God
has made all these Things, He guides and governs them
all . . . for the Power that could make all Things, must
certainly have Power to guide and direct them.

If so, nothing can happen in the great Circuit of his
Works, either without his Knowledge or Appointment.

. . . and if nothing happens without his Appointment, he
has appointed all this to befal me.

Nothing occurr'd to my Thought, to contradict any of
these Conclusions . . .

. . . Immediately it follow'd,

*Why has God done this to me? What have I done to be
thus* us'd?

My conscience presently check'd me in that Enquiry
. . . and methought it spoke to me like a Voice:

'*WRETCH*! dost thou *ask what thou hast done?* look back
upon a dreadful mis-spent life, and ask thyself *what thou
has not done?*'

. . . I was struck dumb with these Reflections . . .   (92)

The importance to Crusoe of the train of thought, the
continual rational inference and conclusions, the conspicuous
use of phrases like 'it follow'd most naturally', and 'these
Conclusions', are self-evident. These are the essence of Crusoe's
experience and progress; but when next we see them at work,
it is once again at the level of the practical, of meeting the
material needs of his predicament:

On the Banks of this Brook I found many pleasant
Savana's, or Meadows . . . I found a great deal of Tobacco
. . . there were divers other Plants, which I had no Notion
of . . . I contented my self with these Discoveries for this

> Time, and came back *musing with myself* what Course I
> might take to know the Vertue and Goodness of any of the
> Fruits or Plants which I should discover; but could bring
> it to no *Conclusion* . . . (98–9)

Before long, Defoe takes up the moral dimension of the narra-
tive, or indeed the religious dimension, once again:

> But now I began to exercise my self with new Thoughts;
> I daily read the Word of God . . . One Morning being
> very sad, I open'd the Bible upon these Words, *I will
> never, never leave thee, nor forsake thee*; immediately it
> occurr'd, That these Words were to me . . . Well then,
> said I, if God does not forsake me . . . what matters it,
> though the World should all forsake me . . .
> From this Moment I began to conclude in my Mind,
> That it was possible for me to be more happy in this
> forsaken Solitary Condition, than it was probable I should
> have been in any other . . . (113)

Thus the process went on, with its 'new thoughts', incessant
inferences, and 'just reflection'. The culmination of it all happens
to be quite especially to the point for the present enquiry:

> Thus I liv'd mighty confortably, my Mind being entirely
> composed by . . . throwing my self wholly upon the
> Disposal of his Providence. This made my life *better than
> sociable* . . . (135)

It is a crucial phrase. There is one amenity which, in the nature
of the case, all Crusoe's successes can never supply him with:
the blessings of society. This is the touchstone against which all
his achievement measures itself. If – *par impossible* – it can
compensate him for this, it can compensate for everything.

By now it is possible to see the bearing of Crusoe's progress
upon the kinds of poem which are discussed in some of the later
chapters of this book. Even considered in advance, as it were, and
in a preliminary way, those poems now suggest themselves as
part of a wider picture. Or at least, this is true of two of the
four new poetic 'kinds' which were briefly catalogued in the
first paragraph of this chapter. If there are poems of which the
purpose is to record the poet's experience, and findings, as he

intently contemplates some particular and as it seems to him uniquely significant object, seeking in it some truth, some enlightenment, as if for the first time, then in view of what has already been said, that cannot any longer seem merely like an individual or chance or isolated innovation. Such poems, and their acts of creation, must present themselves as having to do with the whole conception of Man as empowered to search, and to come to comprehend the human lot, by the concentrated exercise of his unique powers as Man. Poets who write such poems are part of the same story as Descartes, Spinoza, Rousseau in the person of his Vicaire, Defoe's Crusoe. Or again, if there are poems which recount the undertaking of a quest or pilgrimage in pursuit of enlightenment, the same ought surely to be said of them. They too fall within the general theme of the aspiring mind. If, furthermore, there are narrative poems which innovate in that they present their characters as having a quite special depth and resonance, here too the same wider picture may be what gives these poems their context. That special depth and resonance may be what a fictional character acquires, insofar as he or she manifests these unique human powers.

For the present, I put these points quite in a contingent way. It will help the reader to have them in mind as he reads the later chapters, and he will judge for himself to what extent the case is proved. But to speak frankly, I do not know what would really constitute proof in such a case. What is at issue is the strength of an analogy, and if there is some reasonable degree of analogy, that is perhaps of more interest than to determine (if one can) just what degree of analogy would prove the case to the hilt. The fact remains that this conception of the individual as having the power, the right, and perhaps the duty to engage upon a solitary and more or less unaided journey of intellectual or spiritual exploration towards the terms of life and the status of man, is one of the most imaginative and ambitious intellectual achievements of the past five centuries. To some extent, no doubt, such ambitions and such attempts may be traced in all periods; but since the time of Pico, it is no question of one's being able to hunt them out by diligent enquiry. Largely, they become the staple of intellectual and spiritual life. One after another, the outstanding minds show themselves as having, in one medium or another, embarked upon the search for an independent fundamental insight; and the means towards it has been the individual's relying upon his inner powers. That cannot be said of the time before Pico. Perhaps it cannot be said either of the age which is now to begin. It may be that over these five centuries we are looking at something distinctive in the scope and ambitions of mankind.

V

Today, for the individual to have these soaring intellectual ambitions is a little out of favour: often, I think, they are rejected as mere bourgeois manifestations of the capitalist age. There is no need to enter into that controversy, though perhaps it is to the point to remark that if capitalism was a necessary stage of human development, and made a positive contribution for a certain time, the same is likely to be true of the intellectual ambitions which must (according to that line of thought) have been a determined part of the superstructure of such capitalism. Certainly it is to the point to say that there has been no time in the last four or five centuries when the dangers and difficulties, the disabling hubristic potential, of the lone spiritual journey has not been in the minds of those who have concerned themselves with the matter. Briefly, I now illustrate this sense of the difficulties involved. For this purpose I have reserved mention of several authors who would have been useful also as illustrating the spread and continuity of the lone spiritual journey considered in itself.

There has always been what might be called a dark side to the soaring ambitions of the individual seeker after final truth; and lapsing into metaphor like that is to be excused, because it is what one after another of the principals themselves found cause to do, at just this point in their explanations. Hume and Descartes have little enough in common, but when they come to speak of the difficulties and perils of the search of the all-ambitious self, they speak a not dissimilar language. Here is how Descartes, in the third Part of the *Discours*, writes about the need for firm and unambiguous action in the practical affairs of life, even in the middle of such doubts and uncertainties as are brought on by the search for truth:

Ma seconde maxime était d'être le plus ferme et le plus
résolu en mes actions que je pourrais . . . imitant en ceci
les voyageurs qui, se trouvant égarés en quelque forêt, ne
doivent pas errer en tournoyant tantôt d'un côté, tantôt
d'un autre, mais marcher toujours le plus droit qu'ils
peuvent . . . car, par ce moyen . . . vraisemblement ils
seront mieux que dans le milieu d'une forêt.   (56)

Hume, pausing for a moment between the account of judgment
and understanding on the one hand, and on the other, the general
account of human nature which he undertakes in Book II of
the *Treatise,* also writes with an uncharacteristic poetry of the
position in which he finds himself:

Methinks I am like a man, who having struck on many
shoals, and having narrowly escap'd ship-wreck . . . has
yet the temerity *to put out to sea in the same leaky weather-
beaten vessel,* and even carries his ambition so far as to think
of *compassing the globe* . . . This sudden view of my danger
strikes me with melancholy; and, as 'tis usual for that
passion, above all others, to indulge itself; I cannot
forbear feeding my despair, with all those desponding
reflections . . .
  I am first affrighted, and confounded with that forelorn
solitude in which I am plac'd in my philosophy, and fancy
myself some strange uncouth monster, who not being able
to mingle and unite in society, has been expell'd all
human commerce, and left utterly abandon'd . . .   (264)

Hume perhaps flattered himself a little over this eloquent
passage.
  There is of course a much more general idea about reaching
the truth with regard to 'man's estate', and about the difficulties
of so doing. This more general idea has also found expression
through topographical metaphors. If we understand Petrarch's
account of his ascent in 1336 of Mont Ventoux as also a meta-
phorical account of 'the long struggle in his conscience that
eventually led to . . . a higher state of mind' (Cassirer, 28), we
find in him an illustration:

My brother endeavoured to reach the summit by the very

ridge of the mountain on a short cut; I, being so much
more of a weakling, was bending down toward the valley
. . . Again I wandered through the valleys, looking for the
longer and easier path and stumbling only into longer
difficulties.   (39)

Donne uses this metaphor in the third *Satyre*. The detail is
characteristically distinctive, but there is the same sense of
harsh difficulty to be overcome by resolute effort:

> On a huge hill,   (79)
> Cragged, and steep, Truth stands, and hee that will
> Reach her, about must, and about must goe;
> And what the hills suddenness resists, winne so . . .

It could be argued that Donne treats the matter as having rather
more in it of the unexpected, the unconventionalized, than
Petrarch; but he is still on the other side from Descartes and
Hume of a kind of frontier. What their descriptions expressed
was not simply difficulty, not simply need for effort; but
uncertainty, bafflement, isolation and near-despair. This is a
new and crucial strand in the weave of the thought.

In Bunyan's *Pilgrim's Progress*, the start of the journey is
across a 'very wide Field' (10) guided by a 'shining light' of
which the most Christian can say when asked if he can see it
is 'I think I do'. Once the journey is begun, the first thing that
happens to Christian is to fall into the 'Slough of Dispond'. It
is Help who pulls Christian out; and then the author speaks:

> . . . I stepped to him that pluckt him out, and said: Sir,
> Wherefore . . . is it, that *this* Plat is not mended, that poor
> Travellers might go . . . with more security?   (15)

Help replies that it cannot be mended:

> . . . as the sinner is awakened about his lost condition,
> there ariseth in his soul many fears, and doubts, and
> discouraging apprehensions, which all of them get
> together, and settle in this place.

To a limited extent, the passage from Hume quoted above may
be seen as parody of writers like Bunyan. For him, 'Wandering
into such dreary solitudes, and rough passages' is, in one mood,

only a 'philosophical melancholy and delirium'. But the Hume passage is by no means wholly skit. The whole last chapter of Book I of the *Treatise* rests on the idea that there is a natural tendency and bent of the mind towards philosophizing, towards the work of intellectual 'curiosity and ambition' as much as there is towards dining, playing backgammon, or being merry with one's friends (which Hume takes as illustrations of the opposite polarity).

In fact, Bunyan's 'poor travellers' going across a 'very wide plain' and ineffectively led by a 'shining light' form a recurrent metaphor for this dubious and entangling side to the enquiry after the proud knowledge of good and evil. In the opening lines of *Religio Laici*, Dryden too introduces the dubious journey and the shining light:

> Dim, as the borrow'd beams of Moon and Stars (1)
> To *lonely*, *weary*, *wandring* Travellers,
> Is *Reason* to the *Soul*: And as on high,
> Those rowling Fires discover but the Sky
> Not light us *here*; So *Reason*'s glimmering Ray
> Was lent, not to *assure* our doubtfull way,
> But *guide* us upward to a *better Day*.

The Pilgrim's Progress was published in 1678, *Religio Laici* in 1683. Almost mid-way between, in 1680, Rochester published the first text of the poem known as the '*Satyr against Mankind*'. Here the scene reassembles itself. Like Dryden, Rochester is condemning the search for Truth by Reason alone. What is to the point for the moment is not the strictly intellectual position that he takes up with regard to that, but his sense of its human and psychological quality as an experience:

> Reason, *an ignis fatuus* in the mind, (12)
> Which, leaving light of nature, sense behind;
> Pathless and dangerous wandring ways it takes
> Through error's fenny bogs and thorny brakes;
> Whilst the misguided follower climbs with pain
> Mountains of whimseys, heaped in his own brain;
> Stumbling from thought to thought, falls headlong down
> Into doubt's boundless sea, where, like to drown,

Books bear him up awhile, and make him try,
To swim with bladders of philosophy;
In hopes . . .

– mountain, bog, sea, *ignis fatuus* – it is part of Rochester's all-scornful method to jumble them together into an absurd poetical chaos. This makes it only the clearer how they were conventional properties whereby the difficulties and pitfalls of the solitary spiritual explorer could be expressed.

Milton had drawn upon the same idea in *Paradise Lost*; first, in his account of Satan's journey through Chaos. The purpose of this journey is, in a curious inverted or perverted sense, the same as what is at issue here. Beelzebub, in the Council in Hell, speaks of the newly created world, and adds:

> Thither let us bend all our thoughts, to learn   (II.354)
> What creatures there inhabit . . .

The journey that he proposes thither is to be a journey for knowledge; and the difficulties begin to mount immediately:

> But first whom shall we send   (402)
> In search of this new world, whom shall we find
> Sufficient? Who shall tempt with wandring feet
> The dark unbottom'd infinite Abyss
> And through the palpable obscure find out
> His uncouth way . . .

When Satan himself offers to undertake the journey, his words could be a grim parody of the human quest for enlightenment:

> . . . long is the way,   (432)
> And hard, that out of Hell leads up to light . . .

When he at length ventures out into Chaos, the by now familiar landscape reappears in a sort of dreadful mockery of itself:

> . . . that furie stay'd,   (938)
> Quencht *in a Boggie Syrtis*, neither Sea,
> Nor good dry Land: nigh founderd on he fares . . .
> Ore bog or steep, through strait, rough, dense, or rare, (948)
> With head, hands, wings or feet pursues his way,
> And swims or sinks, or wades, or creeps, or flies.

Such images reappear much later, in Blake's accounts of Urizen 'exploring his dens':

Urizen explor'd his dens,
Mountain, moor & wilderness,
With a *globe of fire lighting his journey* . . .

That is the picture at the beginning of chapter VIII of *The First Book of Urizen*. Unmistakably, 'globe of fire' is *ignis fatuus*: Blake has something in common with Rochester. With this passage in mind one may look at 'Night the Sixth' of Blake's *Vala*:

So Urizen arose, & leaning on his spear explor'd his
    dens . . .   (1)

                . . . On his way   (72)
He took, high bounding over hills & desarts, floods &
    horrible chasms.

Infinite was his labour, without end his travel . . .

                . . . he rose   (78)
With pain upon the dreary mountains & with pain
    descended . . .

            . . . Urizen with a Globe of fire   (83)
Lighting his dismal journey thro' the pathless world of
    death.

That the 'dismal journey' is no journey pure and simple, but a search and enquiry for knowledge, is made plain. It is made plain also that the enquiry is unrewarding:

Oft he stood by a howling victim *Questioning in words* (126)
Soothing or Furious; no one answer'd; everyone wrap'd up
In his own sorrow howl'd regardless of his words . . .

Oft would he *stand & question* a fierce scorpion . . .   (131)
In vain; the terror heard not. Then a lion he would
    seize . . .

            . . . *in vain the voice*   (133)
Of Urizen, in vain the Eloquent tongue.

The passage approaches a recurrent kind of despair over just that reason and eloquence which should bring the 'aspiring mind' success.

VI

Taken together, these passages from Milton and Blake are not mere deployings of the metaphors of man's spiritual quest in a context unrelated to man. They suggest that about the quest for that 'proud knowledge' there has always been seen to be a certain ambivalence. The Spinozistic kind of enquiry can perhaps never be quite immune to the accusation of colossal, almost satanic hubris. Milton, at the end of *Paradise Lost*, re-assembles some of the same key ideas in his account of the departure of Adam and Eve from Eden. In doing so he seems exactly to express the theological ambiguity of the occasion and the perennial ambivalence of the 'solitary' quest:

>   from the other Hill   (XII.626)
> The Cherubim descended; on the ground
> Gliding meteorous, as Ev'ning Mist
> Ris'n from a River o'er the marish glides,
> And gathers ground fast at the Labourer's heel
> Homeward returning.

The angelic host seem for an instant wild and errant as a meteor; but at once the image is mutated into, first, a passing suggestion of the *ignis fatuus* which we have encountered before, and then the homely evening valley-mist that misleads no one. As the passage continues, the recurrent properties of the human quest-for-knowledge situation appear one by one. Led forward by the divine sword which is 'fierce as a comet', and watched by the 'dreadful faces' behind them at the eastern gate, Adam and Eve proceed across the 'subjected plain' that lies outside the Garden. The closing words of the poem record that they took *their solitary way*. It is strange to find oneself recalling Hume in such a context, until one considers that Hume and Milton may not in fact be as remote as is supposed (see chapter II below).

That 'solitary way' of the seeker after the proud knowledge is intrinsic to his quest. Usually it is not solitary in the limited sense that held good for Adam and Eve as they journeyed together. It is somewhat different from the position, say, of Vico, as he records this in his *Autobiography*, when he immersed himself in the reading of Latin authors. 'For these reasons

Vico lived in his native city not only a stranger but quite unknown' (134). Such a remark ought first to be related to the traditional theme of the miseries of scholars as we find this amplified, say, in Burton's *Anatomy of Melancholy* (I.2.3.15), or Johnson's *London*. But when Christian and Faithful, interrogated by the magistrates of Vanity Fair, 'told them that they were pilgrims *and strangers in the world*', we have something different. Part of the price paid by the dedicated spiritual pilgrim is this kind of estrangement from all the less dedicated of mankind. Hume, putting to sea in his leaky weather-beaten vessel, and to a greater or lesser extent all those who used the topography of the lost or benighted traveller, also gave expression to this sense of isolation from the generality of mankind. Goethe in *Dichtung und Wahrheit* has a remarkable passage about the intellectual or spiritual ambitions of youth, and how the disappointments that time inevitably brings to them are mitigated by a sense that man is essentially part of mankind, so that an individual's spiritual ambitions, though disappointed personally, will be fulfilled in the communal experience of the Whole:

If the youth of the individual comes at a productive time, when creativity outweighs destructiveness, and early awakens in him the sense of what such a period both calls for, and promises, then causes outside himself will impel him towards a life of active participation. He will make his mark now on one side, now on another, and the desire to be active in many directions will kindle in him. But so many fortuitous impediments collect about our human limitations, that we shall see, here something begun only to be left undone, there, something taken up only to be let drop. One wish after another will fritter itself away to nothing. But if such desires had grown up in one whose heart was pure, and in accordance with the needs of the age, then one can allow things to be left undone or to be let drop, and not feel concern. One may be sure, that such things will necessarily be discovered again and taken in hand again. Not only that, but many related matters that had not caught people's attention nor even come into their minds, will also make their appearance. So, if during the

course of our lives we see things carried out by others that
earlier on we felt a call to do ourselves, we may recall
(and the thought is a precious one) that *it is Mankind
collectively that is truly Man,* and that the individual's
happiness will be fulfilled only when he has the strength
to feel himself part of the Whole.   (II.9)

Goethe, admittedly, is writing in a wide context. He is thinking
about human endeavours more generally than just in relation
to the search for spiritual insight. All the same, he well expresses
how the solitary effort is a near-crushing weight on the indivi-
dual; how his high ambitions are likely in the course of time to
find themselves cut down and limited; and how – the key point –
it will be the sense *of belonging to a community* which will
reinforce his failing power and restore him to confidence and
to happiness. Goethe is identifying what one writer or thinker
after another have turned to, both for relief from the weight of
the 'solitary way', and for renewed strength to pursue it.

This is true of the poets of the English Romantic period. It
has been common enough to think the opposite and to suppose
that those poets were anti-social and self-centred. That is by
now something of a schoolboy error. In chapter VII, several
works which illustrate the sense those poets had of how the
individual draws strength from the social group and fails when
cut off from it will be discussed at length. Here one may recall
the closing paragraph of 'Fears in Solitude': Coleridge finds
the resolution of this poem as he establishes in it the true
relation, for him, between the 'green and silent spot, amid the
hills' that prompted his meditation, and the 'human brethren'
with which it has been concerned and to which when it is over
he is to return. He leaves the quiet recess that he has found in
the Quantocks, and reaches a place where he gets the view of
the low country and the village of his home and family. Then
the poem concludes:

> . . . after lonely sojourning   (213)
> In such a quiet and surrounded nook,
> This burst of prospect, here the shadowy main,
> Dim tinted, there the mighty majesty
> Of that huge amphitheatre of rich

And elmy fields, seems like society –
Conversing with the mind, and giving it
A livelier impulse and a dance of thought!

Solitude is the occasion for thought, but society is the source
of energy:

With light   (226)
And quickened footsteps thitherward I tend,
Remembering thee, O green and silent dell!
And grateful, that by nature's quietness
And solitary musings, all my heart
Is softened, and made worthy to indulge
Love, and the thoughts that yearn for human kind.

One other work must be cited here as showing how English
'Romantic' poets saw the life of the individual interacting with
the force of society. This is Keats's strange poem, 'Lines
Written in the Highlands after a Visit to Burns's Country':
The poem opens:

There is a charm in footing slow across a silent plain . . .

Keats wrote this poem – as no other – in dense, heavy hepta-
meters (occasionally varied as 'poulter's measure'), packed
with meaning and full of tension. It begins as a reverie-poem:
'footing slow' across an old battle-field, or a heath with
Druidic remains, or anywhere else rich with associations of the
distant past will induce reverie, but what will do so most of all,
the poem says, is the long walk towards the birth-place of a
truly great man. Keats energizes what he says by his vividly
observed detail, but what he says in fact is that on such an
occasion the detail is unobserved. There is a deep abstraction of
the mind, for which the metaphor of the pilgrimage, in the full
religious sense, comes naturally:

Light heather-bells may tremble then, but they are far
away;   (13)
Wood-lark may sing from sandy fern, – the Sun may
    hear his lay;
Runnels may kiss the grass on shelves and shallows clear,
But their low voices are not heard, though come on
    travels drear;

Blood-red the Sun may set behind black mountain peaks;
Blue tides may sluice and drench their time in caves and
    weedy creeks;
Eagles may seem to sleep wing-wide upon the air;
Ring-doves may fly convuls'd* across to some high-cedar'd
    lair;
But the forgotten eye is still fast lidded to the ground,
As Palmer's, that with weariness, mid-desert shrine hath
    found.

This condition of rapt reverie, Keats says, is even a little
disquietingly near to madness: if a madman could have a lucid
interval and describe exactly what the coming on of his madness
was like, many who had gone

To find a Bard's low cradle-place about the silent
                     North . . .   (28)

would find his words over-near the knuckle. Such reverie,
intense as it is, does not last long, precisely because if it did,
coming back would be impossible:

Scanty the hour and few the steps, because a longer stay   (31)
  Would bar return, and make a man forget his mortal way:

When Keats tells the reader what prevents that from happening,
he suddenly uses a metaphor which quite changes the poem;
and of all things, it is Hume's metaphor for the pilgrim activity,
it is *the ship on the sea*:

No, no, that horror cannot be, for *at the cable's length*   (39)
  Man feels the gentle anchor pull and gladdens in its
    strength:-

This new idea transforms the effective setting. Over the crowded
landscape of heather-bells and wood-larks is superimposed
quite another *Gestalt*, one which for me effaces the impact of the
former. It is that of the featureless sea, punctuated only by the
image of the pilgrim ship that, however long the cable, is held
safely at anchor. What is the meaning of the 'anchor'? It is man's

---

* 'Convuls'd' is a reference, I believe, to one distinctive part of the ring-dove's
flight, when it glides with motionless wings.

'mortal way'; and this is the 'sweet and bitter world' not of his immediate surroundings, but of the 'well-remember'd face' of brother or sister. In other words, it is society: which leaves the individual scope for creative absorption and reverie, but remains an ultimate controlling and restoring force, a source of joy and in the last resort a defence against disintegration.

VII

It is now possible to see how poems which are based upon the idea of rejecting or satirizing the quest for 'knowledge infinite' fit into a wider framework of ideas. What such works do is dramatize, and accept as preponderant, that dark side, that potentiality for excess, folly or indeed evil, which has steadily been recognized as integral to an activity of which the ambition is near to over-ambition. One may go further. The poems which are to be discussed in chapter VII and which depict what will be termed the decline and regeneration of the Self, seem also to be concerned with this darker side of the enterprise. The soaring and aspiring Self is always at risk. It always falters before the daunting question first put by Beelzebub:

> Who shall tempt with wandring feet　　　　(II.404)
> The dark unbottom'd infinite Abyss
> And through the palpable obscure find out
> His uncouth way, or spread his aerie flight
> Upborn with indefatigable wings
> Over the vast abrupt, ere he arrive
> The happy Ile?

Seeing here the dark side even of the 'wand'ring steps and slow' of Adam and Eve, we can see also the efforts of Wordsworth, Coleridge, Shelley, Tennyson, Arnold, in their poems, to face that dark side and to overcome it.

The kind of poem which is discussed in chapter VIII below also forms another part of the present argument. If the soaring quest for insight is in so unstable a balance, is so likely to bring despair or a flagging of the vital powers, or even a destructive instead of the creative condition of mind, a special interest attaches to all those who, in one way or in another, stand at some opposite extreme of life. To suggest this is not tritely (or

paradoxically) to suggest that a certain kind of interest attaches
to one mode of life, and that something of the same interest
attaches to everything else as well. It is not the mere logical
contradictory of the soaring and aspiring life which is at issue,
nor is it a question of consciously repudiating that life, or of a
poet's writing something like a palinode against it. It is a ques-
tion of modes of life (there seem to be more than one) which
somehow stand at diametrical points of difference and contrast
from the aspiring mind. These are modes of life which have left
it wholly to others, have never so much as glimpsed its
possibility, or have as if chosen *not to know*.

I stress the idea that more than one such mode of life has
occupied the imaginations of writers over the last several
centuries. What is at issue seems to be a complex of concep-
tions, some of them much differing from others, and the whole
having a loose or even problematic unity which some may find
unpersuasive, and which proves in the end to spring very much
a surprise of its own. It may well be that not all who read what
follows later in this book will be persuaded that every one of the
modes of life which are adduced in the discussion really belong
to it. Perhaps it should be pointed out that if this or that one
fails to carry conviction, it does not invalidate the position of
the rest, nor the argument as a whole.

In Gray's 'Elegy Written in a Country Churchyard' there
are two quite different pictures of the humble people buried in
the churchyard – the 'rude Forefathers of the hamlet' (16). On
the one hand they are thought of as men who 'have no memorial'
(save for the 'shapeless sculpture' and 'uncouth rhymes' (79) of
the rustic 'unlettered muse'), but about whom the point is that
for all that, they had or may well have had just such noble and
aspiring qualities as those who became renowned because their
lot was more favoured. Such a 'gem of purest ray serene' (53)
may have withstood the village Tyrant 'with dauntless breast'
(56), or had the powers of a Milton though never the chance to
put Miltonic powers to use.

The other conception shows most clearly in stanzas 19 and 20
of the poem. Here, what comes to the fore is not the idea of men
with hearts 'once pregnant with celestial fire' (46) though never
given a chance to shine, but of those whose life was 'cool' and

'sequestered' (75) whose 'sober wishes' (74) were fulfilled in 'the noiseless tenor of their way' (76). We might say of them: 'they preserve decency and civility in the highest degree, but are altogether innocent of ceremony'.

Those words strike quite another tone, but not a very different idea. They are from Swift's account of the Houyhnhnms. Perhaps Book IV of *Gulliver's Travels* should be read with a recollection of Hume's *Treatise* account 'Of the Reason of Animals' (Book I.iii.16) in mind. Hume offers a proof that beasts reason according to the same principle as men; and he adds 'reason is nothing but a wonderful and unintelligible instinct in our minds'. Certainly this, not the aspiring kind, is the reason manifested by the Houyhnhnms.

> . . . these noble *Houyhnhnms* are endowed by Nature with
> a general Disposition to all Virtues, and have no
> Conceptions or Ideas of what is evil in a rational Creature
> . . . Neither is *Reason* among them a Point problematical
> as with us . . . but strikes you with immediate
> Conviction. (251)

Certainly, the thoughts and reflections of the Houyhnhnms are much other than those who undertake the temerarious voyage in Hume's little 'leaky weather-beaten vessel'. In fact, they are nearer to Thomson's 'plain ox', in *The Seasons*, that is 'harmless, honest, guileless' ('Spring', 362–3) or to the winter cattle that

> from the untasted fields return, ('Winter', 84)
And ask, with meaning low,* their wonted stalls.

'The *Houyhnhnms* have no Letters, and consequently, their Knowledge is all traditional' (257). Their minds, so far as Swift tells us of them, operated in society, not in private meditation; and their discourses were:

> Conversations, where nothing passed but what was useful,
> expressed in the fewest and most significant Words . . .
> Their Subjects are generally on Friendship and Benevolence;
> on Order and Oeconomy; sometimes upon the visible
> Operations of Nature ['visible' here is no idle word], or

---

* 'Meaning low' of course means 'meaningful lowing'.

ancient Traditions; upon the Bounds and Limits of Virtue; upon the unerring Rules of Reason; or upon some Determinations, to be taken at the next great Assembly . . .

(261–2)

This last point once again stresses the social nature of the Houyhnhnms' reasoning. The final item in Swift's catalogue is ' . . . and often upon the various Excellencies of *Poetry*'. The poetry of the Houyhnhnms, however, is no quest for 'knowledge infinite'. It is distinguished only by 'the Justness of their Similes, and the Minuteness, as well as Exactness of their Descriptions' (257); and its usual content is 'exalted Notions of Friendship and Benevolence' (those pre-eminently social virtues) or else 'the Praises of those who were Victors in Races, and other bodily Exercises' (258). With the Houyhnhnms, life is ruled by a total, perfected and infinitely civilized sociability which for me can make the aspiring mind seem, at least for a moment, like the mark of an egregious intellectual *parvenu*.

VIII

Wordsworth is the great example of a poet who saw the integrity, the deep monolithic power, of those who have no part or hand in spiritual adventure after the proud knowledge. His memorable creations are not all of the same kind. The Old Cumberland Beggar (the poem is discussed in detail later on) first appears to us sitting on a stone mounting-block as if that were the plinth for a stone sculpture. He himself is devoid of thought and wisdom about life. What makes him meaningful is that the sight of him, almost like a natural landmark, enables others to see into the ultimate fabric of society, and how it depends upon a reason immensely far from anything speculative or sophisticated.

In 'Resolution and Independence' there comes the figure of the Leech-Gatherer, at once like an animal, and a stone:

As a huge stone is sometimes seen to lie   (57)
Couched on the bald top of an eminence . . .
Like a sea-beast crawled forth, that on a shelf
Of rock or sand reposeth, there to sun itself;

Such seemed this Man . . .

Wordsworth depicts him also as a power in 'life's pilgrimage'
by virtue of his monolithic inactivity; but he is other than the
Old Cumberland Beggar. He does not merely offer wisdom
through what he is. He has it. It resides in his 'gentle answer'
(85), his 'courteous speech' (86), his 'words . . . in solemn
order' (93)

> With something of a lofty uttrance drest –
> Choice word and measured phrase, above the reach
> Of ordinary men; a stately speech;

– but withal 'modest', 'cheerful' and 'complaisant'. Yet those
words are not Wordsworth's at all; they are Swift's. The
Leech-Gatherer's words are English, but his speech is recogni-
zable as the speech of the Houyhnhnms. At the same time, he is
nearer to the Old Cumberland Beggar than appears at first. As
he speaks, his significance modulates, first one way then
another, between what he says and what he is:

> The old Man still stood talking by my side;   (106)
> But now his voice to me was like a stream
> Scarce heard; nor word from word could I divide;
> And the whole body of the Man did seem
> Like one whom I had met with in a dream;
> Or like a man from some far region sent,
> To give me human strength, by apt admonishment.

There is a strange and haunting to-and-fro throughout the later
stanzas of the poem. Wordsworth's sense of the cultivated
human predicament – fear, hope that is 'unwilling to be fed'
(114), human suffering, and above all, the miseries of 'mighty
Poets' (116), those who pre-eminently have tempted 'with
wand'ring feet/The dark unbottomed infinite abyss' – all return
to him. The poet repeats his questions as if his ears were
blocked, as if he did not hear the old man's simple message; but
the Leech-Gatherer, almost with a touch of humour (though he
himself seems unconscious of it) merely tells Wordsworth
again about looking for leeches. There, the poem implies, is the
humble, the true answer to the aspiring questions, the
sophisticated anxieties, which trouble the back of the poet's
mind.

Two of the characters who people *The Prelude* belong to this story. Like the Old Cumberland Beggar, the extraordinarily tall soldier whom the poet encounters on the deserted road at night in Book V is first seen propped against a stone (this time a milestone); he is quite motionless, and is an 'uncouth shape' as the Leech-Gatherer was like a 'huge stone' or a 'sea-beast crawled forth'. In his nature he is ambivalent, even paradoxical. Before he realizes that Wordsworth is watching him, he speaks continuously to himself in 'a murmuring voice of dead complaint'. Perhaps that last word has a musical sense rather than a moral one, because when they enter into conversation, the poet speaks of his 'measured gesture', 'quiet, uncomplaining voice' and 'stately air of mild indifference' (1850, IV. 438–44). As they walk together towards the village, the paradox of his being is manipulated again:

> He all the while was in demeanour calm,   (1850, IV. 472)
> Concise in answer; solemn and sublime
> He might have seemed, but that in all he said
> There was a strange half-absence, and a tone
> Of weakness and indifference, as of one
> Remembering the importance of his theme
> But feeling it no longer.

Calm, measured, stately, the soldier leaves a strange impression: it is of one who is *lost yet wise*. He may be, as Wordsworth calls him at the end of the episode, a 'poor unhappy Man'. Yet when he says:

> . . . 'My trust is in the God of Heaven,   (494)
> And in the eye of him who passes me!'

he knows what is sufficient for his own deliverance.

It hardly seems an accident that the enigmatical Arab of whom Wordsworth (or his friend, in the earlier versions) dreams in Book V of *The Prelude* has his origin in a dream of Descartes himself (see Maxwell, 547). The dreamer is alone in the desert when he realizes that an Arab, mounted on a dromedary, is close at his side. The Arab carries a stone in one hand, a shell in the other. Each of these is, 'in the language of the Dream' (87), a book: the stone is geometry, the shell is poetry.

When the dreamer puts the shell to his ear he hears a passionate ode

> . . . which foretold   (V.97)
> Destruction to the children of the earth
> By deluge, now at hand.

When the Arab departs, it is with a great flood, the deluge itself, pursuing him. 'On he pass'd'. From a certain point of view he represents the enquiring and aspiring mind, 'Wandering upon this quest' (148) with the twin resources of poetry and mathematics in his hand. From another, he seems a little to belong to the group of characters whom Wordsworth found deeply memorable and meaningful precisely because in one way or another they represented a radical alternative to that. He is

> A gentle dweller in the desert, *crazed*   (144)
> By love and feeling and internal thought . . .

Yet to Wordsworth, his disordered mind is no cause for pity. The thought that renders pity otiose is that the very mind which seems to disable one from the quest is what brings one to its goal:

> . . . I have scarcely pitied him; have felt   (149)
> A reverence for a being thus employed;
> And thought that, *in the blind and awful lair*
> *Of such a madness, reason did lie couched.*

It would not be right to argue that some such reversal holds good in every case. It does not in any way hold for the Old Cumberland Beggar. It may do so, on reflection, in the case of the Leech-Gatherer, but it does so much less with the half-crazed soldier. It does not for some of the characters in Browning's poems which will be discussed in chapter VIII; and in the case of one of these, Childe Roland, something like the opposite seems to apply. Roland ostensibly engages successfully in the heroic quest, only for us to find, at the close of the poem, that we have wholly misunderstood. Yet in a way, this very variety and absence of neat pattern is what the argument requires. But once the quest of the aspiring mind for proud knowledge is seen as temerarious, ambivalent, deeply dubious, it seems that a new

interest and at the same time a related interest attaches to any
mode of life, whatever its more specific characteristics may be,
which is in one way or another a polar opposite to the role of
the quest.

It is along such lines that the remaining chapters of this book
are united, somewhat loosely perhaps, under a single wider
theme. It is a large theme, and they certainly do not explore
it comprehensively, even with respect to English poetry alone.
Nor can the various new poetic 'kinds' which figure in the
discussion be seen as sharply separated each from the other.
Several poems which will be discussed in this or that chapter
from its particular point of view, could with only limited loss
(or none) have been considered in some other chapter. This
point will be recalled from time to time, though to do so every
time would labour the obvious.

There is a further point: I make it in the widest terms, before
returning to a more manageable field. If one thinks, not of the
poets discussed in this book, but of Newton, or Kant, or Beet-
hoven, of Rembrandt, or Turner, or Cézanne, of Dostoevsky or
Nietzsche, the theme of the soaring mind seems as if it must be
one of the greatest themes in the intellectual and artistic
history of the past five centuries; but there is some reason to
think that in our own time it is drawing, or may even have now
drawn, to a close.

The last chapter of this book considers the poetry of Hardy as
a writer who rejected the heroic assumptions which in one form
or another seem always to underlie the pursuit of the 'proud
knowledge'; and the Postscript points forward to the great
innovatory poets of the twentieth century, whose place in this
context I hope to discuss more fully as part of another book.

II

Paradise Lost and the Quest for Reality

If we wish to take general stock of Milton's achievement as a writer, and of his place in our literature, our best starting-point is a neglected one. It is the strong link which exists between Milton and Bacon. We think of Milton's strictly poetic ambitions, of his learning in Latin and Greek, of his insistent piety or contumacious republicanism, and all these things encourage us to pass over that link. But the link is there, as a consequence of things at the very heart of Milton's life: his ambitious, perhaps too ambitious, intellectual temper; his incisive interest in government, and his direct concern with it; his position as a senior figure in public affairs; and above all his conviction, over most of his life, that his own time was a time of promise and potential, a moment when the future opened decisively before humanity, and there was little which they could not take into their own hands and solve or re-solve.

Should we wish to strengthen our consciousness of the link with Bacon, there is no difficulty in bringing forward one item after another to show its strength. Alongside Bacon's denial that the present is the old age of the world – rather, he said, it was its youth – we could set Milton's early Latin poem entitled 'Nature Does Not Grow Old', with its eager and eloquent rejection of the traditional commonplace that time devours all things, and its closing reference, in a Baconian or Lucretian vein, to the world as a *machina*. We could cite the passage in Milton's Seventh Undergraduate *Dissertation* which so forcefully attacks vain quibbles in grammar and logic or vain speculation in philosophy. We could notice how the same sentiments recur in the account of the Devil's disputations in Hell (*PL*, II. 557), and also – more censoriously – in the fourth Book of *Paradise Regained*; and we could take stock of how this links Milton with the main traditions of British seventeenth-century thought, running through Bacon, Hobbes, and Locke to Berkeley and Hume, and aiming at a decisive eradication of quibble, confusion, vain words, and useless speculation. Most to my present purpose is a passage in the first Book of Bacon's *Advancement of Learning*. Here, quoting from the Book of Proverbs (25. 2), Bacon describes the chief glory of King Solomon; and he says that it lay not in Solomon's magnificent possessions, but in 'the glory of inquisition of truth': ' "the glory of God is to conceal a thing, but the glory of the king is to find it out" . . . kings could not obtain a greater honour than to be God's playfellows in that game' (86).

Milton cast himself in this kingly role of playfellow. The chorus in *Samson Agonistes*, in their moment of triumphant summing-up, says:

> All is best, though we oft doubt,   (1745)
> What th'unsearchable dispose
> Of highest wisdom brings about . . .

Milton was not insincere in using the word 'unsearchable'. He seems to have been prepared at any point to find that the mysteries of God were mysteries still. On the other hand, his way was repeatedly to search God's dispose to the very limit before admitting that the frontier of Divine Mystery had been reached. His bold references to the idea of justifying God's ways to man come in both *Paradise Lost* and *Samson Agonistes*, and they are too well known to need quoting. King Solomon must have been among Milton's heroes, as he was among Bacon's.

At this point my train of thought encounters a difficulty. 'Here therefore is the first distemper of learning, when men study words, and not matter.' Surely, it will be argued, these celebrated words of Bacon show exactly what sets him at a distance from Milton: it is indeed words, and not matter – the objection will run – with which Milton preoccupied himself. Johnson, long ago, put the point forcefully.

> Through all his greater works there prevails an uniform peculiarity of *Diction* . . . This novelty has been, by those who can find nothing wrong in Milton, imputed to his laborious endeavours after words suitable to the grandeur of his ideas. 'Our language', says Addison, 'sunk under him.' But the truth is, that . . . he had formed his style by a perverse and pedantick principle. He was desirous to use English words with a foreign idiom . . . Milton's style was not modified by his subject . . .   (I. 189–90)

After these well-known observations, Johnson said one good word for Milton; though it has been turned into one more bad one, by the critics who have played variations on Johnson's original tune:

> Whatever be the faults of his diction he cannot want the praise of copiousness and variety: he . . . has selected the melodious words with . . . diligence.   (191)

As will transpire, I stress the link between Milton and Bacon for reasons which go far beyond the matter of Milton's style; but this account of his style certainly stands in the way. As a first step, I must briefly suggest that the matter of what was, or was not, a genuinely English idiom in Milton's time, and what an un-English one – all that is much less easy to settle than we may think. 'Let us not slip th'Occasion', Satan says in Book I of *Paradise Lost*. How easily the modern reader would see this as an illustration of Addison's remark in the context of Milton: 'a Poet should take peculiar care to guard himself against idiomatick Ways of Speaking.' Yet in the very same decade as Milton is writing, almost exactly this phrase turns up in the familiar style of the *Verney Letters*, and Dorothy Osborne's letters too: she, moreover, says quite explicitly that (when the necessary reservations are made) we ought to write letters as we speak. The second edition of Henry Cockeram's Dictionary, dated 1626, has a selection which translates 'vulgar words' in

English into 'more refined and elegant speech' – 'the exact and ample words', Cockeram adds. That word 'ample' is our clue to the literary, the poetic relevance of his list. But it turns out that 'multiply' is refined and ample for 'augment'; 'stupid' for 'blockish'; 'decent' for 'comely'; 'sonority' for – of all things – 'shrillness'. We can see more than one difficulty arising already. Cockeram lists 'vauntcourier' and 'unparalleled' as words in the refined, elegant, ample diction; and so shows us something of Shakespeare's stylistic intentions, when he makes Lear speak of the lightning as vaunt-courier, or calls Cleopatra a 'lass unparallel'd'. *Keen, belt, glow, tug, scope, gruel, rape, prudent*, all turn up in the refined, elegant and ample diction, along with words like *temerity* and *exterminate*; while *disordered assembly, banish, confederate, despiteful,* and others are listed as vulgar. Clearly, the situation is not one in which a modern critic can be both forthright and wise.

But the problem of Milton's style may be seen in a broader light. The truth is (to repeat Johnson, if not to agree with him) that the whole discussion has been bedevilled through the false start given it by Addison. Taking as premiss that in style an epic requires two things only, perspicuity and sublimity, Addison treats perspicuity as wholly a negative virtue; says that (a few venial failings aside) Milton passes under this head; throws the weight of his argument, therefore, entirely upon sublimity, upon *'raising* the Language'; and praises Milton's style because it carried our Language to a greater Height than anyone before or since. What happened next? Later critics who disliked raising as much as Addison liked it, simply stood his praise on its head, and made it into blame. The original diagnosis remained unchallenged: and that original diagnosis was false. One is reminded of Yeats's poem about the horseman slashing his whip at a beggar. The glorious revolution comes, the brutal horseman is unseated.

The beggars have changed places, but the lash goes on.

Dryden said that Milton could be dull and pompous, for a hundred lines together, when he got into one of his 'flats' (Preface to *Sylvae*, II. 32). Dryden was right. But a ruthless, continuous, undifferentiated raising of style is infinitely remote

from Milton's practice. I need not quote from the writings of
Dante or Tasso on the proper style for epic – Milton probably
knew the views of both of them – to show the intrinsic im-
probability of any such attempt. The established conception of
epic style was a radically different one; but it is sufficient simply
to take a straight look at Milton's text. There is too much in
Paradise Lost where he is writing in a way self-evidently
incompatible with any notion of raising style to an unparalleled
height. Do we, in the following passages, find Latinate copious-
ness and melodious amplitude – or do we find a style and use of
words just the opposite of that?

> Too well I see and rue the dire event . . . (I.134)

> Here in the heart of Hell to work in Fire . . . (I.151)

>   but of this be sure, (I.158)
> To do ought good never will be our task . . .

>   Hell (II.719)
> Grew darker at thir frown, so matcht they stood;
> For never but once more was either like
> To meet so great a foe:

> Into this wild Abyss the warie fiend (II.917)
> Stood on the brink of Hell and look'd awhile . . .

>   enjoy thir fill (IV.507)
> Of bliss on bliss, while I to Hell am thrust, . . .
> Yet let me not forget what I have gain'd
> From thir own mouths . . .

> *Adam* shall share with me in bliss or woe: (IX.831)
> So dear I love him, that with him all deaths
> I could endure, without him live no life.

> Thy terms too hard, by which I was to hold (X.751)
> The good I sought not . . .

> . . . but now lead on; (XII.614)
> In mee is no delay; with thee to go
> Is to stay here . . .

It would require some thought, and much learning, to determine
exactly how far, in each of these passages, Milton was con-
forming to the spoken idiom of his time. But in any case this

question draws us only as preliminary to the major one, that of
the actual poetic effect: and in all of them it seems past dispute
that Milton cannot possibly be seeking for elegance and
'raising', for sublimity in any crude and obvious sense. The
terse, close-packed style, blunt and clipped, running line after
line in almost uninterrupted monosyllables, can be seen only as
a deliberate extension of the vernacular. It is a *calculated*
plainness, a calculated commonness, that goes beyond what
those things are in themselves.

The argument naturally reverts to Bacon at this point,
through the famous words in which Thomas Sprat, writing at
exactly the same time as Milton was writing his poem, describes
the policy of the Royal Society in matters of style:

> to reject all the amplifications, digressions, and swellings
> of style: to return back to the primitive purity, and
> shortness, when men deliver'd so many *things*, almost in
> an equal number of *words* . . . a close, naked, natural
> way of speaking. (113)

But although that extraordinary monosyllabic terseness in
Paradise Lost does indeed suggest how Milton comes near to
Sprat, and therefore to Bacon, all the same we must not
simplify. Such bluntness and terseness is itself part also of the
epic tradition. Nor, in Milton, does it come alone: it comes as
part of the variegated spectrum of style over which his poem
continually plays. The passages I quoted just now often had a
context which was the deliberate opposite of themselves.
Equally characteristic of the poem as a whole, and its continual
vehement alternation, an alternation from plain to lofty, and
back again to plain, are passages like:

> But wherefore let we then our faithful friends, (I.264)
> Th'associates and copartners of our loss
> Lye thus astonished on th'Oblivious Pool,
> *And call them not to share with us their part* . . . ?

or (about God's creating the Fowls of the Air):

> Thir Brood as numerous hatch, from the Egg that
> soon (VII.418)

Bursting with kindly rupture forth disclos'd
Thir callow young, but feather'd soon and fledge
They summ'd thir Penns, and soaring th'air sublime
With clang despis'd the ground . . .

'Clang' was the common word at the time for the harsh cry of
birds: the passage enacts its sense, as it does with explosive
vividness, because of the antiphony which the word creates
between one style and another: Formality and sublimity on the
one hand, bluntness on the other.

Again, one must guard against over-simplification. 'Clang'
has been remade in a Saxon idiom, but it is after all a Latin root.
Moreover, in the sense of 'sublimity' where that word implies
formality and magniloquence of diction, 'sublimity' and
'Latinate' are far from synonyms. Milton could perfectly well
have learnt this way of writing, as he learnt so much else, from
Virgil. 'Fit via vi'; 'dant tela locum'; 'arma amens capio'.
Latin does not lend itself to a close and naked style quite as
English does, but beyond question, that close and naked style
shows sometimes in Virgil; and if the contexts where these
terse and pregnant phrases occur are studied, they will all be
found, and especially the last, to illustrate Virgil's power
deliberately to alternate between the magniloquent and its
converse.

Not that Milton needed to go to Virgil either. We have
another critical legend, that Shakespeare wrote only with the
rich immediacy of the vernacular. A glance at some of his finest
passages displays just the same kind of antiphony. Let me quote
a few lines from one of Lear's speeches on the heath:

> undivulged crimes . . .

(we are with Milton's associates and copartners for a moment) –

Unwhipp'd of justice. *Hide thee, thou bloody hand*
Thou perjur'd, and thou simular man of virtue
That art incestuous; caitiff, *to pieces shake,*
That under covert and convenient seeming
Hath practis'd on *man's life.*

The speech keeps up this alternation right to its close:

Close pent-up guilts
Rive your concealing continents, and cry
These dreadful summoners grace. *I am a man*
More sinned against than sinning.

Milton never wrote quite as vividly as this, but his characteristic style – once we take notice of the whole of it, not one part merely – developed what was already well established in our verse, as it is in the natural potentialities of our language; and if, as Johnson alleges, it is a Babylonish dialect, then Shakespeare himself was not infrequently Babylonish too.

To compare Shakespeare with any other poet is temerarious: one is a little likely to be disbelieved, if one fails to say that Shakespeare is better at all points. But to compare him with Milton is certainly to learn a good deal about the later poet's style; and what one learns adds confirmation to the claim that Milton has that strong link with Bacon, and more specifically with the temper of enquiry into fact and reality which Bacon brings into the seventeenth century. Partly, it is a question of succinctness in the plainest sense. Arnold, long ago, pointed to Shakespeare's unrivalled gift of 'abundant and ingenious expression'. With this one must compare not Milton at his worst, in one of his repetitious flats of theology, but Milton the poet of rapid, compressed, vigorous narrative, where fact piles swiftly on fact, and there is a great sense of urgency, economy and power. The baldest illustration of this quality of style would be the closing line of Milton's sonnet on his 'late espoused Saint':

I wak'd, she fled, and day brought back my night.

Beyond this, it seems to me very revealing to compare the passage in *Paradise Lost* where Adam is made to describe his vision of the creation of Eve, and a passage almost of pure narrative which Shakespeare wrote at the height of his powers: Hamlet's account to Horatio of how he discovered that Rosencrantz and Guildenstern carried orders for his own death, and what he did about it. In each of these passages, the narrative interest is wholly dominant; and it so happens that the actual story, in each case, can be brought down to a minimum of about eight or nine facts – go below this, and the event begins to become unrecognizable. So both poets, we could say, had in one sense the same amount of work to do. In Milton, there is nothing of the felicity of Shakespeare's 'my sea-gown scarf'd about me' or 'an exact command/Larded with . . . reason'; nothing like the wit of 'many such-like as-es (that is, asses) of great charge'. On the other hand, Shakespeare takes forty-seven lines for his narrative, and Milton disposes of his in twelve.

The discrepancy is so great, that I think it helps to bring a fundamental point to notice; and this is, that in the commerce which they have through their words with things, with the objects which constitute reality, Shakespeare and Milton at their most characteristic pursue radically different and even antithetical paths. 'Loop'd and window'd raggedness'; 'the heaven's breath/Smells wooingly here'; 'his delights/Were dolphin-like'; 'lackeying the varying tide' – Shakespeare's concreteness, his rich grasp of fact, consists in a wonderful, penetrating imaginativeness that (Longinus-like) seems to light up his subject, in one flash, with a strange and inward light. We would not think of words like fidelity, exactitude, precision as meeting the case of Shakespeare at all. Sometimes even, in his most elaborately figurative writing (I am thinking of passages in *Troilus and Cressida* or in *Macbeth*), what we find is an extraordinary self-proliferating verbal texture, one metaphor continuously giving life to the next, which we delight in for its own sake much more than for the light it casts on things: in fact, Shakespeare's verse seems sometimes to absorb reality more than delineate it.

To some extent, we have cozened ourselves into thinking that Milton lacks any close grasp of fact. When we reject this, our evidence also shows how distinctively Milton used his grasp of fact, how different this use was from Shakespeare's and how on the other hand it brought him close to Bacon. Here is part of the account of the building of Satan's palace:

Nigh on the plain in many cells prepar'd,   (I.700)
That underneath had veins of liquid fire
Sluc'd from the Lake, a second multitude
With wondrous Art founded the massie Ore,
Severing each kinde, and scum'd the bullion dross.

Satan flying through Chaos:

> . . . som times   (II.632)
> He scours the right hand coast, sometimes the left
> Now shaves with level wing the Deep . . .

Adam and Eve at their supper in Eden:

> The savourie pulp they chew, and in the rinde   (IV.335)
> Still as they thirsted scoop the brimming stream . . .

God creating living creatures in the sea:

> Forthwith the Sounds and Seas, each Creek and
>   Bay   (VII.399)
> With Frie innumerable swarme, and Shoales
> Of Fish that with thir Finns and shining Scales
> Glide under the green Wave, in Sculles that oft
> Bank the mid Sea: part single or with mate
> Graze the Sea weed thir pasture, and through Groves
> Of Coral stray, or sporting with quick glance
> Show to the Sun thir wav'd coats dropt with Gold.

It would be confusing to ask 'What quality of *vision* shows here?'
All those passages are too tactile and muscular, too much loaded
with mass and depth and movement, for any word like 'vision'.
But what, shall we say, is the quality of total apprehension?
Johnson noticed Milton's 'ungraceful and unnecessary use of
terms of art' – that is to say, of words and phrases which
belong to particular crafts, kinds of labour, areas of expertise.
It is surprising that Johnson forgot how Dryden earlier had said
'the terms of art in every tongue [bear] more of the idiom of
it than any other words' (I.96). Clearly, 'terms of art' form part
of the distinctiveness of the passages – scum the dross, scour
the coast, Frie, Shoales, glance, dropt with Gold. So it is
frequently in Milton: the tedded grass of Eden, the listed colours
of the rainbow (XI.862), the angels 'squar'd in full Legion'
(VIII.232), the weight in God's golden scales that 'kickt the
beam', the 'grunsel edge' or threshold (I.461), the 'yeanling
kids' (III.434), the 'black bituminous gurge' (XII.41).

Perhaps this is what strikes one, in contrast to the figurative
boldness of Shakespeare; but it is no more than one part of

something much wider than itself; and this is a vividly *direct* apprehension of fact, a determination to search its exact quality and particularity, and render that with responsive vigour and a curious kind of curt delicacy: 'so many things, almost in an equal number of words'. Needless to say, much of Milton's poem is not concerned with such apprehension. It is dialogue, or argument, or explanation, or narrative that rarely stops for detail, or whatever the case may be. But Milton is indeed capable of concreteness of presentation – no English poet clearly more so – and when it is this which is to the fore in him, it takes a quite distinctive form. Above all, it is a determined and direct seizing and mastering of what the fact is like; rather as if, for all his strict meditation of the thankless Muse, Milton also believed that 'all things may be endowed and adorned with speeches, but knowledge itself is more beautiful than any apparel of words that can be put upon it'. And those words are Bacon's.

This whole side of Milton's mind and work may be thrown further into relief, from another standpoint: if we compare his treatment of his theme with that of some of the many other writers who handled it. I should like to do this, however, in the light of Milton's eulogy of knowledge in the Seventh Undergraduate *Dissertation*:

> . . . What a thing it is to grasp the nature of the whole firmament and its stars . . . then perfectly to understand the shifting winds . . . next to know the hidden virtues of plants and metals and understand the nature and the feelings, if that may be, of every living creature . . . and, to crown all, the divine might and power of the soul, and any knowledge we may have gained concerning those beings which we call spirits and genii and daemons . . . So at length . . . when universal learning has once completed its cycle, the spirit of man, no longer confined within this dark prisonhouse, will reach out far and wide, till it fills the whole world . . . to him who holds this strong-hold of wisdom hardly anything can happen in his life which is unforeseen or fortuitous.   (Tillyard, 111–12)

When he wrote those words (in Latin, of course) Milton was

seventeen. I can call to mind no more catholic, eloquent and convincing expression of the belief in knowledge, and enquiry after knowledge, which so much characterized his whole century.

There are several fairly well-known English literary accounts of the creation and fall – we have the Towneley play of the Fall of Lucifer, or the Norwich *Creation of Eve*, or Spenser's 'Hymne of Heavenly Love' – and the noble collection of Watson Kirkconnell gives ready access in translation, and often also in the original, to the foreign versions. It seems to me that only the great Dutch poet Vondel, in his two plays *Lucifer* and *Adam in Banishment*, may be an exception to the contrast between Milton and all the rest, a contrast that stands out clearly and at once. At every point in his narrative, Milton is insistently searching out the exact nuance of the facts. The Fallen Angels found metal in Hell: What did it look like? He tells us: the hillside 'shon with a glossie scurff'. They built the palace of Pandemonium, and crowded into it. What was that moment like? The air was 'Brusht with the hiss of rustling wings'. When Satan begins his great journey, Sin opens the gates of Hell for him. What exactly happens? Sin 'in the keyhole turns/Th'intricate wards . . . '. The gates open. What was that like?

> . . . on a sudden op'n flie   (II.879)
> With impetuous recoile and jarring sound
> Th'infernal dores, and on thir hinges grate
> Harsh Thunder . . .

Satan stares out into Chaos, and then tries to fly. Exactly how did that moment go?

> At last his Sail-broad Vannes   (927)
> He spreads for flight,

but in a moment the story becomes a very different one:

> Fluttring his pennons vain plumb down he drops.   (933)

It is of course a matter of truth not in the strictly literal sense, but in a contingent one. It is not *de fide* that Adam and Eve drank from fruit-rind, or that at first Satan could not fly through the void of Chaos; but if that is true in a general way, Milton's

version of it searches out the exact quality of what it would
have been like in detail.

There is no need to labour how this is more marked in Milton
than elsewhere. The contrast is really so clear as to be truly
astonishing. But it goes much further than I have brought out so
far. Revert to the Seventh *Dissertation*: it was not merely a
knowledge of plants, metals, the heavenly bodies and so on that
Milton craved there; but also, of the feelings and workings of
the soul, and the nature of spiritual beings. And at this point
we encounter a still more remarkable contrast between Milton
and the other writers who have treated his theme. For example:
in Grotius's drama *Adamus Exul*, there is an extended treatment
of the actual moment when Adam decides to eat the fruit. In
effect, he conducts a formal debate with himself, and he weighs
his love for God against his love for Eve. In the end (in
accordance with Genesis 2.24, which states that a man should
leave his father and cleave to his wife – Adam appears to over-
look the fact that since he was then the speaker, he now has no
authority but himself) he decides that he will put Eve first, and
eat the apple. No sooner done, then he goes pale and his head
droops. But he says nothing. The chorus then recites, at great
length, the future sufferings which this action will lead to. Adam
later asks, 'Why have you deceived us?' – but there is no idea of
an answer. In the Italian drama *L'Adamo*, of Andreini, the Fall
itself is treated in the same externalized fashion: afterwards
both Adam and Eve have very long speeches which are, in effect,
simply *recitals* lamenting what they have done. There is no
sense whatever of their striving to comprehend their new
situation, or stretching their minds in an effort to find some
solution to their difficulty.

In 1608, Joshua Sylvester translated the *Seconde Semaine*
which du Bartas had published twenty years before. The
Première Semaine had told the story of the Creation, and this
told that of the Fall. Milton must have known the translation;
but again, the difference between it and his own work is striking.
In du Bartas, both Adam and Eve eat the forbidden fruit simply
without thinking. They are nothing other than stage puppets
acting out the fable which we know it falls to them to act; and
Sylvester, as he translates the opening line of God's speech of

judgment, actually employs a cliché of the early Elizabethan didactic theatre: '*Mark heer*', he writes, mark the consequences of ill-doing. The phrase comes over and over again in the moralizing history dramas like *Gorboduc* or *Locrine* or *The Misfortunes of Arthur* – those diversions of the erudite and masterpieces of tedium. It nudges the audience into an awareness that at this point they are being asked to stand back from the *exemplum* and register how clearly it has exemplified – exemplified a familiar truth.

A familiar truth: that is the point. Again, nowhere does this show more clearly than in a work by John Bunyan: the *Exposition of the First Ten Chapters of Genesis*. This document ought to have great interest for those who study *Paradise Lost*. The two works are almost exactly contemporaneous. Milton and Bunyan of course differed in their religious affiliations, but they agreed more. Yet the fundamental attitude behind the one work is utterly at variance with that behind the other. Bunyan seems never to notice that he himself learns absolutely nothing from Genesis. What he points out, at every step, is that each detail of the story is a 'type' (II.418b, 423b, etc.) or 'figure' (II.427b, etc.) either of some general Christian doctrine, or of some fact in everyday life. 'Adam's wife was a type of the Church', he writes. And so on. Satan tells Eve that to eat the fruit would make them 'as gods, knowing good and evil': 'hence *observe*, that it is usual with the devil, in his tempting of poor creatures, to put a bad and a good together.' We cannot of course learn this generalization from one particular case: the interest of the case is simply to be a clear and memorable *illustration* of a well-established, though perhaps overlookable, fact of experience. Admittedly there are fine moments in Bunyan's piece: 'it is the nature of guilt, however men may in appearance *ruffle* under it, and *set the best leg before*: yet inwardly to make them *blush and fail*' (II.435a); 'hence learn, that so long as we retain the simplicity of the word, *we have Satan at the end of the staff*' (II.429b). But nevertheless, there is also something which to a modern intelligence is distasteful; and this is, that while it brims over with a sense of teaching, it is quite lacking in any sense of learning and enquiry: of wrestling with its subject in order not merely to impart, but also to gain know-

ledge and to advance it. This lack, the modern mind will find
in nearly all sixteenth- and seventeenth-century versions of the
story of the Fall – at least, so far as my own knowledge of them
extends. They may be blessed with poetry, or piety, or both; but
they suffer from a lack of intellectual curiosity so acute as really
to be quite shocking.

   Milton is in another world: and it is our own world. At every
step in the story he seems to be seeking out exactly (to quote
him once again) the nature and feelings of his living creatures,
the power of the soul, the full truth about the spirits and demons
who enter his tale. Why was this done? he asks. What was its
meaning? How did those in the fable understand it? What would
most naturally have happened next? Exactly how was everyone
thinking? Were they right or wrong? These seem to be the
questions in his mind. His answers are exact, thorough,
specific; given self-confidently, sometimes given with a confi-
dence that seems near to arrogance. His difficulties often spring
from this. The individual actions of an omniscient and omnipo-
tent being are probably incomprehensible to us. 'The glory of
God is to conceal a thing.' 'But the glory of the King was to find
it out'; Milton sought that king's glory for himself. It must
never have crossed his mind that he would in due course be
studied by atheists: and, that he especially needed to make
provision for Professor Empson – whose ingenious acumen
would have filled him with (in his own words) infinite wrath
and infinite despair.

   Long before, Milton had written a letter to his friend
Diodati, in which he said: 'my own disposition is such, that no
delay, no thought or care for anything else, can divert me from
my purpose, until I reach my goal and complete some great
cycle of my studies' (Letter of 2 September 1637: Tillyard, 11).
Paradise Lost still bears witness to that; and it does so in one
way which I have not yet noticed. Milton seems, through the
poem, actually to work and strive until he can establish a quite
new fullness of meaning for one great traditional idea: that of
the Fortunate Fall, the *felix culpa*. A. D. Lovejoy has shown that
the Fall, inasmuch as it prepared the way for the Incarnation,
was probably seen as a *felix culpa* as early as the fifth century.
But Milton, while of course he draws upon this idea, also gives a

very noteworthy stress to something which makes the Fall fortunate in quite another sense. And this in its turn is all part of another insistent enquiry, another demand to know about reality, to master it, which emerges in the closing books of *Paradise Lost*. This is Milton's quest to elicit from his fable a *present* rule of life, an insight into how post-lapsarian man must face his fallen world, and his own fallen nature, here and now and all the time.

Spenser, du Bartas, and Vondel all stress how the Fall will be negated, or more than negated, by the Incarnation. But in *Paradise Lost*, we can see Milton searching after a very different layer of meaning, which Lovejoy ignores. It begins to emerge when Adam speaks to Eve:

> . . . to thee
> Pains only in Child-bearing were foretold,   (X.1050)
> And bringing forth, soon recompenc't with joy,
> Fruit of thy womb: On mee the Curse aslope
> Glanc'd on the ground, with labour I must earne
> My bread; what harm? Idleness had bin worse . . .

It grows clearer in Book XI, when Michael tells Adam that God will be as much with him in the world outside, as he has been in Eden –

> and of his presence many a signe   (X.351)
> Still following thee, still compassing thee round
> With goodness and paternal Love . . .

> Farr less I now lament . . . then I rejoyce   (874)

Adam says at the end of that Book – long before he hears of the Incarnation. Certainly, there is another side; just as Milton's sustained desire to understand everything is balanced by his sense that there are firm limits to legitimate enquiry, so the growing conviction that the Fall is Fortunate here and now, is balanced by a conception of the harsher side of life. Admittedly, the world is a wide wilderness: nevertheless, it is one like that in the 23rd Psalm.

I have been arguing that Milton should be seen with Bacon, in that his cast of mind, and so his style of work, reflects the seventeenth-century desire to master reality, to search and probe it to its heart, to elicit truth at whatever cost of effort. Once we notice the force of this conception in Milton, *Paradise Lost* takes on something of a new total shape. More and more, in fact, one comes to sense the poem as a *striving to know*. The less original authors who told the Fall story rehearsed a familiar tale through its well-worn meanings; what Milton rehearses in his poem is something else. He cannot be rehearsing the tale itself and its significance, because his poem gives the sense of a tremendous effort to re-make it, fire-new. What he rehearses, over and over again, is the *activity of enquiry itself*, the quest for insight. First, the Devils seek out the truth of their situation, and what possible remedy it may have. Then, Satan sets out on his incomparable journey; and in the first place, it is a quest for reality, a search for knowledge: he is acting as his own master-spy. Eden is shown, I will not say through his eyes, but wholly as we follow in his footsteps while he reconnoitres. The middle books of the poem are taken up with Raphael's enlightening Adam as to the nature and history of the world and his own place in it. Adam has no small-talk. When he is not putting questions to the angel, his alternative is to offer his own crumb of enlightenment. He supposes, what I wish were true, that after the ladies withdraw men converse to broaden their minds. As soon as they are fallen beings, both Adam and Eve examine their situation with a relentless argumentativeness, an agitated energy, which there is reason (from *Areopagitica*) to think that Milton saw as part of the characteristic nobility of the post-lapsarian state. The tension is maintained to the very end. Adam now combines a desire to know, to comprehend his situation, with fallen Man's almost ineradicable tendency to get things wrong if he possibly can. His comments on Michael's visions and descriptions are those of a man prone to error though striving to learn. But at the end, he is not only 'replete with joy and wonder'; he also says '*I . . . have my fill of knowledge.*' In these words the innermost driving force of the poem reaches its destination.

The necessary note of caution, that Milton in Book VIII of *Paradise Lost,* and more forcefully in the last Book of *Paradise Regained,* recognizes a limit beyond which the pursuit of knowledge is both impossible and impious, does not impair this finding. At the end, Adam says that now he is filled with knowledge

> what this Vessel can containe: (XII.559)
> Beyond which was my *folly* to enquire.

And this is to speak the language of the Chorus in *Samson Agonistes*:

> Down Reason then, at least vain reasonings down.

It is the language also of Bacon on the mysteries of religion, or Pope in the *Essay on Man*. And in one respect, Milton's standpoint was firmly in advance of Bacon. Bacon, and Locke too for that matter, spoke with reserve about religion, when they thought of how it fell to man to find out truth, here and now, by individual and rational enquiry. But Milton vigorously confronts this very task. Arthur Sewell and G. N. Conklin have shown, in their work on Milton's *De Doctrina Christiana*, just how fearless he was in pursuing his conclusions, and just how thoroughly he relied on the typical seventeenth-century empiricist methods: asking only after the plain sense of the words of Scripture, interpreted in the most downright Lockeian manner.*

Whether we think of Milton's link with Bacon and the Empiricists; or of the factualism, the deferential exactitude, with which in his greatest poem he approaches his imagined realities; or of how he stands in contrast to almost all others who attempted his subject, in the vehement insistence of his effort to interpret, understand, and make real at every point what was happening; or lastly, of how *Paradise Lost* has the quest for knowledge as its own recurrent inner ritual – in every case, we are brought back to a great fact about Milton's place in the development not only of our literature but also of our culture. Since the time of the supreme traditonalist, Shakespeare, the European consciousness has undergone a profound modification. Before this modification took place, men believed

---

* A. Sewell, *A Study in Milton's Christian Doctrine*, 1939; G. N. Conklin, *Biblical Criticism and Heresy in Milton*, New York, 1949.

that the great decisive truths about themselves and their place in the cosmos were known. Certainly they had to be imparted to the young and ignorant (as Hooker makes plain): and since human nature was a fallen nature, they had to be rehearsed (as we saw Bunyan doing). But in no way did they have to be sought out: they were already established and known once for all. Between that time and ours, men have changed in this matter. We now believe that the major truths, those which veritably construct the human situation, have only just been discovered; or indeed, are about to be discovered; or most of all, perhaps, that every man must undertake his own personal voyage of discovery and re-discovery. Milton stands at the opening of the new era. He belonged to the older world, the world of Shakespeare, in that his ultimate convictions were the traditional ones. But he did not accept them as mere traditions. He put them to the torture as Bacon said we must put Nature to the torture. He approached them in the new spirit: he fearlessly lent them a new meaning, whenever he thought it right; he found them out once again, as if they were new; and he filled them with an individually realized cogency and life. He was, in a word, the first of our great Moderns. We may begin by noting that he went in for monosyllables as well as poly-syllables, or that he described with his eye, or rather all his senses, on the object; but it is to a conclusion like this, ambitious as it may seem, that we come.

III

The Visionary Gleam

This chapter must begin by suggesting a distinction between two very different kinds of poem, or draw a distinction between a certain kind of poetry – what could be called simply 'poetry about things' – and on the other hand, a certain kind of *poem*, which could be called *the poem about a thing*. This seems to have appeared for the first time in the eighteenth century.

'Poetry about things' has of course been produced from the earliest times. But if one tries to ask in fundamental terms what this poetry about things has actually been like, one comes to see that 'poetry about things' was something distinctive: remarkable for detail and yet at the same time for a significant kind of limitation and restrictedness.

Two stanzas from Spenser's 'Muiopotmos: or The Fate of the Butterfly' make the point clear. The Butterfly is at his 'play', as Spenser puts it; and there are two stanzas of the poem which tell the reader of the flowers that 'make up the pleasures of the paradise' within which he plays:

And then againe he turneth to his play,   (185)
To spoyle the pleasures of that Paradise:
The wholsome Saulge, and Lauender still gray,
Ranke smelling Rue, and Cummin good for eyes,
The Roses raigning in the pride of May,
Sharpe Isope, good for greene wounds remedies,
Fair Marigoldes, and Bees alluring Thime,
Sweet Marioram, and Daysies decking prime.

Cool Violets and Orpine growing still,
Embathed Balme, and chearfull Galingale,
Fresh Costumarie, and breathfull Camomill,
Dull Poppie, and drink-quickning Setuale,
Veyne-healing Veruen, and hed-purging Dill,
Sound Sauorie, and Bazill Hartie-hale,
Fat Colworts, and comforting Perseline,
Colde Lettuce, and refreshing Rosmarine.

These lines are enough by themselves to refute the notion that Spenser's apprehension of sensuous reality lacked immediacy. On the contrary, Spenser's book knowledge of the properties of the flowers is intertwined with a first-hand sensuous apprehension of them; and it is this which creates the strength and firmness of the passage, as well as its depth and intricacy of meaning. If on the one hand Spenser's botanic knowledge from books appears encyclopaedic, on the other, his stored first-hand acquaintance and apprehension seem encyclopaedic also.

Yet, the word 'encyclopaedic' contains in germ everything that sets a limit to what might be called the 'task of apprehension' which the passage sets out to perform. In the first place, this passage is encyclopaedic in the sense that nothing is singled out. Each item in the mass of knowledge is potentially of equal interest: that is why each may follow each, cataloguewise. Moreover, it might be said that to speak of 'apprehension' in this passage distorts the truth; or perhaps it is fair to say that the poem draws on apprehen*sion*, but hardly draws on apprend*ing*. That is to say, it draws on what has presumably been apprehended at some time or other in the past, rather than on any act or process of apprehending which occurs at any single and specific time, and which we are invited to engage with or re-enact as we read the poem; rather as if the poet were engaged in it in the very moment and act of writing the poem. Everything that Spenser has to say about the flowers is said out of what he has learned already: out of what has been for him a real experience, but one completed and closed, and lying now in the indefinite past. The poem is drawing upon the poet's apprehension, a little as it is drawing upon his book-knowledge.

That an encyclopaedic fund of shared knowledge, and more than this, of shared experience and acquaintance, was available to poets of past centuries, and has progressively ceased so to be available, is an idea which has been much explored. Clearly, Spenser's stanzas about the pleasures of the Butterfly's life touch also, in their modest way, on this great guiding conception in the matter of the emergence of the whole situation of modernity. To turn to an early seventeenth-century poem like Vaughan's poem 'Cock-Crowing', is to see another and more important aspect of the same fundamental facts about the past. The first two stanzas of this poem set beyond doubt the glowing first-handedness of Vaughan's encounter, and the marvellous sensuousness, somehow both rich and fluent, which this fact of experience lends to the poet's language.

Yet for the modern reader, there is a perhaps strange discovery to make. It is, that this glowing first-handedness of experience appears not to have been placed by the poet at the heart of his poem, but rather to be the mere preliminary to what is its heart. Vaughan, so far as the process of actually creating his poem is concerned, is not listening at all, in the 'Now' of the poem, to the crowing of the cock. He has listened to that at some time, or many times it may be, in the past. What he is doing now is *meditating* upon that past and stored experience, and thereby taking note of the fact that the familiar cock-crow is an excellent, if only partial, analogy for certain facts, also familiar, in the religious and moral life of man. If the cock can rejoice at the coming of dawn, how can man possibly not rejoice at the coming of God?

> If such a tincture, such a touch, (13)
> So firm a longing can impowre,
> Shall thy own image think it much
> To watch for thy appearing hour?

Or again:

> If joyes, and hopes, and earnest throes, (31)
> And hearts, whose Pulse beats still for light
> are given to birds . . .

Then, the poem argues, surely the corresponding human realities and necessities are dazzlingly clear.

The point which requires stress in the present context, however, is that these moral realities in no way emerge newly for Vaughan, through the process of meditation upon experience; or at least, of meditation on that experience which is the occasion and in part the subject of the poem. Doubtless they have emerged through meditation, in the past, upon other experience. But the experience which directly enters the poem is in no way a revelation of them. Rather, it is simply an *application* of them. Therefore if one tried to estimate the magnitude of the interest which Vaughan finds in the object with which his poem deals – viz, the cock – it would be fair to say that the interest is sharp but shallow. Ultimately, the interest of the cock for him is that by using it as a vehicle, he can say something about another area of experience in which Vaughan's interest is incomparably greater.

In these facts about the task undertaken by the poem, I see signs of two great convictions which have lain at the heart of civilization over long periods in the past, but do so no longer. The first is, that man was the primary entity in the cosmos, and that the other orders of creation were secondary entities of which the significance was in the end derivative. The second, that the great and essential truths which map out the human situation do not await discovery, or even constant re-discovery, but have been established long ago, and once for all. The poet's task is therefore to present truth rather than explore it; and the quality of attention which he brings to his experience reflects that guiding fact.

In the eighteenth century the poetry of objects (whether by that we have in mind generalized accounts as in the passage above from Spenser, or particularized ones as in Vaughan's poem) becomes a common enough kind of poetic composition; but the restrictions of concern which those two poets displayed, usually remain well in evidence. The emotional reverberation of Crabbe, when he is dealing with natural objects, is usually almost the opposite of Spenser; yet his precision of detail may be set beside that of Spenser. 'The slimy mallow waves her silky leaf'. If one asks after the guiding motive behind Crabbe's precision and exactitude, it becomes clear that those qualities actually represent a certain displacement, a kind of relegation, of

C

the objects described, rather than a new potentiality of interest in them. Crabbe is not precise about the slimy mallow out of direct concern or regard for it, but simply in pursuance of a general poetic policy. Whatever its immediate subject matter, the task of poetry is to deal in sober truth, not in fancy picture. If we pursue this point, and enquire why truthful adherence to detail, regardless of what the detail may be, is for Crabbe a pre-eminent virtue, the answer in *The Village* is that man's own life creates the pre-eminent necessity for truth, as well as the decisive justification for it:

> Yes, thus the Muses sing of happy swains,
> Because the Muses never knew their pains: (I.21)

The true poet tells the truth about man; and will tell it best, insofar as truthfulness has become an ingrained habit. That he should be truthful about the mallow plant merely follows. There is probably nothing to learn from close study of the mallow; but any lapse in fidelity to it would be a lapse, though a minor one, from the unfailing practice of truth in the general pursuit of virtue.

However, alongside passages in longer poems which illustrate 'poetry about objects' in the eighteenth century, it is not difficult in this period to find individual poems which concentrate on the treatment of some single object. Here too, much the same mode of apprehension is usually employed as was in evidence in 'Cock-Crowing'. Cowper's poem 'Yardley Oak', and John Langhorne's 'The Evening Primrose' (both written in the last thirty years of the century), afford clear examples. It is possible to read 'Yardley Oak' from beginning to end without noticing that the tree in it might equally well be an elm; but once noticed, the fact seems full of an almost disquieting significance. Cowper's tree, indeed, might be said to be only the ostensible subject of the poem: it is a kind of common place from which the poem *as an argument* proceeds. One quotation will perhaps make clear how much the poetic task Cowper set himself in this poem is the same as what Vaughan had set himself in his:

> . . . at the last (66)
> The rottenness, which time is charg'd t'inflict
> On other mighty ones, found also thee –

The word 'charged' carries the decisive weight. There is no question of discovering the work of time by contemplation of the poem's ostensible object, the oak itself. The work of time is known *about* already, in advance of knowing the tree first hand. That time is 'charged' to inflict rottenness on the things of this world, is a fact which could not possibly be known merely by inspection, however intense and thoughtful, of the things of the world themselves. It must be an article of revelation from a source quite other than sense-acquaintance. Sense-acquaintance might show us what occurs, but it could not reveal to us that something was 'charged' to occur.

No one could tell from John Langhorne's poem 'The Evening Primrose' that an evening primrose looks entirely different from Clare's common primrose (as in fact it does). Certainly they could discover one difference. What interests Langhorne in his evening primrose is the way its blossoms are closed during the day, and open at the evening; as a result of which, few people actually see the flower in bloom at all. Yet Langhorne's case is somewhat like the examples discussed earlier. He has no concern with the sensuous appearance of the evening primrose, whether closed or open. His interest is that behaviour of this kind in a flower (that is, remaining shut by day and opening in bloom when darkness falls) makes an emblem; and that this emblematic quality makes possible a transition to such human and moral realities as are the poem's real (if in this particular case ridiculous) concern:

> Didst thou shepherd never find   (49)
> Pleasure is of pensive kind?

This 'shepherd', an 'aged hind' who lives in Edensvale, would appear to be a simple man. 'In pity's simple thought', he compassionately advises the evening primrose to flower by day; and is corrected by the wise nightingale. What Langhorne makes his nightingale draw upon, however, is a fund of already past experience, like what Spenser and Vaughan drew on.

> *Still* I love the modest mien
> Of gentle evening . . .

In its archaic meaning (always), the word 'still' stresses

precisely the point at issue. The poem is no individualized approach to a sensuous reality, no artefact generated from a pregnant 'Now'. It is a record of accumulated moral experience, and the sensuous reality is merely what it is called at the end: an 'emblematic flower'.

A poem like John Clare's 'The Primrose Bank', written fifty years or so after Langhorne's poem, reveals a deployment of sensibility of a fundamentally new kind. 'The dew is on the thorn . . . ' That image, at the beginning of the poem, at once suspends the reader in a moment of direct, heightened awareness, something that thrusts aside the accumulated past in favour of a momentous if momentary present:

> With its little brimming eye
>   And its yellow rims so pale
>   And its crimp and curdled leaf –
> Who can pass its beauties by
>
> Without a look of love . . .

This writing, at a quite new level of immediacy and detail, repudiates anything in the nature of already stored experience as irrelevant. The poet is writing as if out of a moment of intense apprehension that he seems to be engaged in even as he writes. I say 'as if' because this is one of the poems that Clare had in fact to write wholly out of reminiscence. But this tragic aspect of Clare's own life is not for the moment at issue. He may be writing his poem out of reminiscence, but it is not reminiscence merely of facts recollected generally and in aggregate. It is of a moment of direct experience in all its depth and reality. Some lines in the poem make this wholly clear:

> . . . scores of times
> Have I wished my cottage there,
>
> And felt that lovely mood
>   As a birthright God had given
>   To muse in the green wood
> And meet the smiles of Heaven.

'In the green wood': the moment of contemplation is one which requires the direct presence of the object, and it is no mere cognition of truth, but a 'musing' which is also a 'meeting'. In the last line of the quotation, Clare makes the essential point: The 'yellow blooms' and the 'green light round' in some sense bring spiritual reality before the poet, and so *are an epiphany*.

Possibly, this is the place to notice that (perhaps it is a matter of chance) Clare's response here to the small primrose flowers has a structure significantly similar to that of the scientific writers who, in the century and a half before his poem, concerned themselves with the extraordinary potentialities of the microscope, and the unexpected connections which it was able to establish between the very small and the very great. John Ray, writing in *The wisdom of God manifested in the works of Creation*, speaks of how the mind is 'rapt into an ecstasy of astonishment and admiration' (121) at the spectacle of animalculae and their exceeding smallness.

In his *Spectacle de la Nature*, the Abbé le Pluche also writes about the wonders which the microscope reveals; and the relevance of what he has to say to the train of thought in Clare's poem is obvious:

> We will not begin then with taking a survey of those glorious orbs that roll above us . . . in the first place . . . we'll take the minutest objects into our serious consideration, and afterwards ascend . . . (3)
>
> [Insects] . . . though their minuteness, at first view, may seem a just argument for that contemptible idea which the vulgar entertain of them . . . yet he that views them with due attention, and reflects on the art and mechanism of their structure . . . cannot but discover an all wise Providence. (4–5)

'View' and 'reflect' indicate an articulation of experience remarkably close to the 'meet' and 'muse' of Clare. Later in the same work, the idea of the new and numinous 'world' revealed by the microscope is very clear:

> . . . Here we find a world which is new to us, and find cause to adore our Creator, and acknowledge his power in all things. (IV.256: 'On the Microscope')

One might quote a similar sentiment from George Adams, in a passage where the ideas most relevant to the discussion of poetry ('new scene', 'wonder', 'closeness and attention', 'divine original') are linked particularly closely and clearly:

> . . . the smallest of her [i.e., Nature's] works . . . if we call in the assistance of art, what a new scene of wonder opens to our view? . . . their extreme minuteness . . . however, if we examine them with closeness and attention, we shall soon discover their divine original. (*Micrographia Illustrata: or the Microscope Explained*, London, 1771)

The essential point with regard to these quotations from eighteenth-century works on the newly discovered revelatory powers of the microscope is not simply that by the aid of the microscope one is able to look at the extraordinarily small. The eighteenth century was discovering how, by the aid of some special power of perception, the small could be so looked at as to give insight into the great: the insignificant to give insight into the profoundly significant.

There is a late poem by Wordsworth, called 'A Wren's Nest', which makes the point about the special power of perception particularly clear, by reducing it to its simplest terms. The poet sees a wren's nest built at the foot of an oak tree beside a herbaceous plant. Later, Wordsworth passes by the same tree again, cannot see the nest, and thinks it has been pillaged. Later again, he passes by a third time 'in clearer light'; and *in the clearer light*, he once more sees the wren's nest, which has come to be partly hidden by the plant, as the plant grows bigger. Slowly, inconspicuously, Nature has been protecting her own creatures, and so indeed, herself. The poem has little poetic merit. Its interest is that by means of something like a diagram, it illustrates the recurrent pattern of thought. Deeper insight comes through observation and contemplation even of the lowliest of Nature's objects, provided that that observation is informed with a distinctive, a superior clarity, a 'clearer light'.

One aspect of those quotations from works on the microscope brings out an especially important aspect of this distinctive poetic insight. It is the emphasis upon the wonderful *newness* of the knowledge that the microscope brings. If the 'Muiopotmos' passage and 'Cock-Crowing' are again called to mind, the significance of this will be seen; because (to turn from the microscope, back to poetry) it is easy to find instances, in later eighteenth-century poetry, where the poet's reward for his act of intense contemplation is no mere confirming of some particle of old knowledge, but insight of a wonderful and disturbing newness.

Blake's poem 'The Tyger' is an example. Here the intensity of the apprehensive-contemplative act, reflected in the stark but brilliant imagery, the powerful, sinewy rhythm, is suggested at the very beginning of the poem, by being transferred to the 'Tyger' itself:

Tyger tyger *burning bright*
In the forests of the night . . .

But what that intensity of apprehension and contemplation revealed to the poet, was something beyond the reality of the tiger alone. It was nothing less than the Creator Himself. The poem constitutes an assertion that insight into this Divine Nature is no product of reflection, of intellectualized thinking detached from sensation. Rather, insight is an integral part of the apprehensive act in its glowing individuality. The poem makes this assertion by everywhere interfusing Divine reality and tiger-reality as intimately as it can. This interfusion perhaps shows most clearly in Blake's inspired revision of the third and fourth stanzas of his first draft of the poem; as a result of which the line

What dread hand? and what dread feet?

is left as if in violent suspension, between the Divine and the animal reality.

More than this: in the end it begins to seem that there is something divine about that animal reality; but it also begins to seem that the Divine reality ought somehow to be recognized as *more animal than divine*. No act of contemplation, no work of art, could be further from presenting the Divine Nature in a merely tame and traditional fashion. The perception of the poem (or rather, what one might call the act of preternatural perception which the poem embodies and records) raises a possibility both new and disturbing. It is that the long-credited tale of the all-wise and all-loving Creator is nothing short of a grandiose fraud. The act of Creation comes to seem uncomfortably like an act of audacious, tiger-like ferocity. Nothing could more clearly demonstrate that by the time we reach Blake, we reach a poet who sees the writing of a poem in essentially modern terms: that is, in terms not of re-statement, but re-discovery. Indeed, something much more than re-discovery is at issue. It is *primal* discovery of a truth wholly new, that the past has done nothing short of hypocritically conceal.

This sense of the poet's vocation as a journey in life, the object of which is by no means to master mankind's accumulated wisdom (and to concoct a style as fit rhetorical vehicle for that) but rather to engage in a pilgrimage through experience, so as to win from it a vital and hitherto uncollected insight, marks a profound transition in our civilization. Even in a poet like Wordsworth, in many ways (even in his creative period) powerfully conservative and traditional, there comes this sense of total newness, of a potentiality for pristine discovery, of the poet's trafficking with spiritual realities to which his predecessors were blind:

> . . . for many days, my brain   (I.398)
> Worked with a dim and undetermined sense
> Of *unknown modes of being*;

> . . . I would stand,   (II.326)
> Beneath some rock, listening to sounds that are
> The ghostly language of the ancient earth,
> Or make their dim abode in distant winds.
> Thence did I drink the visionary power.
> I deem not profitless those fleeting moods
> Of shadowy exultation:

> Points have we all of us within our souls,
> Where all stand single; this I feel, and make
> Breathings for incommunicable powers.

In these passages from the early books of the 1805 *Prelude*, Wordsworth claims a place at, or beyond, the frontier of human sensibility. His task is the exploration of the spiritual unknown. The poet works his way into this unknown, laboriously and self-doubtingly, and his words do not merely express the outcome of a search, but are essential instruments operating within the search.

Wordsworth, to be sure, does not always conduct his search by means of an apprehensive-contemplative act directed specifically upon one single object. Often his mode of working is more discursive and extended. But the celebrated passage in Book VI of *The Prelude* (it recounts Wordsworth's crossing of the Alps) manifests with great clarity, though in wider terms, the distinctive structure: particularized, heightened apprehension; profound or intense contemplation; and transition, by the two together, from the individual object to the universal and Eternal.

> . . . The brook and road   (1850, VI.553)
> Were fellow-travellers in this gloomy pass,
> And with them did we journey several hours
> At a slow step.

Here is the sense of a contemplation utterly remote from philosophical reflection on generalities. The lines which immediately follow show how the minds of the travellers are absorbed in what surrounds them in all its sensuous idiosyncrasy:

> . . . The immeasurable height
> Of woods decaying, never to be decayed,
> The stationary blasts of waterfalls,
> And everywhere along the hollow rent
> Winds thwarting winds, bewildered and forlorn,
> The torrents shooting from the clear blue sky,
> The rocks that muttered close upon our ears,
> Black drizzling crags that spate by the wayside
> As if a voice were in them . . .

Perception sweeps over a panorama, but it does so with an extraordinary precision, an eye preternaturally exact and keen for all nature's idiosyncrasy. Then, the culmination of the passage is that all these details, in their togetherness, amount to what can only be called a great directive towards ultimate reality. But it is ultimate reality seen through vision and paradox and appearing in total newness:

> Tumult and peace, the darkness and the light (1850, VI.567)
> Were all like workings of one mind, the features
> Of the same face, blossoms upon one tree,
> Characters of the great Apocalypse,
> The types and symbols of Eternity,
> Of first and last, and midst, and without end.

The passage is discussed again below, from another point of view (p. 99).

Something of this same structure of experience, and same kind of poetic undertaking, is visible in a number of the major shorter poems of Wordsworth's time. Keats's contemplation of the 'Grecian Urn' is no sensuous preoccupation merely. The line 'Pipe to the spirit ditties of no tone', which is addressed to the urn, shows that the poem envisages an act where the outer resources of the senses and the inner resources of the mind join together and become one. When the Urn is received as its mode of significance demands, it proves to be nothing short of micro-cosm: landscape, rural life, the urban scene, society, music, religion, love (something, in other words, like the whole gamut of human life) fuse in a single moment of Attic perfection, a single 'attitude'.

Nothing is here though for reflection or calculation. The one object in which, to the poet's eye, the All resides, expresses merely a 'flowery tale'; and the flowery tale is not 'food for thought', because its essence is to 'tease us out of thought'. Yet, that teasing-out also is distinctive. The urn teases us out of thought *as doth eternity*'. Once again comes the transition from the single object, along a recognizable vector: a movement of mind from the profoundly apprehended small, to the newly comprehended great.

Here it is clear that Keats is operating, and senses that he is operating, at the frontier of awareness. The Urn is an enigma, wonderfully abundant and conclusive in what it yields to poetic awareness, but an enigma for all that. This enigma (from which the poet can tease out a meaning only in the joint apprehensive-contemplative act which is the creative act) does not show only in the well-known closing paradox, the Urn's 'message'. Immediately before that, it is there in the words 'Cold Pastoral', the poem's final account of the sensuous quality of the Urn. 'Pastoral' is the opposite of 'cold'. From one point of view all is a 'flowery tale' of 'mad pursuit' and 'wild ecstasy'. Yet at the same time, enmarbled and in-urned, this acquires a new dimension, such that it becomes a paradox, an enigma – and in the end an epiphany.

In other celebrated poems of this period, the epiphany-experience shades off into modes of poetic creativity. Keats's 'To a Nightingale' is concerned less with what the epiphany-experience yields, than with how the poet finds it progressively taking charge of his consciousness, and then evanescing from it. Yet, at a crucial point in the poem, the 'rich seeming' ('now more than ever seems it rich to die') points towards the preternatural awareness of the epiphany-experience; and the release of the nightingale's song from the limitations of time and then of space, until its ultimate effect is to open for the poet and his reader a 'magic casement' which in its opening reveals a whole transcendent world – this progressive release executes the decisive phase of the epiphany-experience as by now we have become familiar with it.

Shelley's 'To a Skylark' concerns itself with the singing lark as a source of creative *energy*, and with the song as bringing that energy to the poet from the ultimate sources of energy, rather than with the lark as a source simply of creative insight. Nevertheless, it too has something of the recurrent structure of the epiphany-experience. First, there is the characteristically intense and sustained concentration on the subject. This narrowing and concentration is quite explicit: the 'shrill delight' the song embodies is a rapture sharp as an arrow. Once again also, the minutely focused experience, as its full potentiality is realized, spreads out over the whole of experience:

All the earth and air (26)
With thy voice is loud . . .

Finally, in the closing stanzas the song of the lark puts the poet into an immediate intuitive contact with a transcendent reality that makes up a whole world ('what fields, or waves, or mountains . . . ?'), and throws light on the very mystery of death itself.

Shelley's 'Cloud' also is an epiphany-object in the present sense. The poem is cast in dramatic form – the cloud is speaking a monologue – and the intensity of the poet's act of apprehension therefore has to transpire through the clarity and vividness of a mass of sensuous detail which is not presented directly as part of the poet's experience. Yet, for all that, Shelley's own apprehension of sensuous reality is of course what makes 'The Cloud' possible; and at the same time, the poem relates apprehension to contemplation. Shelley's preoccupation with early meteorological science, and his knowledge of the detailed working of the meteorological system of the planet, are made one with his direct intuitive awareness of the sensuous realities through which the planetary cycles present themselves. Then, towards the end of the poem, come the lines (as the Cloud, of course, speaks them):

I am the daughter of earth and water, (73)
And the nursling of the sky . . .

and the reader is thereby invited to see that once again the 'object', intensely contemplated, proves to be an individual reality through which one may have insight into total reality. That is to say, this 'object' also is an epiphany.

For a hundred years after Shelley's time, the epiphany-poem, in one or other of its forms, remained among the basic modes of poetic apprehension and creativity. During that time the world of objects, through science, through exploration, through the visual arts and in other ways, was laid open to the delighted perception of man as it had never been before. The time is now coming when this mode of poetry may well lose its force. In a world where men have almost limitless potentialities for utilitarian mass-production, as therefore also for discarding objects and replacing them with an ease and speed that invites only a casualness of attention, it may well be that intense and prolonged concentration upon an individualized reality will find nothing to do. We can of course find epiphany-poems in the recent past – in Yeats, Williams, Stevens, Rilke for example – but I do not know whether they will long go on being written. Whether their disappearance would be a loss or a gain, there is no need to say.

IV

The Self as Symbol

The subject of this chapter may be seen as a mode of presenting character, or as a mode of developing a narrative; but behind either of these lies a mode of seeing, or rather exploring, reality.

What is at issue shows clearly, if the discussion begins by considering certain passages in Milton, Pope and Thomson. In *Paradise Lost* (XI.825) Michael tells Adam of the Universal Deluge that is to come. First he speaks in general terms, then he describes what is to happen to Adam's original home:

> . . . then shall this Mount (829)
> Of Paradise by might of Waves be moovd
> Out of his place, pushed by the horned floud,
> With all his verdure spoil'd, and Trees adrift
> Down the great River to the op'ning Gulf,
> And there take root an Iland salt and bare,
> The haunt of Seales and Orcs, and Sea-mews clang:

Here there is no attempt at sensuous elaboration for the sake of vividness; yet all the same, there is much precision of the cursive, almost hurried kind discussed in a previous chapter. The mountain of Paradise is 'pushed' by the 'horned flood': the destructive, brutal metaphor behind the blunt physical reality of the pushing need not be laboured. The verdure is 'spoiled' (two senses are at work), the island 'take[s] root', and the sense of precision without detail is maintained by more than the words 'orc' and 'clang' (which Dryden would have called a 'term of art') in the closing line.

Beyond this, something is being singled out for attention. The mountain of Paradise is indeed seen, now, as one item in a world of many physical realities; but it is brought before the reader's mind as something that *stands in isolation.*

Throughout this passage Milton's account is without foundation in Bible legend. The ideas are the poet's own. Nothing is improbable, but all is unexpected. That the mountain of Paradise should be moved, that it should be moved by being washed away by the waters of the deluge, that those waters should sweep it down to the Gulf of Ormuz (the Persian Gulf), that in those desert parts it should become an island 'salt and bare', and that it should become the habitat of the creatures most remote from humanity, those of the open sea, come to the reader as mint-new ideas. As one reads, one senses over these few lines that the poem has begun to grow from within, almost to produce – not reality just, but its own realities: to engender them one by one as if from some originally creative source.

Another passage, from earlier in Book XI of *Paradise Lost*, is even more interesting from a similar point of view. Here, Michael brings before Adam's eyes what disease and death will be like for humanity. The passage is not unfamiliar, and has often been little liked:

> A Lazar-house it seemed, wherein were laid   (479)
> Numbers of all diseas'd, all maladies
> . Of ghastly Spasm, or racking torture, qualms
> Of heart-sick Agonie, all feaverous kinds,
> Convulsions, Epilepsies, fierce Catarrhs,
> Intestine Stone and Ulcer, Colic, pangs,
> Daemonic Phrenzie, moaping Melancholie
> And Moon-struck madness, pining Atrophie,
> Marasmus, and wide-wasting Pestilence,
> Dropsies, and Asthma's, and Joint-racking Rheums.
> Dire was the tossing, deep the groans, despair . . .

One should not mistake the kind of attention the passage invites. It is not like the devils that 'scummed the bullion dross' (I.704) or the newly-created fish-multitudes ' . . . in sculls that oft/Bank the mid-sea' (VIII.402). The oppressive catalogue does not even seek to be description: rather, the primary effect is one of diction. As often in Milton, what one must above all attend to is an effect of contrast: because, after the lavish, encrusted multifariousness of those lines, immediately comes what is their opposite, what is all plainness:

> . . . despair
> Tended the sick busiest from Couch to Couch;

Out of disease's multitude there comes that single, even isolated figure. The words 'busiest from couch to couch', setting the nurse before the reader, continue the note of curt immediacy. Yet once again, if the nurse is Despair, all is unobtrusive surprise. This passage too seems to be possessed of a life of its own. No simple rule of irony will de-code it and leave its meaning as an aggregate that one can mechanically tot up. This is all the clearer from how the passage continues:

> And over them triumphant Death his Dart
> Shook, but delaid to strike, though oft invok't
> With vows, as thir chief good, and final hope.

If Death's triumph is of this procrastinatory kind, a sense begins, at least, to emerge in which Despair might with appropriateness act as nurse. Here, once again, there are turns of the unexpected which lend some kind of independent life to the passage. We look to find that Death is hated, but comes all too soon. Those are the ideas that come most familiarly to us. Instead, death is longed for but comes with tormenting slowness. Despair and Death, isolated out from the *melée* of all the ailments, are not individualized by vividness merely. They have that extra dimension of the individual which comes when we see a character *self-made into an originator*. The character acts not in accordance with overt and predictable schemas, but from an inner and unidentifiable core.

There are more kinds of personification than one: sometimes, one might say, there are personifications which seem to *personify themselves*. Yet this is no matter simply of the unexpected as against the expected. The closing paragraph of Pope's *Dunciad* will make that point clear. In saying that although these lines are perhaps the most memorable in the whole of Pope's writings, they still lack the particular kind of life that has just been traced in Milton, one should not overlook the fact that such life would have belied their meaning. If they recount the collapse of all the arts of civilization, what they enact – it is an enactment of great, because self-defeating, difficulty – is the collapse of the poet's own art. Pope has called on his Muse to aid him in depicting the grandiose dreariness of the advent of universal Dulness:

> What Charms could Faction, what Ambition lull,   (IV.623)
> The Venal quiet, and intrance the Dull;
> 'Till drown'd was Sense, and Shame, and Right, and
>   Wrong –

' . . . drown'd was Sense, and Shame, and Right, and Wrong –'. Those who think that, on the large scale, or the small, they have ever witnessed that contemptible sight all round them will sense the magnitude of the task Pope set himself; and possibly, such readers will also have sensed the unwisdom of presuming that in a world of littleness, faction and dulness one's own insight quite retains its normality. For once, Pope here at the close of his life seems to sense the same. Irredeemable littleness imperils even a dedicated creative power like his.

> O sing, and hush the Nations with thy Song!   (626)

> In vain, in vain –   (627)

The closing paragraph, beginning with those words, has its dramatic place in the whole poem. Could it have an inner and growing life of its own, without to some extent belying the terrible portrait which it tragically concludes?

>   – the all-composing Hour   (627)
> Resistless falls: The Muse obeys the Pow'r.

The Hour which 'composes' all to rest and stupor, by a supreme irony, brings also the composing of the poem to a slowing-down, almost a halt.

> *Fancy's* gilded clouds decay,
> And all its varying Rain-bows die away.

Wit shoots in vain its momentary fires,
The meteor drops, and in a flash expires.

This sunset glow is, one might say, a poetry of Death who predictably shakes his dart, but does not unpredictably delay to strike. Pope superbly sustains the sensuous undercurrent of the lines, the panorama of evening and gathering darkness:

Art after *Art* goes out, and all is Night.

One cannot quite say that surprise is absent: after all, the whole passage is paradox:

See skulking *Truth* to her old Cavern fled,
Mountains of Casuistry heap'd o'er her head!
Philosophy, that lean'd on Heav'n before,
Shrinks to her second cause, and is no more.
Physic of *Metaphysic* begs defence,
And *Metaphysic* calls for aid on *Sense*!

Nothing of this is expected if we think in the abstract. But if we adjust to the perspective in which Pope sees his own time, and in particular, if we recall the detail of his criticism of it over the course of the poem up to this point, then everything may justly be said to be a kind of working out, however brilliant, of ideas and lines of thought that have already been laid down by the poem, or that are among our general heritage of conventions:

Religion blushing veils her sacred fires,
And unawares *Morality* expires.
Nor *public* Flame, nor *private*, dares to shine;
Nor *human* Spark is left, nor Glimpse *divine*!

Vigorous and ranging as this is, and clearly as it at least operates with a kind of concluding quality of energy, all in these lines is really by way of survey, catalogue and summary. It is of the essence that what is personified should not be isolated and individualized: its fate by now is to be no more than doomed part of sickening whole. The Cave of truth, philosophy's first and second causes, the sacred fires of religion, are conventionalized items and (like what is said about physics, metaphysics and mathematics) the statements they comprise are epitomes of what the poem has said in detail already. They cannot – as in the passages from Milton - be ideas growing and taking shape newly with an independent life of their own.

For a long time after Milton, it is difficult to find a poet who writes in anything like his creative, self-creative mode:

> . . . from surge to surge,
> Stalked the tremendous Genius of the Deep.
> Around him clouds in mingled tempest hung;
> Thick flashing meteors crowned his starry head;
> And ready thunder reddened in his hand,
> Or from it streamed compressed the gloomy cloud.

Those egregious lines from Thomson's *Liberty* (IV.395) show what is the commoner thing: personification is scarcely individualized at all, the description is amplified, aggrandized, grandiosified, for emphasis and display, and the details are obvious and predictable in general terms, and incomprehensible when attended to in particular. Indeed, they must be predictable, if self-evident grandiosity is what is sought. One need not even mention how life or growth from within is absent. Such a mode of composition leaves it no better than plague-stricken by self-advertisement.

Blake's earliest narrative poems bring this long period after Milton to a close. Consider *Thel* (1789: written 1787). At the very start, the youngest daughter of 'Mne Seraphim' (which doubtless was intended to mean 'the sons of the Seraphim'*) separates herself off into an isolated figure with something rather like what is called an identity crisis. But almost from the start of the poem, and certainly as soon as her lament for ephemerality comes to be answered by the 'Lilly of the valley', we find already a Miltonic texture of inconspicuous surprise, a texture of development from within.

That impression extends down into the details: 'he that smiles on all' (19) does not touch the lily when he visits it each morning. Nothing is banal or blatant. 'Over me spreads his

---

* Cf. Kathleen Raine, *Blake and Tradition*, Princeton, 1968; Routledge & Kegan Paul, 1969, I. 103.

hand'. (20) The lines could refer to God, or to the sun, about equally well: they leave the reader with a fluid sense of opening possibilities, uncircumscribed potentiality. The brilliant, magisterial delimitedness of the *Dunciad* is far away.

Of course, there is nothing of the startling or sensational in this unexpectedness. There is a constant if uninsistent sense of the undetermined, the now-being-created; or better, the now-creating. Thel says that the Lily gives 'to those that cannot crave' (29): there is a moment of puzzlement, until the reader sees how the lowly lily gives to those who are the very humblest in the scale of creation. So remote is the moment described from anything that is human, the Lily can smile on the lamb even as the lamb eats it. Again, does Thel have a 'pearly throne' (37) because she is descended from the Seraphim, or merely because for a moment she imagines herself as a cloud created at the moment of a pearly dawn? This poem does not summon a reader to legislate among such delicate dubieties. Yet all the same, it has its unexpectednesses, its moments of uninsistent drama. Thel likens herself, in her helpless and useless ephemerality, to a morning cloud, but the comparison is exactly what makes against her. The glittering pearly cloud is not a meaningless ephemerality at all.

> 'Queen of the vales,' the Lilly answer'd, 'ask the tender cloud, (38)
> And it shall tell thee why it glitters in the morning sky . . .

Why can the Lily summon the Cloud and have it come? The reason lies impacted before us, but emerges only gradually. It begins to take shape as the Cloud (pointing out crisply enough to Thel that if she becomes the food of worms that is the contrary of being what she thinks, of being 'without a use') proves able to summon the Worm just as the Lily could summon the Cloud. When the Worm comes, it can sit upon the 'Lilly's leaf' (68). The reciprocity is uninsistent, but it ramifies all the time.

Thel sees the Worm as a child. She thinks that the Worm cannot speak. In this she is mistaken. There is another quiet and quite unemphasized movement of the unexpected. She thinks that, unable to speak, it can weep as if it were an infant. Then she thinks the infant is an orphan:

And none to answer, none to cherish thee with mother's smiles.   (75)

But Thel is again mistaken. The Worm can indeed speak. What hears it, though, is not Thel: it is another surprise, it is the Clod of Clay, that rears up over – no, what it rears up over is not the Worm at all now, in the first place, but 'the weeping infant', and the Clod of Clay offers it, mother-like, the nourishment of milk. Seemingly it is the Clod of Clay that speaks next:

My bosom of itself is cold, and of itself is dark;   (81)
But he, that loves the lowly, pours his oil upon my head . . .

and when 'He' speaks, it is the Clod of Clay that he addresses: 'Thou mother of my children' (83). Yet all the same, a few lines further on Thel is saying that she did not know that God cherished 'a Worm' with (milk and) *oil*; and it seems both right in itself, and another touch of unexpectedness which runs through the poem, that the slippery Worm is as it is because it is the Worm that God cherishes by the pouring out of his holy oil. Here would be one further touch in the picture of interfusing sacralized innocence and gentleness which the poem so far has created for us. But 'interfusing' is a word essential to that statement. More and more, as the poem proceeds, the reader becomes conscious of how the series of events, of viewpoints, even of speeches, extend beyond themselves, reflect in each other, invite him to sense that more is conveyed than is said, that the tissue of unobtrusive surprises and unexpectednesses begins to branch and grow with a life of its own. It is this sense of self-growth and independent meaning on the one hand, and of fluidity and relative indeterminacy of meaning on the other, which makes one unwilling to accept the categorical quality of statements like 'The theme of the poem is a debate between the Neoplatonic and the alchemical philosophies', or 'Thel herself is a nymph from Porphyry's myth; she is looking down from the Galaxy into the cave or grave of generation' (Raine, op. cit., 99, 100). Certainly it is clear that many ideas and associations from Neo-Platonic and other traditions are somehow present in the poem; but they are present in a work which is as far as possible from merely rehearsing them. Rather, it releases them into some kind of interplay in a free state, and within a shaping and growing idea that comes fully into being in this poem and nowhere else. Only one further example of this fecund fluidity need, I hope, be cited. The matron Clay says:

'Wilt thou, O Queen, enter my house? 'Tis given thee to
    enter   (96)
And to return: fear nothing, enter with thy virgin feet.'

The eternal gates' terrific porter lifted the northern bar:
Thel enter'd in & saw the secrets of the land unknown.

The northern gate is indeed the way out of Porphyry's Cave for the new-born: it is the gate of birth. But one cannot assert that at this point Thel therefore descends by birth into the realm of materiality (ibid., 111). It is as easy, from the point of view of the local context, to see her as entering the realm of the dead, but backwards by the gate of birth, not as is normal by the gate of death: so that she may learn the secrets of that realm even though, by a unique privilege, it is given her to return to the world of the living.

Unexpectedness and self-growth are by nature inclined to be one. Over the course of the poem *Thel*, both those things become progressively more animated and prominent. The inconspicuous surprises seem to come more frequently and to be always a little more striking as the poem proceeds. In the closing incident of the work, it seems that there comes the surprise indeed: the tension and drama of the work reach a climax. What Thel hears from the 'hollow pit' of her own grave-plot is a voice which calls her kind of sacralized innocence altogether in question:

Why cannot the Ear be closed to its own destruction? (108)
Or the glist'ning Eye to the poison of a smile? . . .

Of set purpose no doubt, the speech which begins with these lines is sybilline and enigmatical. From the first, though, as we read it, we recognize the idea that for humanity at least, the senses and the world of the senses lack the perhaps slightly wan gentleness of the world of Lilly, Worm and matron Clay. What makes Thel one with them is in her particular case somewhat less bland and innocuous than their own mode of being:

> Why are Eyelids stor'd with arrows ready drawn? . . .
> Why a Tongue inpress'd with honey from every wind?
> Why an Ear, a whirlpool fierce to draw creations in?
> Why a Nostril wide inhaling terror, trembling, & affright?

It is traditional for the afterworld to be a place from which wisdom about this world may be obtained. What the 'voice of sorrow' offers Thel by way of wisdom is in fact that the sentience which unites her to the lowly creatures of the early part of the poem is a sentience of disturbing vehemence and ambivalence. Not that the non-human part of created nature is allowed, in this crescendo of excitement, quite to disappear from view. How can one read:

> Why a Nostril wide inhaling terror, trembling & affright?

without recalling the war-horse of the Book of Job? ('Hast thou given the horse strength? . . . the glory of his nostrils is terrible. He paweth in the valley . . . he mocketh at fear, and is not affrighted . . . He saith among the trumpets, Ha, ha; and he smelleth the battle afar off'.) All the same, it is not the animal creation, and it is not the 'five senses' merely, which the passage reaches in its climax. It is the fact that what unites Thel, *as a woman*, to the world of Lily, little Cloud, and weak Worm in a regimen of reciprocal abundance, is almost awesomely other than their own ostensible quality:

> Why a tender curb upon the youthful burning boy?
> Why a little curtain of flesh on the bed of our desire?

Thel. Tenderness, one may say, is not enough. It may well be that the name has its connection with the Thalia of Vaughan's 'Lumen de Lumine', and that Thalia is from θάλλειν (which means, to blossom), as also that it has 'perhaps also an overtone of Lethe (reversed)' (ibid., 114). But there is another Greek root which is nearer still to this virgin's name, and that is ἐθέλω, the meaning of which is the very last word of that same sybilline speech – *desire*. What justifies the ingenuous virgin's existence as one among the realm of nature, and what her consciousness has been altogether remote from recognizing, is the part of her nature which is confirmed by her very name. It is no wonder that the final and greatest surprise of the poem seems now to have emerged, that the poem has resolved itself, or that Thel herself starts from her seat with a shriek; but in fleeing back to where she has come from, she leaves at least an intimation that she has received her message and is fleeing into reality, into being what she is: a creature of, besides everything else, 'burning' and 'desire'.

At this point in the discussion it is to the purpose to recall the passages from Milton. Milton isolated out Despair and Death from the throng, enacted in diction, of the ailments of mankind. By that movement of the unexpected in their action he endowed them with a dimension of innate self-growth and autonomous reality: if personified at all, they were self-personified, and could not appear to be like the summarizing personifications of the *Dunciad* passage or the merely decorative and expatiatory personification of *Liberty*. Yet at the same time, of course, Despair and Death were in no way and to no degree characterized. They did not come to possess individualities. No idiosyncrasy entered into them. If one refers to them as personifications, that is as a rhetorical figure, not a fictional achievement.

Surely, these same three characteristics are found in Thel. That she is isolated out is self-evident. She isolates herself at the beginning of the poem because she 'sought the secret air' instead of being like her sisters and 'leading round' her 'sunny flocks'. Her interlocutors are from the other kingdoms of nature and have contact with her only in a momentary and ritualized way. But next, the poem in which she appears is a texture of unpredictability and self-growth. It is not (like the Pope passage) the summary of anything; nor the mere expansion of anything, like that from Thomson. Finally, though, Thel has no idiosyncrasy. She is not endowed by the poem in which she appears with the verisimilitude of a personality. More than virginity as abstraction, she is not more than 'the virgin'.

There is something else about Thel, something which could not show, one way or another, in the brief snatch from Milton about Despair and Death: though it may indeed be seen in the lines about the final fate of the Garden of Paradise, and perhaps it was its presence in Pope's paragraph ending 'universal darkness covers all' which called it to mind, even if only for a moment, in the present context. This something else is what Shakespeare makes Lear respond to as he contemplates the naked and destitute Edgar at the hovel on the heath:

Is man no more than this? Consider him well. (III.iv.101)

When he does so, what he sees is a creature at the very nadir of the scale of humanity. By comparison with such a creature, his knight, his Fool, and himself all sink back to take their place among the ordinary multitude of the world:

Thou ow'st the worm no silk, the beast no hide, the sheep no wool, the cat no perfume. Ha! here's three on's are sophisticated! Thou art the thing itself . . .

Then, finally, the significance of what Edgar is, as against everything 'sophisticated', is brought out:

Thou art the thing itself: unaccommodated man is *no more* but such a poor, bare, forked animal as thou art.

There is nothing beyond Edgar. He is the ultimate case, going to an extreme beyond which there is no going at all.

Is not the same true of *Thel*? In two ways, the answer is surely, Yes. From the Lily, which is alive and grows up in the air, to the Cloud, which though not alive grows in the air ('a faint cloud kindled at the rising sun'), to the Worm which, though alive, is confined to the darkness of the earth, to the dark earth itself, and from that to the 'hollow pit' of the grave in the dark earth, is a movement, it seems, always to what is lower and lower in the scale. What could Thel explore, in her search for enlightenment and consolation, after she has listened to the voice of her own grave? It is impossible to think that there is anything. She has reached the ultimate.

She does so also, however, in another sense. There can be no greater *reversal* than that which Thel encounters. First she supposes that all is meaningless discreteness; only to find, instead, universal reciprocity and fertilizing service. Then she discovers that if you are not a Lily or a Worm but a virgin, fertilizing service means burning youth and the bed of our desire. Her case is indeed pursued to the final, revelatory moment.

Thel, as we saw, is no personification either of virginity or of anything else. She may have no 'character' and no idiosyncrasy, she may be 'the virgin', in some generic sense, but undoubtedly she is individualized as an achievement in a fiction. *Thel* is a narrative poem, a 'tale', in a plain and real sense. It has transpired, though, that this tale has several quite distinctive features. It is isolating of its protagonist; it is autonomous and self-creating in its growth; it presents an individual, who is all the same not a 'character'; and it carries its situation to the extreme and ultimate point.

We have identified, in fact, a distinctive kind of poem, a distinctive mode of composition in words.

Wordsworth wrote two poems, 'Michael' and 'The Ruined Cottage' (in effect an incident included in Book I of *The Excursion*), which throws further light on that mode. They do so, moreover, in significantly different ways. 'Michael', the poet describes as 'a domestic' tale (22), a 'history/Homely and rude'(34–5). He also says that it is a 'story' which is *'unenriched with strange events'* (19). 'The Ruined Cottage', he speaks of in rather similar terms:

> 'Tis *a common tale*,
> *An ordinary sorrow* of man's life,
> A tale of silent suffering, *hardly clothed*
> *In bodily form.*—

'unenriched with strange events'; 'hardly clothed/in bodily form'. The likeness between the two introductory phrases is unobtrusive but too strong to be ignored. Wordsworth understood what he was doing.

'Michael' may be 'unenriched with strange events'. It is not unenriched with detail and distinctiveness such as make it unique and self-unfolding:

> You will suppose that with an upright path   (3)
> Your feet must struggle: in such bold ascent
> The pastoral mountains front you, face to face.

This is the strange setting for the beginning of the tale, and in particular for the ruined sheep-fold which is its central image. At once, those opening lines perform the isolating function: above the seemingly vertical face of the mountain slope is a 'hidden valley' (8), an 'utter solitude' (13) which is the story's essential *local*. Michael himself, from the start, receives similar treatment. That he was 'prompt/ And watchful more than ordinary men' (46–7) is particularized in that he had 'learned the meaning of all winds/,/Of blasts of every tone'. Yet such lore is not any kind of 'characterizing' idiosyncrasy. True enough, it is unique; but part only of Michael's unique *generic* rôle as mountain shepherd. Moreover, it isolates him. The storm winds which drove the traveller to shelter,

> summoned him   (57)
> Up to the mountains: he had been alone
> Amid the heart of many thousand mists,
> That came to him, and left him, on the heights.
> So lived he till his eightieth year was past.

At first, to be sure, the shepherd is not isolated away from his family: but collectively, they were isolated from the rest of the society of the place:

> . . . as it chanced,   (131)
> Their cottage on a plot of rising ground
> Stood single . . .

The light from the cottage where this family that is all benignity and affection live is so distinctive, as it hangs high and isolated above that landscape, that it has come to have its own special name of symbolic remoteness: *the Evening Star*. Wordsworth is explicit as to how one should think of it:

> This light was famous in its neighbourhood,   (129)
> And was a public symbol of the life
> That thrifty Pair had lived.

When, beginning to grow up, Luke the son joins his father in their work in the mountains, one passage determines that both of these characters are characters of self-growth and autonomy:

> that from the Boy there came   (200)

Feelings and emanations – things which were
Light to the sun and music to the wind . . .
And that the old Man's heart seemed born again . . .

This is manifested over the course of the story, as for example when in an unpredictable moment, sudden but unhurried, Michael asks Luke, just before he leaves, to lay the first stone of the sheep-pen that they were to have built together. Again, the act is a generic and ritual act, invited by the *mythos* as a whole and not to embellish the personality of Michael; but its unpredictable, autonomous quality is clear.

As the tale proceeds, the isolating function within it becomes more prominent. Ostensibly, Michael depends for nothing on those outside his isolated family circle. His sole contact with others seems to be that – long ago – he stood surety for the debt of someone else. But now, that 'unlooked-for claim' falls upon him (217); this means that his one link with what is outside becomes a link of estrangement and burden. Later on, another link begins to form. Then that also is severed and lapses. Luke 'gave himself/To evil courses' (444–5) in the far-away city, and goes overseas to hide. The news ceases to come, the distant kinsman fades from view. When tragedy overtakes Michael, his isolation becomes total. The neighbours' hearts are all filled with pity for him, but he has no remaining contact either with them or with his wife. The impression left with the reader by the closing lines is that he in effect withdraws to the mountain heights, still labouring to care for the sheep, yet losing effective contact even with the sheep-fold which once bound him to his son, but to which he cannot now bring himself to set a single stone. He is *unsophisticated*, if one may use Shakespeare's word, of everything. His isolation has reached finality.

'Michael' is a memorable poem. Perhaps one can now see something of why the impression it leaves is utterly different from that left by memorable prose fiction of the nineteenth century. It belongs to another mode of composition. Separation from society instead of immersion in it; distinctiveness and growth from within which all the same are remote from 'characterization' and idiosyncrasy; and movement on to an ultimate point beyond which there is no going, all seem to be *moments*, as it were, in this distinctive mode. They did also in the case of *Thel*. One is looking, I believe, at what inclines fictions towards *myth* instead of towards novel.

'The Ruined Cottage' amplifies this account of the matter, by – at the same time – showing a partial divergence from it. In 'Michael', there is one incident which appears suddenly to strike some kind of alien or even false note. This is the moment when Michael's wife, speaking of the letters that come from Luke in his good days in the great city, said that these were 'The prettiest letters that were ever seen'. It is not clear that she is saying this to Michael. It seems more likely that the narrator knows she said it, because she said it up and down the valley to the neighbours. At this late stage in the fiction, that particular interpretation does harm. On the whole, it seems a pity that the narration does not somehow provide against it; for it leaves the sudden impression of a valley society of gossip and neighbourliness to which Michael and his wife belong after all. The isolating function suddenly seems not to have been performed after all: we are slipping into a Mrs Poyser-like garrulity, a novel-world a little after the style of *Adam Bede*.

In the fiction of 'The Ruined Cottage', several features leave a similar effect. In the end, we seem to have a narration which is intermediate in status. To be sure, this too is a fiction which proceeds to an extreme. The family in the cottage falls on evil times, their social productivity and the gaiety of their domestic life are both brought to an end. Next, the cottage wife loses her husband because he goes away to enlist. The wife sinks deeper and deeper into poverty. The elder child is sent away to work on a 'distant farm', one younger child dies. Finally, the wife dies in total loneliness, and the cottage falls into ruin.

But on the other hand, this fiction does much less than 'Michael' did to isolate its protagonist. The cottage wife has a contact all the time (albeit an intermittent one) with the Wanderer who tells the tale. He knows its details because he keeps returning to see the cottage and converse at length with its inhabitant. On one of these occasions, he finds the cottage wife away from the house (she has begun to ramble aimlessly about the countryside), but there is someone about (a 'stranger' to him, but it must be a neighbour to her) who can tell him about her, why she is absent, how she will soon enough return. Even towards the end of the story, we read how she is always asking the tramping soldiers who pass, or the beggars, or the passing horseman she would hold the gate open for, about news of her husband. Also, she has acquired a small child, from some other family we must infer, to turn her wheel while she spins the hemp-thread. The isolating function process proves to be partial and intermittent.

Finally, there is a recurrence of novel-like 'characterization' in 'The Ruined Cottage' to which there is no parallel in 'Michael'. When the workless husband whistles 'merry tunes/ That had no mirth in them' (*Excursion*, I.569–70), or carves 'uncouth figures on the heads of sticks', or begins to fall, because of his idleness and uselessness, into 'a petted mood/And a sore temper' (580–1), we see Wordsworth beginning to psychologize, to render for us this man and no other. Similarly when he describes how, later on, the unhappy wife gives a very idiosyncratic welcome to the Wanderer on one of his later visits:

> when she at her table gave me food, (793)
> She did not look at me. Her voice was low,
> Her body was subdued. In every act
> Pertaining to her house-affairs, appeared
> The *careless stillness* of a thinking mind
> Self-occupied; to which all outward things
> Are like an idle matter.

'Stillness' means silence. As a piece of psychologizing, 'careless stillness' is acute and thought-provoking. Yet, not very characteristic of Wordsworth, it seems to look towards George Eliot or indeed Dickens. It belongs to the 'study' of character and its ins and outs which is part of the great achievement of the fiction of the nineteenth century. What we have been looking at in this chapter has in fact been the emergence, or rather of course the re-emergence, of narrating a fiction (a *mythos*) so that it invites the word *myth*. I believe that when this word enters critical discussion, it comes as a feeling towards the recognition of narration of a quite distinctive kind: narration subject to several quite distinctive conditions which have to be maintained more or less throughout if the full effect is to be secured. In several respects, they are not maintained throughout 'The Ruined Cottage'.

Perhaps one may briefly add the suggestion that this distinctive mode of narration is probably no historical freak or individual writer's whim. More likely, it has its substantial connection with movements of mind and with psychic needs which have been touched on in earlier chapters and which will appear again in subsequent ones. When a narrative approaches to the condition of myth, it is not being narrated for summary nor for mere idle amplification. Hence there must be that sense of inner depth, of autonomy, from which the tale is unfolding. Also, there must be a texture of the unexpected, the self-authenticating, to sustain this. Wordsworth himself gives an account of what he saw of value in a mythos like 'Michael'. What he says has affinity with first a newer, and then an older, anthropologists' conception of myth:

> this Tale . . .
> . . . led me on to *feel*   (30)
> For passions that were not my own, and *think*
> (At random and imperfectly indeed)
> On man, the heart of man, and human life.

They are interesting lines. They show how Wordsworth was not seeing his tales as mere illustrations of well-known truths. Hence the need for that quality of the realized and self-growing. But also, whether the myth-poem represents an attempt to enter in sympathetic *feeling* into what at first seemed alien and closed, or to explore in *thought* and to comprehend, there is in either case a definite need, written into the purpose that the tale seems to its teller to serve, to isolate this experience out from the rest of experience; to rid it of idiosyncrasy and so to encounter it in its essential form; and to pursue to an extreme point whence it can be pursued no further. Blake and Wordsworth had in common with Milton (though in detail their position was no doubt a very different one from his) the sense and conviction that insight into human truth had to be pursued afresh, had to be pursued as if from the very start. There is good reason why, in this respect as in others, the work of the earlier poet can throw light on theirs.

V

The Odyssey
and the Quest

I

The transition from a higher to a lower condition, and the
converse transition, that from a lower to a higher condition:
these two may be numbered among the fundamental orders to
which the literary work may conform. Over the whole course
of literary history, drama lends itself a good deal more directly
and naturally to the former than to the latter. This results from
the limitations of the stage. About the splendid formalities of
the court of Lear or Cleopatra, or the potent, grave and
reverend seniors of the opening scene of *Othello*, there is
always likely to be a touch, at least in the theatre of the past,
with its limited physical resources, of the unreal – the *staged*.
There are always likely to be signs of excessive demands on the
resources of wardrobe or scenery, or even on the dimensions of
the stage itself. This touch of unreality may remind the
spectator that he is after all watching a play. But the closing
and climactic scenes of a tragedy concentrate upon what Lear
called 'unaccommodated man'. The spectacle is likely to
represent men more in their nothingness than their grandeur;
and the strain on the resources of the theatre is likely to be
less. So, we may perhaps say that to a certain degree, the literary
mode of transition towards disaster finds in the theatre a
natural medium.

In saying this I am not contrasting tragedy with comedy such as that of Aristophanes or for that matter Molière, which has no relevance to the present discussion; but rather with the literary mode which is represented above all by Dante's *Divine Comedy*. The drama is a literary form which tends naturally towards sweep and integration, towards brevity, climax and resolution. There is sweep, integration and a decisive event as climax in the *Divine Comedy*, but of another kind; and this other kind is, the decisive arrival at a condition higher, grander and more expansive than that from which one started, or through which one has passed over the course of the work.

Here it is reasonable to take note of some other literary facts of a general kind, and to allow the *Odyssey* to enter the discussion. On the one hand, the *Odyssey* is relevant because it too depicts a transition from lower to higher, from Odysseus half drowned on his raft to Odysseus the restored king of his country. It is not, though, a poem of transition from the reality of everyday to some reality higher and grander than everyday. Also, in the *Odyssey* one encounters another and this time profoundly non-theatrical aspect of literary creation: how, in certain works, resolution does not emerge from any brief and selective set of preliminary incidents. It is part of the nature of such works that they resolve themselves out of what is multitudinous, exhaustive. Odysseus' tribulations are so many and so diverse, it seems they could not be added to. The hero has had to pass throughout the gamut of human trial and vicissitude. Doubtless, if we stand back from the work we recognize this as an illusion. There may always be one more tribulation, however many there have been already. That, however, is not to the point. The nature of the work is to create in us the sense that Odysseus passes through the gamut of tribulation (rather as it is integral to *King Lear* to seem to show us Lear and Edgar and Gloucester as reaching the extremity of tribulation). Likewise with Dante:

> . . . oramai   (*Inferno*, XXXIV.68)
> E da partir, *che tutto avem veduto* . . .

'Tutto avem veduto': that is what Virgil says to him as they escape at last from the chastening horrors of the *Inferno*. In recalling this fact, we cannot but see that we are approaching the crowded and multitudinous territory of the novel.

The novel also, of course, will provide the spectacle of sweep and integration and resolution; but prose fiction is perhaps not the most natural literary mode in which to expect resolution by transition from a lower condition of reality to a higher. To point this out is not to assert that such a structure is impossible in prose fiction, any more than it is impossible on the stage. We have *Wilhelm Meister*, and Hölderlin's *Hyperion*, and on the other hand we have Shakespeare's last plays (though these have not infrequently been seen as somehow straining the theatre to its limits) to confirm that. 'Prose fiction', however, has come to mean more than simply the use of prose. It includes a whole series of conventions about the language in which the novelist conducts the narration in his own voice, and about the use of dialogue and incident from everyday life, and the creation and multifarious development of individual character more or less as it occurs in everyday life. Transition to a reality finer and grander than the everyday therefore begins, of its very nature, to move somewhat outside the established territory and conventions of the novel. The novel introduces presuppositions which incline against such a development. Rather, it is in the long narrative poem that one should seek such a form and such a resolution. To say that the author has chosen verse is to say that he has freed himself to use a language more animated than that of ordinary life, and to distance himself and his work from the multiple conventions of normality, of everyday-ness, upon which prose fiction is for the most part designed to depend.

If *Paradise Lost* is considered with those points in mind, we see, more than ever, the remarkable distinctiveness and originality of the poem. To begin with, the great irony of the title. It was not the case that Milton said nothing in this poem of 'Paradise Regained'. That is what the last two Books are about; and they make the culmination of the poem. More than this is the unique position of Adam himself in those two Books. He is not only the character *about* whom the regaining of Paradise through the mercy of Christ is recounted, but also the character *to* whom it is recounted. It is his own decisive comprehension of it which is the culmination and resolution of the work. That comprehension itself concludes a movement through the work far wider than simply that of Adam's fall, because it is a movement which begins as soon as the reader first encounters him. This movement is Adam's persistent and inexpugnable desire (discussed more fully above, in chapter II) to comprehend his situation. It is this which initiates his conversation with Raphael, taking up the whole central section of the poem (Books IV–VIII). The reader sees him still pursuing it (albeit 'with faltering steps and slow') even throughout the temporary disintegration of the Fall itself.

There are as it were two dimensions to this quality of Adam. Together they mark out something very distinctive. Partly, it is a matter simply of what Adam *desires*. He desires to comprehend. Besides that, it is a matter of what he is called on to *do*. He is summoned, by a higher power, to pursue comprehension. This is the essence of his nature. It is what makes possible his redemption as well as his fall. There seems to be no real parallel to this in earlier English literature. The desire for knowledge and ultimate comprehension that Marlowe's Faustus manifests is a caricature of the real thing.

In this respect as in others, *Paradise Lost* provided a great model for some of the more ambitious poems of the early nineteenth century. It magisterially prefigured that search for comprehension of the human condition, in general terms, which seems to have become increasingly powerful (and increasingly necessary perhaps) as the eighteenth century wore on. To be sure, Milton's solution to the problem was more traditional than was to satisfy some of the poets of the later period. It was by no means traditional altogether. Christianity provided him with an answer in his own distinctive terms, and in particular those terms were the terms of an intense energy of individual search, required of man (as of Adam) equally by an outside, fore-ordaining authority, and by his own determination and innermost nature. This search, on the one hand a search for knowledge, self-knowledge and self-mastery, is also incorporated into the poem at the level of literality: the dénouement of the fiction of *Paradise Lost* is that Adam and Eve are not in any simple sense expelled from the Garden. They are *released* from it in a manner which frees them to engage in what can only be termed a *quest* over the earth for a place of rest which is at the same time the key to comprehension of their state.

One must add that the quest is also an *Odyssey*. It is a searching for man's true home: not his initial, idyllic, tutelary home, rather the place which is his true home because it requires him, and so enables him, to realize his own permanent and highest nature. This notion of the poem as Odyssey will recur.

Dante's *Divine Comedy* was more than the first great example of the quest-poem, it was a direct and pervasive influence throughout the later eighteenth and earlier nineteenth centuries. Southey read right through the poem in the middle 1790s. Cary's translation of the *Inferno* appeared in 1805–6, and of the *Purgatorio* and *Paradiso* in 1814. Wordsworth and Coleridge were acquainted with the poem, as was Byron. Its profound influence on both Shelley and Keats need not be elaborated. What may require emphasis is that the poem introduced something new into English poetry not only in respect of style, but also through its constant rhythm of encounter and interlocking dialogue, and more still through certain of its other most basic features. What were these? First, Shelley and Keats could acquaint themselves with no English poem that so deeply and directly *involved the writer himself* as protagonist (one must of course remember that neither of them ever saw Wordsworth's *Prelude*: while Pope's *Epistles* and *Satires* belong to quite another context). The quest of the *Commedia* is the quest of Dante himself in the most direct sense and with passionate involvement. Again, it is a journey in search of knowledge. It has a clearly defined goal and *terminus ad quem*. Above all, it is a quest which is prescribed and ordained.

> Più lunga scala *convien* che si saglia   (*Inferno*, 24.55)

– the reticence yet force of 'convien' must not be missed, and the force of the same idea for Keats will transpire later.

If there is no need to labour the importance and novelty of Dante for this period, there is perhaps also no need to say much about the place of the literature of travel in the background of the poetry of the time. Already in *Paradise Lost*, there are indications that Milton knew of the English sailings to the White Sea, the 'caney waggons light' of the 'Chineses', and the place of Ormuz in the ancient trade routes to India and the Far East. Since this is not a history of literary background, a few isolated examples must serve to recall the point at issue. Wordsworth says that the idea of his poem 'The Forsaken Indian Woman' came from Samuel Hearne's *Journey from . . . Hudson's Bay to the Northern Ocean* of 1795, a work which Coleridge possessed and annotated. Wordsworth had a copy of Frederick Marten's *Voyage to Spitzbergen and Greenland* of 1614, one of the many travel works which Coleridge drew on, albeit unconsciously, in writing 'The Ancient Mariner'. Coleridge was also familiar with the two great early seventeenth-century travel collections by Samuel Purchas: *Purchas his Pilgrimage* (1617) and *Purchas his Pilgrims* (1625). He is known to have drawn the idea of 'Kubla Khan' from them. The importance of travel writings to the literature of the time need scarcely be argued in detail.

One poet gives quite special evidence of interest in travel literature and wide reading in it. He has a quite special significance for the period, in part because – wisely, it must be admitted – he is now read little. This is Robert Southey. Southey was not read little in his own time. Newman, writing as late as 1850 of one of Southey's works, said 'it has ever been, to my feelings, the most sublime of English poems'. Southey's *Common-Place Book* records passages in his reading from a wide variety of travel works, especially those about travel in the Orient. He knew Purchas's collections, the *Travels* of Marco Polo and Mandeville, Karsten Niebuhr's account of his 1763 expedition to Arabia (at least in Robert Heron's translation: *Travels through Arabia*, Edinburgh, 1792) and the work of Ibn Battuta, the great fourteenth-century Arab traveller. He shows also in his *Common-Place Book* that he was familiar with a number of writings on Oriental mythology, among them Pierre Sonnerat's *Voyage aux Indes Orientales* (the original was published in Paris in 1782, but Southey appears to have used the first volume of F. Magnus's translation, published in Calcutta in 1788: he refers to this work simply as Sonnerat's

Hindu Mythology), as well as Edward Moor's *Hindu Pantheon* (1810), and the writings of d'Herbelat.

Out of this mass of reading Southey created two poems which in a sense it is our good fortune to have forgotten. It must be conceded that they are ridiculous works. Yet paradoxically, for an understanding of the poetry of the time they must be recognized as key documents. These two poems are *Thalaba the Destroyer* (1800), which draws upon Southey's reading in Arabian mythology, and which he alleges is based upon 'a continuation of the Arabian Nights'; and *The Curse of Kehama* (1810), which is based upon the richer and stranger mythology (insofar as Southey understood it, which was not very far) of Hinduism. Keats and Shelley were not themselves widely read in the travel literature of their time. But these two poems mediated that body of writing to them; and Southey's poems also help to explain the remarkable contrast in style between the earlier English Romantic poets and the later ones.* True enough, Shelley, and to some extent Keats, and in particular Byron, all admired and studied Wordsworth, and quarried in his works; especially in *The Excursion*, the poem which presented Wordsworth to them as a major poet. Yet these allegiances in larger terms of consciousness went with a sharp contrast in style. Wordsworth's plainness is not followed. There is lavish description and colourful sensuous opulence instead. It is Southey's work which explains this fact.

II

This discussion ought now briefly to consider *The Prelude*. The poem may be seen from three different points of view, each as it were more inward than the last. It may be seen simply as a biography of external events in the poet's life: his childhood, years at the university, visits to London, travels on the Continent. More significantly, it may be seen as an apologia: in fact, this side of the poem is surprisingly, almost disquietingly prominent. Wordsworth seems almost unduly anxious to excuse his idleness at Cambridge and to engage in what is

---

* I have discussed this briefly in an earlier book, *Widening Horizons in English Verse*, Routledge & Kegan Paul, 1966.

known nowadays as an 'auto-critique' in respect of (to con-
tinue in the same language) his formalist errors in the period
of the early French Revolution. Possibly this note of self-
extenuation, which runs through the work, stems from a sense
of guilt and failure having more to do with Annette Vallon and
the confused and helpless sonnet 'On Calais Sands' than with
any political issue.

Third and most important, the poem invites reading as a
spiritual autobiography, a 'pilgrimage', in its own words,
towards 'highest truth'. This strand of the poem's meaning
takes the form of meditation and recollection, but at the same
time the sense of a quest is present too, in part directly, in part
through metaphor. It is a quest for knowledge of ultimates, and
it is pursued with as high a sense of calling as Milton shows in
his own epic:

Be mine to follow with no timid step   (XII.249)
Where knowledge leads me: it shall be my pride
That I have dared to tread this holy ground,
Speaking no dream, but things oracular . . .

Life for Wordsworth is a progress not an accident. 'I would
trace /The progress of our being', he says early in the poem
(II.238). A significant passage in Book II depicts the transition
from life as accident to life as an ordained and imposed searching
after a higher reality:

Thus, day by day,   (250)
Subjected to the discipline of love . . .

(an indication, of course, of how gentle and psychically creative
is that subjection and imposition) –

His organs and recipient faculties
Are quickened, are more vigorous, his mind spreads,
Tenacious of the forms which it receives.

From the child's mother, in the first instance, there comes:

A virtue which irradiates and exalts   (259)
All objects through all intercourse of sense.

Under this creative influence, life becomes not a vagary merely, but what is ordained by a superior call to the individual:

No outcast he, bewildered and depressed:
Along his infant veins are interfused
The gravitation and the filial bond
Of Nature that connect him with the world.
Emphatically such a Being lives,
An inmate of this *active* universe;

(That is to say, there is an activity which works upon him from outside, and which at the same time renders him active from within):

From nature largely he receives; nor so
Is satisfied, but largely gives again . . .
Even as an agent of the one great Mind,   (272)
          . . . Such, verily, is the first
Poetic spirit of our human life.

The upshot of this passage is to bring out how Wordsworth sees growing up as transition to activity which, for all that it is activity, is also one with the 'wise passivity' of early childhood.

A later passage introduces the vocabulary characteristic of this poetic mode as a whole:

          . . . from the firm habitual *quest*   (IV.278)
Of feeding pleasures, from that eager zeal,
Those yearnings which had every day been mine . . .

The search of life had been for 'feeding' pleasures in the sense that they nourished what was other than themselves. They ministered to spiritual progress rather than merely enjoyment. It is interesting to see how exactly the passage quoted justifies the word 'quest': something more ambitious, more dedicated than a search merely. It is the word 'zeal' which makes clear that 'firm' in the passage above does not qualify 'habitual' only, or even chiefly. It is not doing duty just for 'firmly'; in the end, it is the quest itself which is 'firm'. The firmness is doubtless in part a matter of habit; but more than that, it is one of deep desire ('yearning') and of zeal. Custom is reinforced by a major movement of the mind.

The Prelude cannot be seen as recounting any quest in a literal sense. At that level, it is a meditative autobiography, and the travels it records were those normal enough for a young man in Wordsworth's social position. All the same, this does not bring out how the incidents and phases of the poem are treated. Recurrently, the idea of a journey enters the climactic Books of the poem (XI–XIII in the 1805 edition) *as metaphor*; this is true of Wordsworth's phase of aberration, and one of the metaphors he uses must by now be strikingly reminiscent:

My business was *upon the barren sea,*   (XI.55)
My errand was to *sail* to other coasts.

Yet was I often greedy in the chase,   (XI.190)
And roamed from hill to hill, from rock to rock,
Still craving combinations of new forms,
New pleasures, wider empires from the sight . . .

Once again the metaphors delimit precisely: the *hunter* (he who is engaged in a 'chase') has a goal which means that his course, his 'errand', is determined from something outside himself – but at a fuller level of analysis, it is determined rather from within, and by choice and dedication.

The quest, the ordained journey, enters the poem also as metaphor for what Wordsworth does when he follows the narrow but saving line of rightness:

          . . . O Friend, for whom   (XI.390)
I *travel* in these dim uncertain ways;
Thou wilt assist me as a *pilgrim* gone
In search of highest truth.

The search after insight is a recurrent idea:

Long time *in search of knowledge* desperate,   (XII.20)
I was *benighted* heart and mind;

Disposes her [i.e. the mind] . . .   (XII.37)
To seek in man, and in the frame of life,
Social and individual, what there is
Desirable, affecting, good or fair
Of kindred permanence . . .

> sanguine schemes, (XII.65)
> Ambitious virtues, pleased me less; I sought
> For good in the familiar face of life . . .

Moreover, although Wordsworth's 'search for good' is not a literal, physical quest, the idea of a quest or journey is present, literally, through much of the poem. Here is an example: the lines

> A favourite pleasure hath it been with me, (IV.363)
> From time of earliest youth, to walk alone
> Along the public way . . .

open one of the best-known passages in the Book describing Wordsworth's 'summer vacation' from Cambridge, and we soon find that the 'walk' has more of the quest in it, of a response to some kind of summons, than appeared at first:

> While thus I wandered, step by step *led on,* (400)
> It chanced a sudden turning of the road
> Presented to my view an uncouth shape
> So near . . .

The tall, desolate soldier is himself a walker on the 'public way'. In Book V comes the incident in which the dreamer meets the Arab who will be 'a guide /To lead him through the desert' (82). The Arab *pursues his journey* in what seems like deep absorption of mind:

> On he passed (117)
> Not heeding me . . .

In Book VI, Wordsworth writes 'my poem *leads* me' (334) to 'wanderings of my own'. While at Cambridge, he and a fellow student

> staff in hand, on foot pursued our way (341)
> Towards the distant Alps . . .

They sound like pilgrims, and as they go through Switzerland that is what Wordsworth calls them, in a passage which emphasizes how the pilgrimage is one in search of major truth:

> we could not choose but read (474)
> A frequent lesson of sound tenderness,
> The universal reason of mankind,
> The truth of young and old. Nor, side by side
> Pacing, two brother *pilgrims* . . .

The celebrated moment of semi-mystical illumination that Wordsworth experienced as he descended the Alps on the Italian side is not the outcome of a quest for illumination, in the literal sense; but it is closely bound up with pursuit of the pilgrim journey. In fact, it is almost as if the poet has a sense of this. The two travellers lose their way. Then they find it again. Having re-discovered their fore-ordained route, they pursue it in a mood of solemnity and dedication:

> Downwards we hurried fast, (VI.551)
> And entered with the road which we had missed
> Into a narrow chasm. The brook and road
> Were fellow-travellers in this gloomy pass,
> And with them did we journey several hours
> At a slow step.

The passage which follows (ll.556–72) is a celebrated one. It depicts the details of what this dedicated journey spread out before the travellers. Its intricate syntax and periodic structure ought not to be overlooked, and it is from these details that Wordsworth makes emerge his moment of vision. As the structure of the sentence at last unfolds itself, the long catalogue of impressions prove to be:

> . . . *all* like workings of one mind, the features (VI.568)
> Of the same face, blossoms upon one tree . . .

The pilgrim journey is precisely what transforms life to a higher power of itself.

Much later, in the resolution of the poem, the idea of the road re-appears:

> I love a public road: few sights there are (XII.145)
> That please me more . . .

Wordsworth goes on to speak of the fundamental illuminative

power, and movement towards the open, transforming kind of knowledge, that the idea seemed to him always to have:

> . . . such object hath had power
> O'er my imagination since the dawn
> Of childhood, when its disappearing line . . .
> Was *like a guide into eternity*,
> At least to *things unknown and without bound*.

As he grew up, the power of the idea realized itself for him:

> When I began to enquire   (XII.161)
> To watch and question those I met, and held
> Familiar talk with them, *the lonely roads*
> *Were schools to me* in which I daily read
> With most delight the passions of mankind,
> There saw into the depth of human souls . . .

'School' emphasizes the idea of learning and knowledge, but the passage quoted last but one makes clear ('a guide . . . to things unknown and without bound') that the knowledge is a new knowledge, a searching-out of the mysterious and open-ended. The visionary nature of the whole experience shows in a later passage. Wordsworth says (XII.305 ff.), that he has hoped to write a poem which 'Proceeding from the depth of untaught things', might be 'A power like one of Nature's': be, in other words, revelatory at a radical, primal level. Then he goes on to recount an occasion when those hopes became uniquely strong. He was a traveller on Salisbury Plain, going over the Downs with no track to guide him, or

> along the bare white roads   (XII.316)
> Lengthening in solitude their dreary line . . .

The precise nature of the image should be noted. The road is long and empty ('bare'), there are no distractions and there are no alternative routes (the road before him is 'lengthening in solitude'). The atmosphere of the walk is melancholy and solemn. These things are what make up the structure of a journey which is a quest. Wordsworth indicates the psychic consequences of such journeying:

> . . . While through those vestiges of ancient times, (XII.318)
> I range, and by the solitude o'ercome,
> I *had a reverie and saw the past* . . .

Influenced by the sight of Stonehenge and perhaps some of the other prehistoric monuments of the Plain, Wordsworth's vision in this setting is of Stone Age times; but the essential point is that here, once again, the image of the road and of the ordained journey, the quest, leads forward into a sense of visionary, preternatural insight.

Wordsworth's poem thus proves to have a distinctive structure. It is not the poem it seems. It by no means simply recounts, and meditates upon, such various experiences as made up the first thirty or so years of the poet's life. Underlying these experiences, or often as a literally constituent part of them, is an idea which seems to be sleeping throughout the whole poem, and at the same time constantly to start into life in it. Nor is this just the idea of the road as 'image'. It is more structured and dynamic than that. It is the idea of a journey which is solemn, which is ordained, and which at the same time is the route to knowledge and self-mastery. In other words, the idea of the quest. Wordsworth's poem assimilates, and deeply, covertly embodies, a structure which proves to be more explicitly utilized elsewhere.

The quest for knowledge and self-mastery may lead men to remote and strange places. It can also lead them home: quest turns out to be Odyssey. The inter-action between the two conceptions is of much interest for poetry between Wordsworth's time and the present; and in view of how the quest-poem seems to owe something to the European explorations of the seventeenth and eighteenth centuries, it is of interest in trying to comprehend the whole development of Western European culture over that period. Looked at more and more closely, *The Prelude* came to seem more and more like a quest-poem, though indirectly so; but there comes a point when we realize, because Wordsworth realizes, that this poem's quest is an Odyssey:

> Shall I avow that I had hope to see, (XI.57)
> I mean that future times would surely see,

The man to come, parted, as by a gulph,
From him who had been . . .

This 'seeing' would be the product of a quest for knowledge
which led forward into unknown regions. Everyone knows
how in the end, the poem recognizes that idea as the central and
irremediable aberration. It is 'life's familiar face . . .' (1850,
XII.62), the goal of Odysseus, which is the true goal of the
enquiring spirit.

The point is confirmed by the *local* in which *The Prelude* is
written. The opening of the first book describes Wordsworth
making a journey, freely chosen by himself, back to the known
and familiar places of his childhood; and it stresses how he has
hopes that this very fact will release his major poetic powers.
The poem, which opens with an echo of the closing lines of
Paradise Lost: 'The earth is all before me . . .' (I.15), comes to
rest in the 'house and fields' (83) which the poet can see in his
mind's eye before he reaches them, and which will be the
'hermitage' (115) where the poem will come to fruition. This
is Wordsworth's idea, in *The Prelude*, of (to quote Milton's
lines again) '. . . where to choose'.

III

Robert Southey's early long poem *Madoc* may be called a
quest-poem insofar as it recounts the legendary history of the
early Welsh peoples who (as legend had it) were the first
Europeans to reach America. Once again the quest is akin to an
Odyssey, in that the emigrant tribes prove, as the narrative
advances, to be in search of a homeland, albeit a new one. The
poem is a medley of warfare, rhetoric and fulsomely lush
description of nature, but the radical pattern shows beneath
that. *Thalaba the Destroyer*, and *The Curse of Kehama*, are quest-
poems much more clearly. Each of them narrates the wanderings
of the hero for the purpose of escaping the powers of evil and
enlisting the powers of good.

Not even Southey could write two such long poems and
achieve nothing at all. There are a few descriptive passages of
merit, and Southey's marked prosodic facility and variety of
style (there is something of a contrast here with the long

poems of Wordsworth and Coleridge) has a certain technical interest in itself and a certain interest also for a poem like *Prometheus Unbound*. But in the main, those two poems more or less fulfilled for their time the function fulfilled in recent times by films in gorgeous technicolour of the Orient, and by science fiction and possibly by a novel like *The Lord of the Rings*. Scenery, romantic affairs, fantastic travel, cosmic warfare, other grandiose but trifling thrills, make their stock in trade. The poems deserve study, despite their shortcomings, for the part they played in the development of Shelley and Keats, and their poems *Alastor* and *Endymion*.

There are one or two what might be termed 'properties' recurrent in the quest-poem. One of these is the little boat which the quester finds to help him at one stage of his journey. Alastor finds a 'little shallop' on the shore of a lake. It is a ruined boat:

> its sides   (301)
> Gaped wide with many a rift

and there is no sail, so that to catch the wind Alastor has to spread his coat on the bare mast. In *Thalaba the Destroyer* the hero found a 'little boat' (Book XI, Section 31 . . .), with a Damsel at the helm, as in Spenser. In *The Curse of Kehama* (XX.7) there is another little boat, and this one is nearer to Shelley's:

> There in a creek a vessel lay . . .
>   Through its yawning side the wave
> Was oozing in; the mast was frail,
> And old and torn its only sail.

Shelley would doubtless have known the incident in Spenser's *Faerie Queen* (II.6) where the knight travels across the lake in a 'shallop'. But Spenser's incident does not at all match with Shelley's treatment as Southey's does; and this not only in respect of the shallop but also of the context of that. If we pursue this image of the 'little boat' (the boat which carries the hero) back to its original sources, we come to Charon and the souls he ferries across the Styx (*Aeneid*, VI.410–16). But between them and Spenser stands the 'nave piccioletta' of the

Inferno, Canto VIII, in which Dante and Virgil cross the River Phlegethon so as to enter the City of Dis. Swift as it is, this boat resembles Southey's dilapidated little boat at least in its 'antica prora' (VIII.29). It is piloted by Phlegyas, ageless guardian spirit of the river, as Charon was of the Styx. Southey was reading through Dante only a year or so before he wrote *Thalaba the Destroyer*.

Perhaps, therefore, Southey owes to Dante the connection between dilapidated ancient boat and ancient guardian spirit: at all events, Southey's hero enters a little boat, crosses the sea in it, and then sails on into a mysterious cave (XII.9). This time (as in Spenser's incident) there is a 'damsel' who acts as crew; but when she brings the little craft to the edge of the sub-terranean waters, Southey introduces a new 'property':

> Reclining on a rock beside
> Sate a grey-headed man.

This incident also supplied Keats with something for his poem *Endymion*.

In the course of Book III of that poem, Endymion journeys to the depths of the sea. There he meets a man of measureless age. This derives from Southey, because in *Endymion* (234) the Old Man gets up from his rock and greets Endymion with the words 'Thou art the man!': it is Glaucon, victim of Circe, and doomed to wait a thousand years to be released from her evil spell. Endymion is the man fated to release him. But likewise in *Thalaba*: here the 'damsel' greets the age-old man with markedly similar words: 'Is it the hour appointed?' As in Keats's poem, the 'hour' is when the Old Man can be released from a spell put on him as a lover long before. Needless to say, Southey is soon showing us that it is indeed the hour appointed. Thalaba is 'the Man', as Endymion was to be in his turn, in imitation of Thalaba.

So much for the 'properties' of the little Boat and the enchanted Old Man. Continuities between Southey's poems and those of Shelley and Keats extend somewhat further than this, even in matters of comparative detail. When he met the Old Man, Thalaba was on a journey to the underworld of the sea. Kehama (section XV) makes a similar journey: he walks down, and the waves 'rise above his head'. It is at the end of Book II of *Endymion* that the hero of Keats's poem also walks down into the sea and finds it close over him: 'He saw the giant sea above his head' (1023). Early in Book III of the poem, Endymion sees the wonders of the sea-bed, including the remains of the first men (ll.130 . . .). The passage is reminiscent of the account of the world under the sea in *Prometheus Unbound* (IV. 285 ff.) and of the first men as described in *Alastor* (110 ff.). After this, Endymion enters the palaces of Neptune: once again, *The Curse of Kehama*, with the 'thousand palaces' of its under-water city, does not seem far away;* and there is a curiously close echo to confirm that. Those thousand palaces stand, says Southey's poem, 'in *sunlight* and *sea-green*' (XVI.44). In Keats's *Endymion* there is a '*gold-green* zenith' (III.878) above the palace of Neptune.

There are a few other respects in which details show the continuity between Southey's poems and poems by Keats or Shelley. The 'Arabian Maiden' who escorts the hero in *Alastor* has her counterpart in *Thalaba*; the Indian setting of *Kehama* may at least possibly have occasioned the 'Indian Maid' who escorts Endymion. Shelley's supernatural chariots are from Southey, and his phrase 'The magic car moved on' in *Queen Mab* (207) combines two characteristic phrases of Southey's, one from *Thalaba* and one from *Kehama*† (one may also note 'the car is fled' at the end of the vision of Apollo in Keats's 'Sleep and Poetry'). It may be that Shelley also drew from Southey's poems two of the more substantial ideas which effect crucial stages in his narratives. When, in *The Curse of Kehama*, the wicked Rajah drinks the cup of immortality (XXIV, sections 14–18), he thinks that it is bringing him the moment of ultimate triumph; on the contrary – to the wicked, what it brings is an immortality of punishment, and this climactic reversal is instantaneous. In *Prometheus Unbound*, there is a

---

* Cf. also Keats's *Hyperion*, I. 176 ff:
His palace bright . . .
Glared a blood-red through all its thousand courts
Arches, and domes, and fiery galleries . . .
† Cf. 'The fated fire moved on', of *Thalaba*, II. 206; 'the magic car begins its course', IV. 591; 'The ponderous Car rolls on', *Curse of Kehama*, XIV. 66; 'The Car . . . Moved on', XXIV. 301–2.

moment when the tyrant Zeus thinks that his ultimate triumph has come; but it too proves, immediately, to be the very moment of his disaster. Again, in section XIV of *Kehama* there is a juggernaut procession which is intended to celebrate the universal triumph and rule of tyranny. But suddenly, a spirit of good appears, and everything is transformed. There is a clear similarity to another juggernaut procession, that which opens Shelley's *Mask of Anarchy*, and its equally sudden dissolution when the giant angel of good appears.

These points of detail have their interest for the historical continuities of the period and its poetry. By setting up a frame for *Alastor* and *Endymion*, they help one to see these poems as it were in relief. But Keats, if he took over something of Southey's quest-design, intended to give it more meaning than Southey himself ever did. Southey's protagonists pursue a quest, certainly; in each case, though, it is for a personal and private goal, the woman each is in love with. Endymion's Moon-goddess is more than herself. She is a symbol of what might be termed adequate poetic inspiration. The quest for her is the quest for an adequate sense of life and approach to it on the part of the poet.

To comprehend the structure of the seeming-structureless *Endymion*, one needs to recognize how the poem is organized into a quest, therefore; and also what sort of quest this is. Out of the shifting scenes of Book I, what emerges is that Endymion himself, after a kind of preparatory period of unconscious dedication as a 'marble man' who keeps a 'fixèd trance' (403–5), assumes a 'resolvèd course' (488) and has a 'voyage prepared' (772) – prepared, notice. By the end of the Book, he is engaged, 'patiently' (973) and in 'a calm round of hours' (983) on a 'pilgrimage' which has a very distinctive goal: it is a pilgrimage 'for the world's dusky brink' (977). In other words, it is some-how to take the protagonist on a journey of comprehension over the gamut of experience and to its limit. More than in such details as the 'little shallop' (423) which Peona uses to take Endymion to her bower, we see in these things the outlines of the quest-poem.

The quest-journey begins in earnest in Book II with Endym-ion pursuing a butterfly (61). It is an unexpected beginning to such a journey, though there will prove to be a point in this very detail. Yet the seriousness of the quest and the journey is made plain enough. Peona says to Endymion:

> . . . thou must wander far
> In other regions, past the scanty bar
> To mortal steps . . .   (II.123)

This is before his quest can be accomplished. The voice from the cavern tells the same tale:

> He ne'er is crowned   (II.211)
> With immortality who fears to follow
> Where airy voices lead . . .

Where the 'airy voices' lead, though, is into the 'vast antre' (230) or cavern of the interior of the earth.

This is no foray into the randomly fanciful. It proves to be the first phase of a journey which will take Endymion systematically through the whole of created Nature, the whole therefore of potential human experience. This is the structure of the journey, and it will take shape progressively throughout the rest of the poem.

Endymion now explores the 'dusky empire' (224) of the underworld. He manages to 'acquaint himself' with 'every mystery' there (270), and when at last he sits down to rest, has 'raught' (i.e., reached; cf. III.856) 'the goal of consciousness' (II.283). He meets the presiding deities of the 'dusky empire' – Venus, Adonis, and lastly the universal Mother-goddess Cybele (640), loses 'his way' (656), is helped back to it by an eagle, and at the end of Book II enters a further stage in the journey through all experience by passing (as we have seen) into the world of under the sea:

> The visions of the earth were gone and fled –   (II.1022)
> He saw the giant sea above his head.

'Far had he roam'd', we find early in Book III (119): what directs Endymion onward is the power of love, and we read (92):

> O love! How potent hast thou been to teach
> *Strange journeyings!*

The opening lines of Book III make clear why the journey in question has to be a strange one. Keats contrasts the false great ones of the earth and their tinsel and 'baaing vanities' (l.3), with the 'throned seats unscalable' (l.23) – unscalable save to those who by patience, dedication and supernatural help can:

> . . . make a ladder of the eternal wind (l.26)

and thereby ascend into the heavens. But for what purpose? Once again the link between a quest such as Endymion's and a meeting with reality and profound comprehension of it is made clear. The purpose of ascending into the heavens is indicated exactly:

> To watch the abysm-birth of elements . . . (l.28)

to see, that is, into the formative secrets of reality.

Most of Book III is taken up with the account of Glaucon, Scylla and Circe. This has directly to do with the over-riding purpose of the poem, but may be left aside for the moment. The structure of Endymion's quest as a progress through all reality is completed in Book IV. At the bidding of Mercury, two jet-black Plutonian steeds spring up out of the earth and complete Endymion's progress by transporting him and the Indian Maid into the upper air. Here, asleep on the sleeping horses' outstretched wings, Endymion in fact completes the exploration of reality by dreaming that he 'walks/ On heaven's pavement' itself (407); and it is now that the quest, identified for the reader once again as it is, seems to go beyond itself and reach its goal. Endymion sees Diana, the Moon-goddess not just the moon, as she 'rises crescented' (430): and the response is:

> . . . Good-bye earth, and sea, (IV.431)
> And air, and pains, and care, and suffering.
> Good-bye to all but love!

The arduous pilgrimage through the whole of reality is over, and its achievement and culmination, one supposes, is at hand.

It is not at hand. The dreamer awakens even as he springs towards the Moon-goddess. The dream somehow re-assembles within waking consciousness, but once more the essential part of it slips from the seeker's grasp.

> . . . Is there nought for me,   (460)
> Upon the bourne of bliss, but misery?

When the moon rises in reality (as contrasted with the
appearance of the Moon-goddess in the dream), there is a
curious sequence of events in the poem: the reader is perhaps
beginning to see where it will lead. At first the moon, which

> put forth a little diamond peak,   (497)
> No bigger than an unobserved star

is described, exactly and vividly, as it might be seen in fact:
when, for example, the tip of the new moon's crescent appears
from behind a mountain on a particularly clear night. Im-
mediately, though, the physical object is transmuted into the
goddess: she is pausing in her ascent to tie her sandals, is
bowing her 'timid head' (503). At the same time as the physical
moon is thus being transmuted into a woman, the Indian Maid
who is journeying with Endymion is evanescing, is fading away
in the 'cold moonshine' (508). In a moment, Endymion is
alone.

Endymion recovers the Indian Maid, however, after his soul
(though not his body) has sojourned in the 'Cave of Quietude'.
It is a strange place to form part of a pilgrimage, almost a
denial of the very idea of pilgrimage:

> . . . Enter none   (531)
> Who strive therefore: on the sudden it is won.
> Just when the sufferer begins to burn,
> Then it is free to him . . .

If Endymion had not been overcome with the quietude and
torpor of the Cave, we are told that he would have heard the
'skyey mask' singing a prothalamium for the Moon-goddess's
marriage (563–611). But the outcome is very different. The
supernatural horse lands him on earth again, he is re-united
with the Indian Maid, and he renounces the moon-quest.

> . . . I have clung   (636)
> To nothing, loved a nothing, nothing seen
> Or felt but a great dream! Oh, I have been
> Presumptuous against love . . .

>   . . . against the tie
> Of mortals each to each . . .
>   . . . thou redeemèd hast   (649)
> My life from too thin breathing. Gone and past
> Are cloudy phantasms. *Caverns* lone, farewell,
> And *air* of visions, and the monstrous swell
> Of visionary *seas!*

The panoramic pilgrimage through earth, air and sea – the text is quite specific, if we will let it give us its message – and its celestial culmination, are renounced for a substantial reason of the poet's own:

> Enskied ere this but truly that I deem   (772)
> *Truth* the best music in a first-born song.

Yet if Endymion cannot truthfully be 'enskied', he also cannot be

>   . . . caught   (760)
> In trammels of perverse deliciousness . . .

– caught, that is, in the sensuous pleasures of wedlock with a partner wholly of the earth. This is as impossible a solution for him as the one he has ceremonially rejected. It would bring, as the Indian Maid hints in line 754, only 'gorgon wrath'. There is some kind of significant *impasse*, both sides of which Keats is trying to develop throughout this long section of the poem.

Inconspicuously, the Indian Maid feels pleasure as she sees him nonplussed by his predicament. Speaking in his own voice, the poet-narrator says:

>   . . . Oh, treachery!   (797)
> Why does his lady smile, pleasing her eye
> With all his sorrowing? He sees her not.

But 'It is no treachery' (804). She perceives, joyfully, that he is coming to realize how the earthly solution is no better than the 'enskied' one. Endymion comes to sense that the quest which he began with the chase of a butterfly (II.61: see p. 106 above) has in the last analysis been no better than the wanderings of a butterfly:

Why, *I have been a butterfly*, a lord   (937)
Of flowers, garlands, love-knots, silly posies,
Groves, meadows, melodies, and arbour roses.
My kingdom's at its death, and just it is
That I should die with it.

Such existence has no meaning beyond summer transience.

The complementary movement sets in for the last time.
Endymion's 'soul was changed', as we read in the draft version
of the poem (Allott, 282n.); and as he recollects that he has not
been 'king of the butterflies' (952) only, but:

                    . . . I did wed   (957)
Myself to things of light from infancy . . .

His mood is transformed once more:

                    . . . he inwardly began   (961)
On things for which no wording can be found,
Deeper and deeper sinking . . .

This meditative hour is what discovers the mystery and the
secret. When his sister returns and asks him what his dying
wish may be, he says:

                    . . . Sister, I would *have command*,   (975)
If it were heaven's will, *on our sad fate* . . .

'At which', the poem says, with point, the Indian Maid fills
with elation and is apotheosized into the Moon-goddess herself.

Now, at last, the story of Glaucon may be resumed from
Book III. Here are the culminating words in Glaucon's spell:

                    If he utterly   (III.696)
Scans all the depths of magic and expounds
The meanings of all motions, shapes and sounds,
If he *explores* all forms and substances
Straight homeward to their symbol-essences,
He shall not die . . .
A youth, by heavenly power loved and led,   (706)
Shall stand before him, whom he shall direct
How to consummate all. The youth elect
Must do the thing, or both will be destroyed.

Just so, Endymion himself, and the Indian Maid, will be destroyed at the end of the poem if he does not 'do the thing' which consummates all. What 'thing' is this? It is to recognize that man's 'fate' is not butterfly-like but tragic. The right response is neither sensuous evasion nor evasion by seeking to be 'enskied'. It lies in comprehension, sad but wise acceptance, mastery.

Endymion with his quest, Glaucon with the unending exploration and scanning he must engage in if he is not to perish – there is a subtle equipoise in structure. How ought the reader to see Endymion, Phoebe and the Indian Maid on the one hand, and Glaucon, Circe and Scylla the nymph on the other? One certainly cannot identify Circe and the Indian Maid as both representing the attraction of the sensual powers of life. The Indian Maid is far from doing so in any case, and one is human and moral while the other is semi-divine. Circe and Diana of course cannot be assimilated, straightforwardly, because Diana is a goddess and Circe (see III.500 and 555) is a witch. Yet: there are the two seekers, Endymion and Glaucon; the Indian Maid and Scylla, both humble and lowly consorts; and Diana and Circe, who are more than human and whose pursuit is profound illusion. That there is some implication in this direction, as well as in the contrary one, cannot be missed. At the end of Glaucon's quest and tribulations, there comes a re-generation into life. Glaucon is rejuvenated, Scylla is restored to life (III.771–82). At the end of Endymion's quest, which is at the end of the poem, there is a similar movement as it were at a higher level. Endymion's death is averted, and the Indian Maid is raised from the human to what is more than human.

That Keats intended the transformation to be seen as an apotheosis is clear at once, if the passage is set side by side with the later apotheosis at the end of *Hyperion*, when Apollo assumes the role of Sun-god. First *Endymion*:

> . . . as she spake, into her face there came (IV.982)
> Light, as reflected from a silver flame:
> Her long black hair swell'd ampler, in display
> Full golden; in her eyes a brighter day
> Dawn'd . . .

Apollo's transformation is more masculine, and of course more
solar in quality. But in *Hyperion* the likeness is plain:

> Soon wild commotions shook him, and made flush (III.124)
> All the immortal fairness of his limbs –
> Most like the struggle at the gate of death;
> Or liker still to one who should take leave
> Of pale immortal death, and with a pang
> As hot as death's is chill, with fierce convulse
> Die into life. So young Apollo anguish'd:
> His very hair, his golden tresses famed,
> Kept undulation round his eager neck . . .
>   . . . at length
> Apollo shriek'd; – and lo! from all his limbs
> Celestial Glory dawn'd: he was a god!

Keats never quite finished the passage. 'Phoebus . . . he was the
God', '[Celestial] Glory dawn'd: he was a god!', and 'Celestial
. . . and godlike', were attempts in the manuscripts. But there
is no doubt, surely, that this was to be the moment at which
Apollo was intended to replace Hyperion and become the god
of the sun.

Keats was thus right to call *Endymion* 'a regular stepping of
the Imagination towards a Truth' (letter to Taylor, 30 January
1818: M. Buxton Forman, 90); and the quest which made up
that regular stepping turns out to be both a quest and an
Odyssey. It is an Odyssey, because what begins as a 'high
employ' seeking through the whole of reality for possession of
that more-than-human which lies beyond the frontier of
experience, ends as renunciation of such grandiosity and an
opting for the lowly and the everyday. Eternity resides in the
humble Indian Maid much as Blake saw it in the grain of sand
('Auguries of Innocence': Keynes, 431). In this sense, the goal
of supreme endeavour lies, as it did for Wordsworth in *The
Prelude*, at home.

At the same time, one may see that the quest-poem, for
Keats as for Wordsworth, is in its own way a regeneration-
poem. The journey back through the total range of experience
towards home again, is a journey towards the finding and
restoration of the self. The 'drear . . . delaying' (*Endymion*,

IV.988–9) of the fond quest is finally resolved for Endymion in an 'unlook'd for change' in which he is 'spiritualiz'd' (992–3). The journey of the whole poem through experience, the climax at the end, and the complex parallel-in-difference of the Glaucon story in Book III, all fall into place as parts of what in the end must be seen as a comprehensive order in the poem, an order, it may be added, profoundly in accord with the deepest attitudes in the poetry of its time.

Yet if this is so, does a further question not remain? This further question is the question: why is the design so hard of access? – why does the poem at first or second reading leave so strong an impression of almost inextricable divagation and chaos?

Here, as elsewhere in his work, Keats shows that he yearned to be a lofty and ambitious poet of the human destiny in a profound sense; whereas his spontaneous inclinations and strongest talents were for something less lofty and more sensuous. He understood something of what it meant to be lowly wise; but he was not lowly wise enough. The Dantesque but, it must be admitted, always in his case a trifle laboured grandeurs of the scene in *The Fall of Hyperion* between Moneta and the poet ('. . . purge off, Benign, if so it please thee, my mind's film': 145–6) were what drew him, more than what he was to achieve in the ode 'To Autumn'.

One finds this sad if noble movement of his mind reflected in *Endymion*, sharply and unexpectedly, in one particular respect. The fact is, that if one begins to note the places in *Endymion* where the writing is weakest, they seem surprisingly often to be places where what is prominent in the text is some step forward in the action, the movement of events, which constitutes Endymion's quest and journey; while if one begins to notice where the writing is at its strongest, that seems surprisingly often to be where quest and journey have been, for a moment, suspended. This is not a contrast simply between description of what Endymion sees as against description of what he does; though that is a perhaps not wholly unrelated matter. But what is at issue for the moment is the more precise contrast between those events which promote, and those which deliberately suspend, the journey itself.

Here there cannot but be some uncertainty. It is not always a simple thing to say whether such-and-such particular lines carry forward the quest, or suspend it. This part of the discussion must also be illustrative, and suggestive, not a comprehensive survey and a statistical result. Very early in *Endymion*, in the 'Hymn to Pan', we already find the god spoken of as the

> Dread opener of the mysterious doors   (I.288)
> Leading to universal knowledge . . .

When the 'little shallop' begins to journey with Endymion and Peona, we read:

> And soon it lightly dipped and rose, and sank,   (425)
> And dipped again, with the young couple's weight –
> Peona guiding, through the water straight,
> Towards a bowery island opposite . . .

Those lines have surprisingly little to say about either the boat's individual, or its recurrent movements. It dips 'lightly', and its recurrent movement is merely to rise and fall. 'Young couple', 'weight', 'opposite' and even 'bowery' are all much the same in quality. Suddenly, the treatment has become generic, even diagrammatic. Keats's usual sense that everything 'hath a purpose and its eyes are bright with it' (Forman, 316:March 1819) has momentarily evanesced.

In contrast to this may be set a passage where, through metaphor, Keats touches on a sea-idea to explain not progress, but *a pause in the journey* so as to contemplate the scene. The plants Endymion sees in Book II when he halts his journey were like

> . . . when heaved anew   (II.347)
> Old ocean rolls a lengthened wave to the shore,
> Down whose green back the short-liv'd foam, all hoar,
> Bursts gradual, with a wayward indolence.

The interest of these celebrated lines far exceeds the fulness and aptness of the descriptive words. Their most rewarding feature is how that luxuriant fullness is created by the necessity that the reader recurrently feels his mind curve back on its tracks in order to seize the exact sense of the words. The wave is 'lengthened' only because it comes from a 'heave', an upward movement of the sea: otherwise 'lengthened' could mean only something different or nothing at all. 'Down its . . . back' makes sense only because the wave is lengthened. 'Short-liv'd' explains itself as one's attention reverts to the word 'anew', two lines before, and one remembers that the next wave will soon obliterate this one (though essentially the pattern is unchanging). The 'burst' can be 'gradual' precisely because it takes place down the 'lengthen'd' back of the wave, and the 'indolence' can be wayward because the burst is gradual. All in all, the convolutions implicit here in the reading process do not merely embody the local meaning: they create and compel the whole sense of arrest, of halted movement, which is the more than local meaning, because it is the meaning called out by the developing structure of the poem itself as it particularly transpires at this point.

Perhaps a few examples of what happens when *Endymion* is conspicuously moving forward will be enough to settle the point. Here are some passages where the 'quest' goes forward. To me, their shortcomings as verse are inescapable:

> . . . A golden butterfly, upon whose wings   (II.61)
> There must be surely charactered strange things,
> For with wide eye he wonders, and smiles oft.

> Lightly this little herald flew aloft,
> Followed by glad Endymion's claspèd hands:
> Onward it flies. From languor's sullen bands
> His limbs are loos'd, and eager, on he hies
> Dazzled to trace it in the sunny skies.
> It seemed he flew, the way so easy was . . .

> Free from the smallest pebble-bead of doubt   (II.149)
> That he will seize on trickling honey-combs –
> Alas, he finds them dry; and then he foams,
> And onward to another city speeds.
> But this is human life . . .

>   . . . by all the stars   (II.184)
> That tend thy bidding, I do think the bars

That kept my spirit in are burst – that I
Am sailing with thee through the dizzy sky!
How beautiful thou art! The world how deep!

> . . . lo! the wreathed green   (II.516)
> Disparted, and far upward could be seen
> Blue heaven, and a silver car, air-borne,
> Whose silent wheels, fresh wet from clouds of morn,
> Spun off a drizzling dew, which falling chill
> On soft Adonis' shoulders made him still
> Nestle and turn uneasily about . . .

> there crossed   (II.657)
> Towards him a large eagle, 'twixt whose wings,
> Without one impious word, himself he flings,
> Committed to the darkness and the gloom,
> Down, down, uncertain to what pleasant doom.
> Swift as a fathoming plummet down he fell
> Through unknown things . . .

The vague and diagrammatic quality of these lines ('large';
'without . . . one . . . word'; 'flings'; 'uncertain'; 'unknown')
surely needs no proving; but all the same, Keats's faltering
touch here shows up particularly clearly if the lines are set
against two passages in the *Divine Comedy* which may well have
been (in translation) at the back of his mind. First, the eagle
which transports Dante within his dream on the first night in
Purgatory:

> Poi mi parea che, poi rotata un poco,   (IX.28)
> Terribil come fulgor discendesse,
> e mi rapisse suso infino al foco.

Cary's translation (which is what Keats would have known at
this stage) lost the hovering 'poi . . . poi', but otherwise
retained a great deal of the sense of double movement and
sudden snatch in the original:

> Therwith, it seem'd   (25)
> A little wheeling in his aëry tour,
> Terrible as the lightning rush'd he down,
> And snatch'd me upward even to the fire.

The other passage is in *Inferno* XVII, where Dante embarks on the back of the monster Geryon that is to take him down to the Eighth Circle.

> Io m'assettai in su quelle spallacce: (91)
>   si volli dir, ma la voce non venne
>   com'io credetti: 'Fa che tu m'abbracce'.
> Ma esso, che altra volta mi sovenne
>   ad altro forse, tosto ch'io montai
>   con le braccia m'avvinse e mi sostenne . . .

Cary rendered this:

> I settled me upon those shoulders huge,   (87)
> And would have said, but that the words to aid
> My purpose came not, 'Look thou clasp me firm!'
>   But he whose succour then not first I prov'd,
> Soon as I mounted, in his arms aloft,
> Embracing, held me up . . .

Perhaps Dante's involuntary silence here is the background to Keats's 'without one impious word' in the *Endymion* passage. But if so, how great is the loss! Of Dante's so characteristic tautening and tensening of the sequence of event (here, for example, Dante does not get, tamely, what he asks for, he finds that he has got what he wanted but was powerless to ask for), nothing is left save a gesture of silence and the quite gratuitous idea of impiety. Why, after all, should Endymion have uttered an impious word? Dante's marvellous insight into the powers of dialogue and of silence seem in fact to be closed to Keats both here and henceforth.

The association in *Endymion* between sudden loss of detail and resumption of the onward movement of the poem is really quite striking. In the passages which follow, the italics are of course mine:

>   out he strayed   (II.873)
> Half seeing visions that *might have* dismay'd
> Alecto's serpents . . .

> He turned – there was a whelming sound.
>   He stepped –   (II.1018)
> There was a cooller light; and so he kept

Towards it by a sandy path, and lo!
More suddenly than doth a moment go,
The visions of the earth were gone and fled –

This, from the standpoint simply of the narrative, is perhaps the most striking step in the quest: Endymion's journey takes him below the waves. When Glaucon recounts his life, we find:

at once I visited   (III.391)
The ceaseless wonders of the ocean-bed.
No need to tell thee of them, for I see
That thou hast been a witness – it must be . . .

So from the turf outsprang two steeds jet-black,   (IV.343)
Each with large dark blue wings upon his back.
The youth of Caria plac'd the lovely dame
On one, and felt himself in spleen to tame
The other's fierceness . . .

. . . they   (IV.486)
Thus sprang direct towards the Galaxy.
Nor did speed hinder converse *soft and strange* –

Endymion rejoins the Indian Maid back on earth once more; again, it is a key movement in the whole narrative:

Ah, me!   (IV.622)
It is thy voice – divinest! Where? Who, who
Left thee so quiet on this bed of dew?

It is hardly too much to say that at such points the poem regularly inclines to the inarticulate. Such a criticism is no glancing blow. For Keats at this stage, the whole activity of the pilgrim journey was a 'call' but not a vocation. It seems to have been uncongenial to him.

In the moments when the pilgrim journey is suspended one sometimes finds a sudden access of exactitude, and a sudden springing to life of the rhythm. The chorus begins its song in Book I while

. . . gummy frankincense was sparkling bright
(I.229)
'Neath smothering parsley, and a hazy light
Spread greyly eastward . . .

Peona watches over the sleeping Endymion:

> . . . as a willow keeps　　　　　　　　　　(446)
> A patient watch over the stream that creeps
> Windingly by it, so the quiet maid
> Held her in peace: so that a whispering blade
> Of grass, a wailful gnat, a bee bustling
> Down in the blue-bells or a wren light rustling
> Among sere leaves and twigs, might all be heard.

In Book II Endymion, benighted in the labyrinth of under-world caverns, calls upon Diana to deliver him. While he asks to be transported elsewhere, Keats is at his worst:

> If in soft slumber thou dost hear my voice,　　(II.329)
> O think how I should love a bed of flowers! –
> Young goddess! let me see my native bowers!
> Deliver me from this rapacious deep!'
>
> Thus ending loudly, as he would o'erleap
> His destiny, alert he stood . . .

Then the poem turns from the histrionics of o'erleaping destiny to what Keats is masterly at, in the astonishing lines:

> when　　　　　　　　　　　　　(II.334)
> Obstinate silence came heavily again,
> Feeling about for its old couch of space
> And airy cradle . . .

Later in Book II, after proceeding with 'slow, languid paces' (872), Endymion sits down beside a vast grotto filled with

> . . . crimson mouthèd shells with stubborn curls,　(880)
> Of every shape and size, even to the bulk
> In which whales arbour close, to brood and sulk
> Against an endless storm.

This image may have something of the grotesque about it; but precisely in saying so, one touches on an open, many-sided strength in the lines which was sadly to seek when Adonis got splashed with dew by chariot wheels, or Endymion chased the butterfly (pointed as that was in itself), sailed through the dizzy sky, placed the lovely dame on the steed's back, thought the world was deep, or otherwise found himself left a trifle under-insured against the ridiculous.

Perhaps, therefore, *Endymion* has a certain special interest, one which comes to it even through its defect. Keats was justified in referring to it as 'a regular stepping of the Imagination after Truth'. It shows a poet shaping his work in accordance with one of the major and formative poetic conceptions of the time. It recounts the quest of the creative spirit, throughout the whole range of experience, so as to identify with the authentic source of poetic insight and creation. Then, however, its resolution takes the form of a discovery that the true poetic quest can only be a certain kind of Odyssey. Insight and creativity reside within the commonplace. They become manifest when questing is abandoned. Keats wished to use the quest-poem and the quest-structure for something that went beyond itself. One cannot say, 'contrary to itself', because if a quest turns out to be an Odyssey, that is both dramatic and illuminative. Yet at the same time, Keats's ulterior design to reject the quest-pattern, or perhaps one should say to transcend it, cannot be separated from the recurrent tendency in the poem for him to be at his worst when the quest is to the fore, and his best when it is suspended. The sureness or unsureness of touch in the most local grain of the poem seems at one with the contrast between its ostensible design and its ultimate statement.

IV

Shelley's *Alastor* is a baffling poem of extraordinary interest. Many will begin by doubting this suggestion, but it is to be hoped that even a brief discussion may convince them.

That *Alastor* is a poem constructed on the pattern of the quest does not need arguing. It is the tale of a Solitary and Poet who

> left (75)
> His cold fireside and alienated home
> To *seek strange truths* in undiscovered lands.

In quest of them, he pursued 'Nature's most secret steps' (81) as closely as if he were Nature's shadow, and wandered 'obedient to high thoughts' (107). His route is an interesting and perhaps significant one. Briefly, it is a rough approximation to the route taken by Alexander the Great in his conquest of the Middle East and the Orient, save that it runs in the reverse, counterclockwise direction: after Greece, the Levant and Egypt, it runs through Arabia and southern Iran (Carmania), then into India and the 'Vale of Kashmir' (Alexander himself fell short, though only by a little, of Kashmir). It is in the Vale of Kashmir that the Poet has a crucial experience, in a dream which appears to transform his journey from a quest for something, into a retreat ('. . . He *fled.*' 237). To begin with, this flight takes him along something like Alexander's outward, northern route; save that instead of returning home to Europe via Hyrcania and the South Caspian shore, the Poet follows a route across the River Oxus, much like that which Alexander took on his excursus into Sogdiana (though more to the west than that), until it reaches the marshland of Chorasmia (272) on the eastern shore of the Caspian. Alexander's excursus towards the central Asiatic steppes came to nothing. He retreated the way he had come. The protagonist of *Alastor* does not return from Chorasmia. There is a sense in the poem that he crosses the Caspian in his little half-ruined boat, and that his journey ends amidst the mountains and forests of Caucasia. After the 'lone Chorasmian shore', however, the geography of the poem moves increasingly outside the realm of what is natural and can be located.

A first reading makes it plain enough that the quest described is much like that in *Endymion* for 'universal knowledge' and 'command . . . of our sad fate'. In the introductory passage the writer of the poem says in his own voice (as distinct from that of the protagonist, the Poet whom the poem depicts) that he has put 'obstinate questionings' to Mother Nature herself in the hope that a messenger from her would

> render up *the tale* (28)
> *Of what we are.*

The wandering Poet himself travels 'obedient to high thoughts' (107), and in his sleep has a vision of a 'veiled maid' who speaks to him of 'knowledge and truth and virtue', as well as of liberty and of poetry itself. The journey continues with the traveller 'Following his eager soul' (311), and

> Obedient to the light   (492)
> That shone within his soul . . .

No one can mistake or dispute the sense of dedication to – in some sense – a quest in respect of some high purpose, which is ordained (albeit self-ordained) not selected as a matter of free choice and gratification.

The first paragraph of Shelley's Preface confirms all this, at the same time as it points out that the vision of the 'veiled maid' from one point of view marks a further stage, and also a most significant transmutation, in the object and meaning of the quest. The protagonist Poet, it states, is 'led forth', and 'drinks deep of the fountains of knowledge'. His concern is 'contemplation of the universe'. The veiled maid has a mind filled with the same concerns as the Poet. She too cares for knowledge and truth, liberty and poetry. For the Poet, however, she represents more than these things in the abstract. She is their human embodiment in 'an intelligence similar to himself', and so she seems to afford him the opportunity for 'intercourse' at every human level, 'the intellectual faculties, the imagination' and also 'the functions of sense'. The second part of the Poet's journey, after the visionary dream, therefore represents a quest for something which brings the object of the first part to a higher power of itself: the 'obstinate questionings' and high thoughts now prove to belong to human communion and contact in the richest, fullest sense. On this view the poem might be said to be a tragic poem recording the failure of a quest in search of a single, comprehensive, consistent idea.

Yet there is a dimension in the poem quite alien to all this. Perhaps the simplest way to see how that is so, is to consider the passage where, after the vision, the wandering Poet seems for some reason to make only fleeting and distracted contact with the cottagers, the 'mountaineer', the children with their mothers, and the 'youthful maidens' who apparently comprehend, at least in part, what he stands in need of, and who offer it him by calling him friend and brother (254–71). Here the Poet seems to be less one who is in search of adequate human contact, than one debarred, one who cannot enter into it when it lies before him.

Closer acquaintance with the poem reveals much more of a similar kind. Before the visionary dream the poet travels in 'joy and exultation' (144), his hand is 'innocuous' (101) and his looks 'gentle' (101–2). The dream once over, his hand is 'listless' (250) and his whole body 'wasted' (268). Why is this? The fact is, that the 'spirit of sweet human love' who sent him the dream (203) did so in a spirit far from that of sweetness and love. From this point of view, she is no embodiment of the idea of fullest human communion at all. Rather, she is a siren-figure, a 'fair fiend' (297), like a poisonous 'serpent' (228), a retributive and destroying *ignis fatuus* sent to the Poet a little in the spirit which Euripides depicts as that of Aphrodite towards Hippolytus. The Poet has given no thought to the 'Arab maiden' (129–39) who ministered to his needs, and the outraged spirit of love has sent a malignant though beautiful vision in order to destroy him. Hence the 'insatiate hope' (221) that felt like despair, the 'two eyes' (489) that enigmatically 'seemed with their serene and azure smiles' to beckon the Poet onward, and the 'one voice' – a disembodied voice – which led the Poet on into the place of his death, and is apparently the voice of the 'veiled maid'. This would appear to be correct not only from the general movement of the narrative but also from some of the details. The 'loveliest among human forms' is confirmed as the Poet by the reference to the 'dark and drooping eyes' (601), which recall the 'dark eyes' of the Poet in line 254. One detail which was perhaps unconscious on Shelley's part seems to confirm the general suggestion of the narrative that the 'voice' is that of the vision. The voice that '. . . hither came, floating *among the winds*' seems a conception essentially similar to what the veiled maid is like, in the vision itself, when she springs up and the Poet sees

> Her glowing limbs beneath the sinuous veil (176)
> Of *woven wind* . . .

There is a clear continuity here of the idea the Poet is working with, though it is also true that the idea is generally and characteristically Shelleyan.

So there seem to be two quite distinct shaping conceptions in the poem. In the first place, the Poet embarks on a 'high' and praiseworthy quest for ultimate truths, until (as the Preface says) there comes a time when these 'cease to suffice' him, and he extends the goal of his search. He now goes in quest of an equal (and opposite) humanity in whom those ultimates shall be embodied, and the poem ends sorrowfully since the search is fruitless. In the second place, however, the Poet embarks on a quest characterized by what the Preface, in its second paragraph, refers to as 'self-centred seclusion'; spurning the spirit of human love, and so provoking the spirit to dispatch a punitive siren-figure that lures him to his doom.

These two interpretations are not present in the poem as alternatives between which the reader is to make a simple choice. Nor are they present as distinct but reconcilable 'levels of meaning', either or both of which he may enjoy, depending on how comprehensively he reads. They are present as fluidly inter-penetrating, within a work in which the writer is exploring his own thoughts as he writes and has not fully determined them. That this is so is surely confirmed by how Shelley set the first and second paragraphs of his Preface baldly side by side, although they offer two quite different accounts of the poem. Given that fluid inter-penetration, therefore, it is reasonable to see the poem as not merely juxtaposing those two formative ideas, but as genuinely inter-relating and permuting them: and this means, as offering in all *four* possibilities of meaning.

On this basis, the narrative would be one which depicts, first, how the quest for ultimates will extend into that for humanity (even though this latter is unsuccessful); second, how 'self-centred seclusion' provokes self-destructive retribution; then, third, how self-centred seclusion will prove inadequate and will lead to a search for what is more fully human than that, something by way of 'intercourse' in every sense. Finally, something more disturbing: the fact that that third possibility of meaning integrates so easily and completely with the first and second surely confirms the justice of contemplating the poem in this way, and then also of bringing forward the fourth and last combination of ideas. But this fourth combination is a surprising one. The reader may have identified it already, as it lies implicit in what has been said. It is nothing less than that the quest for ultimate truths, gazing into 'the thrilling secrets of the birth of time', wandering 'obedient to high thoughts' and so on, will itself provoke a retributive self-destruction, provoke 'the furies of an irresistible passion pursuing . . . to speedy ruin'.

It is at this point that what one is a little inclined to see as the secret of *Alastor* stands revealed. The poem is obscure and confused, at a certain level anyhow, because Shelley is releasing in it something that he has glimpsed, but is far from believing and adopting. Within and through its lines, and contrary no doubt to the writer's conscious convictions, is expressed the price which is to be paid in human and social terms for the Romantic ideal of profound and masterful insight into 'the tale / Of what we are'. The risk is, that this price is likely to be a terrible but self-engendered self-destructiveness: we see that it is self-engendered when (489 ff.) the two 'starry eyes' that lure the Poet on to destruction 'hung in the gloom *of thought*'. Paraphrasing this at the opening of the next paragraph, Shelley writes that the protagonist now pursued his quest

> Obedient to the light (492)
> That shone *within his soul* . . .

The *ignis fatuus* is internalized; just as it was an internalized prohibition of destructive self-isolation that had earlier on prevented the Poet from decking himself with the flowers that surrounded him:

> . . . on his heart its solitude returned (414)
> And he forbore.

The whole idea of an individual re-exploration of the human condition, an ultimate re-opening of the springs of truth by the superb individualized effort and vatic striving of the seer-Poet, was fraught with disastrous risk of self-isolation, self-incarceration – and self-immolation. Shelley must often have sensed this, though he never accepted it and acted on it. Once penetrated, the rich tangle of *Alastor* gives it reverberating expression. The poem is ostensibly a quest: inwardly it calls all such ideas deeply into question. If I did not wish to retain the term 'anti-quest' for a poem of another kind, I should use it here.

What has just been said stands confirmed, if one takes note of a certain regularity of sequence in the poem. Over and over, there comes some phrase which emphasizes the continuance of the quest. These signs of continuance of course fit into a general descriptive texture which runs through the poem. But there is an implicitly tell-tale feature as there was with Keats's poem. If one traces the substance, and also (often enough) the poetic quality, of what follows *immediately after* such phrases about continuance, the result is significant, and the pattern is a rather too regular one to be thought of as accident.

This series of linkages begins at line 75:

> When early youth had past, he left
> His cold fireside and alienated home
> To seek strange truths in undiscovered lands.

So far, the reader is doubtless prepared to find that the 'undiscovered lands' may be of any kind whatsoever. In fact, they are of a distinctive kind.

> Nature's most secret steps (81)
> He like her shadow has pursued, *where'er*
> *The red volcano overcanopies*
> *Its fields of snow* and pinnacles of ice
> With burning smoke, or where *bitumen lakes*
> *On black bare pointed islets ever beat*
> With sluggish surge.

The next reference to the journey of the protagonist comes at line 106:

> His wandering step
>   . . . has visited
> The awful ruins of the days of old:

Part of what is to be seen in the 'awful ruins' seems to be continuous with that landscape of fire and ice in the lines quoted just now:

> wild images (117)
> Of more than man, where marble *daemons* watch
> The Zodiac's brazen mystery, and *dead men*
> Hang their mute thoughts on the mute walls around . . .

The journey is resumed in line 140:

> The poet wandering on, through Arabie
> And Persia, and the wild Carmanian *waste*,
> And o'er the aërial mountains which pour down
> Indus and Oxus from their icy caves . . .

Only to a limited extent, one inclines to think, could the Poet have pursued his course through such landscapes in the spirit that the next line says he enjoys: 'In joy and exultation'. The succeeding phase of the poem is the vision of the 'veiled maid'. Then:

> Roused by the shock he started from his trance – (192)
> The cold white light of morning, the blue moon
> Low in the west, the clear and garish hills,
> The distinct valley and the vacant woods,
> Spread round him . . .

It is a curious passage, and its stark assemblage of a few clear-cut items into a juxtaposition which is also a remoteness seems more Surrealist than anything else. Perhaps the essential point is that 'garish' hills and 'vacant' woods (vacant of what? of life?) do not make up a natural landscape: though they might, a nightmare one.

The Poet then 'eagerly pursues' (205) the vision – but to no avail. The text asks whether it is the 'dark *gate of death*' (211) that leads to the state of sleep in which the vision was first seen. Before long, a remarkable transition has occurred. Pursuit of the vision seems more like flight than pursuit. Yet, once again, there is something noteworthy about the country it passes through. First we have:

> He fled. Red morning dawned upon his flight . . . (237)

The next time the journey is stressed comes when the Poet finds the Dantesque 'shallop' (299) and

A restless impulse urged him to embark . . .   (304)

It proves to be with something very distinctive in mind:

> . . . embark
> And *meet lone Death* on the drear ocean's waste;
> For well he knew that mighty Shadow loves
> The slimy caverns of the populous deep.

Soon the shallop passes through the great forest:

> One vast mass   (421)
> Of mingling shade, whose brown magnificence
> A narrow vale embosoms . . .

The Poet seeks

> in Nature's dearest haunt, some bank,   (429)
> Her cradle, and his sepulchre.

– and he sees that besides cedars, ash and acacia, there is other and less attractive vegetation in the forest:

> Like restless *serpents*, clothed   (438)
> In rainbow and in *fire*, the parasites,
> Starred with ten thousand blossoms, flow around
> The grey trunks . . .

There is no need to point out either the source, or the trend, of all this. The embosoming vale of line 422 is an echo of how Milton's fallen angels in *Paradise Lost* are like

> . . . Autumnal Leaves that strow the Brooks (I.302)
> In *Vallombrosa*, where th'*Etrurian* shades
> High overarch't imbowr . . .

What follows that is an echo of Milton's account of Chaos:

> The Womb of nature and perhaps her Grave . . .   (II.911)

Finally, the parasite-plants like serpents recall Satan as snake in *Paradise Lost* Book IX (Milton also, in IX.634, likens the serpent, as Shelley implicitly does the 'veiled maid', to the *ignis fatuus* by now familiar to us). The point may impair Shelley's originality, but it makes clear the direction his poem is taking all the time. That direction shows once more when the Poet addresses the stream whose course he is following:

> O stream! (502)
> Whose source is inaccessibly profound,
> Whither do thy mysterious waters tend?
> Thou imagest my life . . .

The stream is from 'depth', presumably, to depth: and that is where the journey is to take the Poet. Once again, his 'rapid steps' (522) take him where:

> tall spires of windlestrae (528)
> Threw their thin shadows down the rugged slope . . .

which could well be an unconscious re-working of Milton's account of the serpent:

> . . . his circling Spires, that on the grass (IX.502)
> Floted redundant.

('windlestrae', windlestraw, is dried grass). The Poet 'still pursued' his journey (539), until at last the stream leads him into what might perhaps be called the terminal landscape of the quest. What is that terminal landscape like? –

> Lo! where the pass expands (550)
> Its *stony jaws* . . .
> . . . wide expand
> Beneath the wan stars and descending moon
> Islanded seas, blue mountains, mighty streams,
> Dim tracts and vast, robed in the *lustrous gloom*
> Of leaden-coloured even, and *fiery* hills
> Mingling their flames with twilight, on the verge
> Of the remote horizon.

There is now a steady tendency and direction in the poem. The islands and mountains of this last landscape mutate into a country of volcanoes and darkness, just of a piece with the other landscapes of ice-mountains and mysterious rivers, smoke and bitumen lakes, daemons and the spirits of the dead. The sequence is unmistakable. The one landscape different from the others (l. 192 above) is a harsh, non-natural, Surrealist picture of pro-Hades, ante-Hades rather than Hades itself. For otherwise, the regular, perhaps the compulsively regular, sequel in Shelley's mind to the thought of pursuing his Poet's knowledge-quest to its end is to penetrate to a foretaste, or indeed to the reality, of Hell. The poem works out the idea of a Faustian, a Promethean quest, but what it says all the time at its heart is, after all, what Marlowe said: that that quest is a diabolic one.

VI

The Quest Repudiated

I *Childe Harold's Pilgrimage* and *Don Juan*
It is not easy to believe that when Byron wrote *Childe Harold's Pilgrimage* he had a clear idea of what he was doing. The last word of the title of the poem is a reminder of the works which were discussed in the previous chapter, and there is a good deal in the poem to make one think this work may be another quest-poem. We find in Canto I, stanza 28, a reference to the 'goal' where the pilgrim is to rest from his 'pilgrimage'. In I.93, Childe Harold is 'doom'd' (i.e. ordained, fated) to continue his 'pilgrimage' in 'other lands'. In the lyric 'To Inez' which follows stanza 84 of Canto I, the poem asks how any 'Exile' can 'flee . . . from himself' when 'pursued' by the demon thought. All these remarks suggest that the idea of the poem is to portray a protagonist engaged in the sort of ordained, stressful, teleological quest already traced elsewhere. Canto I says (stanza 27) that the Childe, in his journeying, came under the guidance of Reason and learnt to meditate and to moralize; and also speaks (I.23) of how 'fresh lessons to the thinking bosom' are provided by some of the sights that Childe Harold was able to observe. This also appears to follow the by now familiar pattern.

Yet it is not possible, for all these passages, to see *Childe Harold* as a quest-poem like the other ones. True enough, it displays familiarity with the idea of the quest-poem as an ordained ('doom'd') pilgrimage with a goal consisting in some form of enlightenment. Periodically, it makes a gesture in the direction of that kind of poem. This is not enough, though, to determine the *genre* of the poem or even its intended *genre*; and in fact *Childe Harold* can hardly be seen at all as a poem written with any one clear intention in mind. Byron's 'Addition to the Preface', dated 1813, makes this plain enough: the Childe ' . . . never was intended as an example, further than to show, that early perversion of mind and morals lead to satiety . . . and that even the beauties of nature and the stimulus of travel . . . are lost on a soul so constituted'.

Probably one ought not to say that Byron was uncertain over what he wanted to do: likely enough, he wanted to do what he in fact did, which was to write a poem that suggested any or all of a number of rôles for itself, and invited the reader to approach it in any of several ways. Its multi-valency, easy many-sidedness, relaxed amplitude, make it what it is. Also *Childe Harold* is, quite simply, a travel poem. 'The *scenes* attempted to be sketched . . . ', we read in the original 'Preface to the First and Second Cantos' (1812). The reference in Canto I.6 to Childe Harold's need for 'change of *scene*' rather pointedly uses the word again, though here the context is somewhat ambiguous: we read that Childe Harold ' . . . e'en for change of scene would seek the shades below', which does not sound like a travel-sketch poem so much as a poem of inner crisis. On the other hand, in Canto II.88, Childe Harold in Attica presents the reader with yet another modulation of feeling:

> . . . the sense aches with gazing to behold
> The scenes our earliest dreams have dwelt upon:

Here one on the whole reverts to the travel-poem and to scene-sketching, though there is a suggestion of psychic crisis as well. In Canto II.43, there is another ambiguous passage where the word 'scene' appears. Harold arrives in Greece, at that time the beginning of the Muslim world, a ' . . . shore unknown,/Which all admire, but many dread to view'. Again the reader finds the pleasure of travel, amalgamated to the inner pang:

> His breast was arm'd 'gainst fate, his wants were few;
> Peril he sought not, but ne'er shrank to meet:
> The *scene* was savage, but the scene was new;
> This made the ceaseless toil of travel sweet . . .

For the pilgrim, the 'travel' that he undergoes can only in a limited sense be called 'toil'; and if anything might be said to make it 'sweet' (which is doubtful) it would not be novelty.

Other strands of suggestion also are woven into the loose and copious fabric of this work. In Canto III.3, Childe Harold is described as 'The wandering outlaw of his own dark mind'. In stanza 70 of that Canto there is something of a suggestion that there are perhaps many who 'walk in darkness' as 'wanderers o'er Eternity', and for whom 'life becomes a hopeless flight'. This implies that one aspect of the poem is to record neither travel nor pilgrimage nor even Odyssey, but something like the helpless and undirected wandering of a spiritual refugee. On the other hand, there are a number of passages (for example, the 'fresh lessons to the thinking bosom' envisaged in I.23, the 'reveries' of III.109, or the poet's desire to 'ponder boldly' in IV.127) which incline the work towards the well-established eighteenth-century continuity of moralistic meditation-poems, with travel, of whatever kind, rather subordinate to that.

By the beginning of Canto IV, however, and to some extent earlier, the poem has begun quite to change its nature. The change is familiar enough, and is simply that as the poem proceeds, the 'I' of the poem becomes the central figure, and Childe Harold recedes into unimportance – until in IV.164 he suffers a momentary and most unceremonious recall, and an immediate dispatch. This change is deep and pervasive. Gradually, inconspicuously, it works a total change in the poem. One good way to see this is to notice how the *tenses* are modified so as to shift the reader's attention from past moments of directly witnessing 'scenes', to a present moment in which the poet is composing his poem, reflecting simply upon places that are now distant and recollected, rather than once present to a character at a definite past time. Canto IV opens with a simple preterite: 'I stood in Venice . . . ' The substitution of the poet for Childe Harold as observer is already of course clear, but there is as yet no grammatical embodiment of the fact. However, such a grammatical embodiment has already occurred ('I *have not loved* the world, nor the world me', III.113), and by IV.8 comes again, once more with the present perfect tense:

I've taught me other tongues, and in strange eyes
Have made me not a stranger . . .

This tense, of its very nature, subordinates the events recorded to
the interest of the moment at which someone is recording them.

Other syntactical changes also help to mark the depth and
pervasiveness of the change, and the centralization in the poem
of the poet as he writes. In stanza 152 of Canto IV, the reader
is addressed, I think for the first time, in the imperative mood:

Turn to the Mole which Hadrian rear'd on high!

'Man' (mankind) has already been addressed directly, in the
second person, in stanza 109. In stanza 178 of Canto IV, the lines

I love not Man the less, but Nature more
From *these our interviews* . . .

are exceedingly suggestive. On the one hand, they make clearer
still the poet's direct communication, as he speaks his poem,
with the reader. On the other, they show the poet as having in
effect *taken over* what were originally Childe Harold's *past*
experiences (the 'interviews' with nature).

Childe Harold's Pilgrimage, clearly not a poem with a single
intention and a single principle of structure, may be seen as
fluctuating between one conception and another, and as pro-
gressively becoming less and less of a poem centred upon a
questing protagonist, and more and more one centred upon the
persona of the composing poet. It seems to put the conception of
the quest-poem into play, rather than in fact to take it as a
genuinely shaping principle. At least two others of Byron's
works in fact depend more upon the conception of the quest than
does *Childe Harold*. In the drama *Cain* (1821), Lucifer takes
Cain upon a cosmic journey in the course of which he sees Hades
and the 'pre-Adamite' world, and Cain himself is given lines to
speak which put him indisputably among the visionary pilgrims
of Romantic verse:

          . . . thou canst not   (I.i.243)
Speak aught of knowledge which I would not know
And do not thirst to know, and bear a mind
To know . . .

Milton's Adam could barely have said more. In *Manfred* (1817) it turns out that the protagonist has also engaged in 'lone wanderings . . . enquiring after death itself and searching its cause in its effect' (II.ii.81); and thus, to have engaged in a quest for knowledge of precisely the profound and all-embracing kind that has characterized the quest-poem:

> lone thoughts and wanderings,   (109)
> The quest of hidden knowledge, and a mind
> To comprehend the universe . . .

It seems, moreover, that Manfred has not failed in his quest: or at least, has not failed in the straightforward sense. We are led to believe that he has indeed sounded the whole depth and range of experience and acquired all that wisdom has to offer to man. Yet something else is indeed missing. 'The Tree of Knowledge is not the Tree of Life', we find him saying. The Faustian task of the protagonist now seems to bring no true satisfaction even when it has been completed.

If, with this note of something like scepticism or disillusionment in mind, one looks back again to *Childe Harold's Pilgrimage*, it turns out that one line, as it were, in the varied spectrum of that poem still remains to be identified. Reflecting, for example, upon the fallen glories of Rome, the poet recognizes, in two swift acts of thought, first that the tale of Rome is 'the moral of all human tales' (IV.108), and then that because of this, history has in essence 'but *one* page'. The record of history – knowledge, that is, of the human condition at its broadest – becomes just a little trite. 'Away with words!' we read at the end of the stanza. One single, complex act of perception will be enough to seize the human paradox:

> . . . Man!   (IV.109)
> Thou *pendulum* betwixt a smile and tear . . .

Here is something which might be the next step in such a response: if mankind is an eternal paradox, something of detachment is called for in viewing his case. Of this, one finds a certain intimation once or twice at earlier points in the poem:

Childe Harold at a little distance stood (II.72)
And *view'd*, but not displeased, the revelrie . . .

This is the pilgrim's detached and a trifle equivocal response to
the spectacle of some rather aggressively masculine Suliote
dancing. Later on, a similar *persona* is adopted, this time by the
poet himself, when he increasingly speaks in his own voice. 'In
the crowd', he says:

I stood (III.113)
Among them, but not of them . . .

Intimations of this kind are not at all frequent in *Childe Harold*.
It is useful to take note of them, because they afford yet one
further variety of poetic *persona* and therefore of organizing
principle in the poem. But the fact is, they make it clearer still
that in none of these individual *personae* should one look for the
essential conception of the poem. Rather than any such thing, it
is in the sense an unambitious poem, and to pass in relaxed
fashion from one mode to another is of its nature:

. . . for these words, thus woven into song, (III.112)
It may be that they are a harmless wile, –
The colouring of the scenes which fleet along,
Which I would seize, in passing, to *beguile*
My breast, or that of others, for a while . . .

Childe Harold has its own distinctiveness and special quality,
which is to mingle the rôles of quest-poem, travel-sketch-poem,
quizzical reminiscence, or moralized meditation: to mingle them
with a certain air of almost genial, long-drawn-out casualness, a
distant reminiscence of Spenserian leisure (but without the
ulterior seriousness of Spenser) that begins sometimes to get
within sight of the effects of Absurdist art. Few in our own
anxious and time-saving age will care unreservedly for these
engagingly dilute *longueurs*.

Childe Harold was a traveller, and Don Juan, in the poem of
that name, was a traveller too; but there the resemblance ends.
True enough, there is a certain sense in which Don Juan's
journeyings may be thought of as a quest for enlightenment:
but not for long. It is Don Juan's *mother* who, after his notorious

escapade with Julia, sends him off to travel as part of her own
penitential programme over that event:

> . . . then, by the advice of some old ladies, (I.190)
> She sent her son to be shipp'd off from Cadiz.
>
> She had resolved that he should travel through
>   All European climes, by land or sea,
> To *mend his former morals, and get new,*
>   Especially in France and Italy
> (At least, this is the thing most people do.)

Donna Inez supplies her son, when he departs, with a letter of
good advice. He never reads it (II.9). There is no question here
of a conception of the poem which is put forward at first in some
seriousness and is modified later. The initial impression is one
of complex jest. We do not need the good offices of the un-
worldly old ladies (maybe, indeed, they are not at all unworldly)
nor of Don Juan's sanctimonious mother, to make the situation
clear. The hero's legendary name is enough. We know what
sort of quest Don Juan goes on. It has always been the same
one, and in itself it is simply a mockery of the 'quest' idea of the
poems discussed earlier. *Don Juan* is a kind of anti-art; I should
like to call it an anti-quest poem. The hero's getting 'new'
morals, which after all is a central idea of the Proud Knowledge,
is here the basic joke of the poem. The conception of the sus-
tained and dedicated quest for insight is brushed aside not only
by the succession of amorous escapades – Julia, Haidee,
Bulbayez – that makes up the staple of the poem, but also by the
way that, through its constant digressions, the poem as it were
on second reading rejects the idea that it has any staple or
continuity at all. The jest is given one further turn by the
solemn profession, in the opening stanzas, that (by contrast with
the self-indulgent medley style of the conventional epic) order
and sequaciousness are the very being of *Don Juan*:

> My way is to begin with the beginning; (I.7)
>   The regularity of my design
>   Forbids all wandering as the worst of sinning . . .

This is one of the many places in the poem where one can see
that digression does not occur either in spite of, or in pursuit of,

the poem's dedication to an order or to a higher truth. Such
ideas are kept in play precisely so that the poem can be a
constant rejection of them, a 'send-up'.

This shows clearly at IX.41 where, after a brief reference to
one of the favourite natural-history ideas of the time, that of
successive creations and cataclysms as the key to the story of
life on the planet, we find:

> I quite forgot this poem's merely quizzical,
>   And deviate into matter rather dry.

Early in the same Canto, the search for knowledge is set aside
in other terms:

> ('Que sçais-je?' was the motto of Montaigne . . .   (IX.17)
> There's no such thing as certainty, that's plain . . .

Later in the poem Byron contrasts himself with one of the great
mythical figures associated with the dedicated knowledge-quest,
at the same time that he condemns the quest itself as
unrealizable:

> I'm not Oedipus, and life's a Sphinx.   (XIII.12)

'Life's a Sphinx'. Earlier on, the same point has been made
about the perennial 'deepest questionings' over the human lot
(the italics are Byron's):

> What are we? and whence came we? what shall be (VI.63)
> Our *ultimate* existence? what's our present?
> And questions answerless, and yet incessant . . .

At this point in the poem, Byron has just been complicating the
stance he takes up, by purporting to be in pursuit of knowledge:

> My tendency is to philosophize   (VI.63)
>   On most things, from a tyrant to a tree;
> But still the spouseless virgin *Knowledge* flies.

'Tyrant' and 'tree' are not without their literary point: doubtless
they invite the reader to recall such poems, among many, as
Gray's 'The Bard', Cowper's 'Yardley Oak' (see p. 58 above)
or Wordsworth's 'The Thorn'. At the same time, Byron's bald
phraseology intimates that the themes of such poems are a

solemn absurdity. Philosophizing is noted as something of an absurdity, even as (self-deprecatingly?) it is admitted for a 'tendency'. Knowledge flees from a world of which one may write (Byron's italics):

> . . . I hope it is no crime   (VIII.2)
> To laugh at *all* things – for I wish to know
> *What*, after *all*, are *all* things – but a *show?*

– flees, that is, from a world of fake and unreality, just as the virgin Astraea fled from a world of wickedness. The involutions of the passage progressively transpire. The hope that it is no 'crime' to take nothing seriously adjusts itself as a not quite serious hope. If all is a 'show', crime will not be the one thing different, it will be a show too. Then, having settled for universal laughter, even the 'wish to know' itself becomes a passing quirk, a cause for laughter, in its turn. Nothing is immune.

What begins to emerge, from these passages and others, is in fact something like a new and striking poetic *persona*: a new posture (though one, as we saw, occasionally present in germ in *Childe Harold*) which the poet is constrained to take up, as speaker of his poem, towards reality, by the tendency of his findings with regard both to reality and to himself.

> Thrice happy he who, after a survey (XI.69: Byron's italics)
> Of the good company, can win a corner,
> A door that's *in* or boudoir *out* of the way,
> Where he may fix himself like small 'Jack Horner',
> And let the Babel round run as it may,
> And look on as a mourner, or a scorner,
> Or an approver, or a mere spectator,
> Yawning a little as the night grows later.

The logic, or rather what is a kind of anti-logic of the poem, is of much interest. Here, 'good company' takes on a somewhat modified and extra sense ('I see what the good Berkeley would be at', Kant said) from what follows it. Jack Horner putting in his thumb and pulling out a plum sustains ideas both of the guest at a party who turns to the food because the people are so dull, and also of the situation of one who withdraws from the *melée* and 'fixes himself' in some secluded boudoir. But 'mourner', and the words which follow, all contribute to the demolition of this incipient sense of satisfactions that the guest *à part* can manage to find for himself. This particular Jack Horner would be as bored with 'what a good boy am I' as with anything else. Whatever is said is undermined as soon as said. It is not enough to call this *persona* that of the quizzical by-stander, though that is what it begins by being. Over and over, the structures of thought intimated by the poem are such that this, like every other articulated conception of *persona*, is half-disintegrated almost as soon as created.

As a further stage of the argument, it is fair to say that even this instantaneously and continuously disintegrating *persona* remains a *persona* of a kind. Once the poet as quizzical bystander turns his detachment and quizzicality upon himself, there has to be a multiple, an endless reiteration of the movements both of submission before dubiety and at the same time of rising above it through the very act of registering it: and if the structure of the experience is logically a boundless one, the image of a personality that it casts is in the end both emphatic and coherent. Certainly that emphatic and coherent personality makes its presence felt in this poem; and in doing so, it establishes what is a sort of palinode to the quest-poem as a poetic kind. At the same time, from another standpoint, it may be seen as a sort of resolution of the quest from an unexpected angle – unexpected, that is, in the given context, though the more general idea that insight is to be found at the moment of ceasing to seek it is of course perennial in another one.

I shall not consider, in any detail, how the poetic *persona* that Byron creates in *Don Juan* has a history in the poetry of the nineteenth century and beyond: merely suggest that it indeed does so, by reference to two poems. Arnold, first, was responsive to its power in a poem like 'Resignation'. Here, the poet 'leans upon a gate' and watches 'life unroll': but this act of detachment does not prevent his retaining a characteristic 'sad lucidity of soul' while he does so. That, at least, is his own version of the matter. The woman who is with him, when she smiles her quiet smile at his words, calls them a little in question, and constructs the second movement of the structure of scepticism somewhat as was done in *Don Juan*, though without Byron's economy of means, and with a sort of bald and 'sad lucidity' of her own that is perhaps a measure of Arnold's seriousness of purpose and of his limitations as an artist here as well. Secondly, T. S. Eliot's 'Love Song of J. Alfred Prufrock' is a striking case of the *Don Juan persona* re-appearing. Of course the character of Prufrock, considered as a totality, is altogether different from that of Don Juan. That is not to the point. It is not the total personality, but merely one particularized *persona* organized as it were over the top of that, which is at issue. As it happens, there is a perhaps graphic short way to suggest how much of the Byron of *Don Juan* has got into 'Prufrock'. It is simply to display how, with scarcely a change even of punctuation, some lines of the latter may be re-arranged until they could almost be inserted into the former.

> I am not Prince Hamlet, nor was meant to be:
>   But deferential, glad to be of use.
> After the cups, the marmalade, the tea,
>   Politic, cautious and meticulous;
> Among the porcelain, talk of you and me
>   Full of high sentence, but a bit obtuse.
> Though I have seen my head upon a platter,
> I am no prophet – and here's no great matter.
>
> And would it have been worth it, after all
>   (I shall wear white flannel trousers, on the beach!)
> To have squeezed the universe into a ball?
>   Have heard the mermaids singing each to each,
> The voices dying with a dying fall?
>   Shall I part my hair behind, or eat a peach?
> I have seen the moment of my greatness flicker,
> The eternal footman hold my coat, and snicker.

Perhaps this will be thought an unpardonable liberty; but it seems to make, briefly, a striking point which I at least could otherwise make only less well and in more words.

II *Paracelsus* and *Dipsychus*

Browning's *Paracelsus* has as its subject a man whose energy, copiousness and variety of thought are far in excess of what the thought achieves. Unfortunately, the poem mirrors, in its own

texture, that pointless over-abundance. The brackets marked in
the following passage I think make the pleonastic nature of the
writing clear enough (the round brackets indicate the repetitions
of one idea, the square brackets those of another):

> So long as God would kindly (pioneer   (IV.566)
> A path for you), (and screen you from the world)
> (Procure you full exemption from [man's lot],)
> [Man's common hopes and fears], on the mere pretext
> Of your engagement in his service – (yield you
> A limitless licence) (make you God, in fact),
> (And turn your slave) –

The same melancholy quality shows elsewhere. In fact, once the
reader is alerted to it he readily detects it everywhere: to
labour this fault would be to ape it. Browning did not dramatize,
but succumbed to, the endless ill-directed garrulity of his
protagonist (the lines quoted above are not spoken by Paracelsus
at all, but by Festus his opposite, the man free from the curse of
the 'proud knowledge'). He paid the price of disabling his poem;
and since repetitiveness almost inevitably leads to dilution
and banality (that is amply illustrated above) he paid it twice
over. Those who write about this poem have not to follow its
example.

There is no need to illustrate at any length how *Paracelsus*
partakes of the nature of the quest-poem as that has been dis-
cussed. From the beginning, Paracelsus the man displays the
appropriate powers:

> You, if a man may, dare aspire to KNOW . . .   (I.282)

and appropriate personality:

> What fairer seal   (I.333)
> Shall I require to my authentic mission
> Than this fierie energy? – this instinct *striving*
> Because its nature is to strive? . . .
>   . . . the restless irresistible force   (340)
> That works within me?

He seeks knowledge 'in strange and untried paths' (I.399) and,
like Childe Roland in a better poem, is

Like some knight traversing a wilderness . . .   (I.476)

Ideas of striving (I.335; II.368–9; III.229 etc.); of 'setting out'
(IV.179), of being a 'wanderer' (IV.259), of one who had
'probed the inmost truth' (V.145), all recur. Paracelsus looks
exactly as if he were going to be a quest-hero. The initial,
ostensible similarity between this poem and poems like *Alastor*
is not in doubt.

One may recall in passing, though, that if Browning had
caused his poem to endorse this conception of life and of man, it
would have stood apart from the rest of his work. The author of
'Bishop Blougram's Apology', 'The Statue and the Bust',
'Cleon', and 'Abt Vogler' (not to name poems discussed else-
where in this book) is not the poet we should expect to find
celebrating the grand, triumphant success of man's striving
nature or enquiring mind. *Paracelsus* is almost the opposite of
that. If Byron's *Don Juan*, and *Paracelsus*, are considered
together, Byron's poem takes shape as a quizzical, half-
indifferent avoiding of the quest-myth – it is quietly, subtly
dropped – while Browning's amounts to an anxious, deeply
pondered, and laboured rejection of it.

Browning has almost no share of Shelley's vague and doubtful
sense that quest brings the quester somehow to major truths.
What Paracelsus finds throughout most of the poem is in effect
that so far as major truths are concerned, so far as in the widest
sense the 'proud knowledge' is concerned, his search brings
nothing but manifold increases in his predicament.

> . . . since they strove I strove. Then came a slow   (I.501)
> And strangling failure . . .
> While I was restless, nothing satisfied,   (506)
> Distrustful, most perplexed.

When, in a moment of detachment at Constantinople, Paracelsus
looks back over his life, what he sees is:

> A stranger wandered long through many lands   (II.27)
> And reaped the fruit he coveted in a few
> Discoveries, as appended here and there,
> The *fragmentary produce of much toil*,
> In a dim heap . . .

Intent on gain to come too much to stay
And scrutinize the little gained: the whole
Slip't in the blank space 'twixt an idiot's gibber
And a mad lover's ditty – there it lies.
And yet those blottings chronicle a life –
A whole life, and my life!

The 'one tyrant all-absorbing aim' destroys him; and surprisingly enough, he expresses his realization of this through the traditional metaphors:

> . . . this working sea (II.170)
> Which parts me from that happy strip of land:
> But o'er that happy strip a sun shone, too!
> And fainter gleams it as the waves grow rough,
> And still more faint as the sea widens; last
> I sicken on a dead gulf streaked with *light*
> *From its own putrefying depths* alone . . .

Here, Paracelsus adopts the metaphor of the voyage, and as it develops it even comes near to that of the *ignis fatuus* (notice the last two lines above). 'I have thrown my life away' is his conclusion in the first movement of the poem. Moreover, if one explores how this is an exaggeration on his part, one finds that the poem (even, I mean, before its different and final resolution) delineates a significant further stage. Paracelsus has thrown his life away in that his high ambitions have proved themselves folly. But something less ambitious has not:

> I possess (III.922)
> *Two sorts of knowledge*; one, – vast, shadowy,
> Hints of the unbounded aim I once pursued:
> *The other* consists of many secrets, caught
> While bent on nobler prize, – perhaps a few
> Prime principles which may conduct to much . . .

What Paracelsus has acquired is not nothing, but – manifold, miscellaneous or else preliminary – it is quite other than the knowledge he sought, the knowledge that his quest was intended to produce.

At the moment of his death, however, Browning's Paracelsus

turns a 'new knowledge upon old events' (V.507). Marred as the long final scene is by the verbosity that mars everything, there is a transfiguring moment, a regeneration of the self. Paracelsus' companion Festus is astounded to see him arise from his death-bed and proclaim that after all the moment when he dedicated himself to the quest was the supreme happy moment of his life. Everything that has seemed vainglorious folly is somehow to be vindicated after all.

Yet that vindication, in the form it takes, distances the poem over again, and even more decisively, from its predecessors in the quest-mode. In a passage that is full of interest, Paracelsus asserts his own self-justification in something like the terms of the early part of the poem: but, even as he elucidates those terms, he implicitly transforms them. He was from the first, he begins, a chosen spirit. Others, he says, if, 'searching and impetuous', might come in the course of their lives consciously to learn that the task of the quest existed,

But this was born in me; I was made so . . .   (V.622)

Save for just such a modicum of doubt as saved him from dangerous pride, he could say:

I stood at first where all aspire at last   (636)
To stand: the secret of the world was mine

('at first' has its common archaic meaning here of 'from the first'). By these words, Paracelsus declares himself to have been a unique, a God-filled man. He has felt 'at every pore' (the expression is his own) 'what God is, what we are,/What life is' (642).

Yet those words turn out to be a colossal act of *legerdemain*. In saying that, I do not wish to raise issues of theology. What I refer to as legerdemain may or may not be cogent when set out as theological argument, and for the present purpose that matter has no importance. The word legerdemain is justified by the unexplained and unargued superimposition, within the poem, of one conception upon another which is quite different from it, which is in fact its opposite. To feel 'what God is' may be the prerogative of the man who is God-filled and unique; but to feel 'what life is', turns out to be, feeling not how God partakes of the whole world (' . . . God tastes an infinite joy/In infinite ways': 643–4), but *how the whole world partakes of God*. This latter is what the passage as a whole describes. Existence, even 'in its lowest form', includes God. Even the natural fire within the planet does so as it works upward from the depths, transforming the earth and rising into the sunlight. Volcanic cataclysm is succeeded by Ice Age; that by a renewal of vegetation. But then, both of these extraordinary events are transmuted, as Paracelsus's account proceeds, into the ordinary perennial cycle of winter and returning spring, where one after another, plants, insects, birds and mammals come to life again. Next, protracting the central ambiguity of the passage, but so that it is hardly to be noticed, God not only 'tastes a pleasure' (664) in the most primitive of these things as much as he 'renews/His ancient rapture' (680–1) in the last and highest of them, but also (the text adds at once) he *'dwells in all'*. The syntax of this expression is closely matched even at the very moment when the poem gives expression, at the beginning of the upward impulse, to what is virtually its opposite – 'dwells in all': 'joys therein'. But the likeness of syntax expresses a contrariety of meaning. In the first of those, God is in the world as a spirit is said to be 'in' a body, but in the second the body is 'in' the spirit in the sense that body (the cosmos) is the content of the spirit's thought, that is to say God's thought. The splendour and variety of nature is warrant at one and the same time for God's *pleasure* in nature, and also for God's *presence* in it: His presence, not only up from mollusc to animal, but on into the highest sphere of all:

> From life's minute beginnings, up at last   (682)
> *To man* – the consummation of this scheme
> Of being, whose attributes had here and there
> Been scattered o'er the visible world before,
> Asking to be combined . . .

The quest-hero is culmination of the whole impulse of natural history, the evolutionary process itself.

Yet this is utterly to transform the original conception. The quest-hero disappears if he turns out to be none other than Everyman. Paracelsus's unique potential, his dedicated difference from other men, is simply not there at all, once it is transformed into not just man's common nature, but the common nature of everything, highest to lowest. One may now see quite a new sense in some lines quoted earlier (p. 143 above), a sense brought out by new italics:

> What fairer seal
> Shall I require to my authentic mission
> Than this fierce energy? – this *instinct* striving
> Because its nature is to strive? . . .

'Instinct' in those lines did not mean what it at first looked as if it meant. Earlier on, it looked as if it had a rather special though quite standard meaning: an innermost, individual drive. In reality, it meant (once the end of the poem comes into view) the impulse of the whole of nature: 'instinct' as what all share. This is not to argue that Paracelsus remains indistinguishable from his fellow-men. Of course he is distinguishable from them. But what the poem comes to rest on is that thinking the distinction fundamental is the error of errors. Any contrast between the quest-hero and other men (other beings, rather) is an ostensible difference over a basic identity. Quest for the proud knowledge is, at the level of man in general, the form taken by a cosmic evolutionary drive. The heroic figure, God-filled, is God-filled only in that all mankind and all of nature are God-filled. Uniqueness turns out to be at bottom universality, the age of the Hero turns out to be the age of the Common Man.

Paracelsus loses at least part of its tedium, when we see that it transmutes a Romantic myth into a Victorian one.

Fifteen years after *Paracelsus*, the publication of Clough's *Dipsychus* seems to have taken the disintegration of the quest-myth a stage further. The merits of this poem, obvious enough no doubt, form no part of the present discussion, nor even does a general review of its nature;* and the briefest note on one aspect of Dipsychus, considered in isolation, is all that is intended. What is significant from the standpoint of the quest-poem is simply that Clough is able to use the Faust-legend, long a major vehicle for exploring the myth of the quest and its

---

* I have discussed this poem at some length in *TLS*, 10 January 1975, p. 37.

glories and its dangers, as if it had no such provenance. Dipsy-
chus in the earlier drafts is called 'Faustulus': 'Faust the Little'.
He has shrunk from the stature of the heroic enquirer and seeker
to that of diminutive mannikin, all doubt and hesitation, with
no more than the weakest incipient glintings of larger ambition.
Yet the change from the traditional Mephistopheles to the
'Spirit' whom we encounter in *Dipsychus* is greater. What, over
and over, the 'Spirit' tempts Dipsychus towards, is not a
pilgrimage of learning that moves towards higher things, nor
even a fallacious pilgrimage of pseudo-learning of which the
ultimate inspiration is diabolical; but a brisk and cynical, even
callous, dismissal of all such nonsense.

> Could I believe it even of us men   (III.64)
> That once the young exuberance drawn off
> The liquor would run clear . . .
> Could I indeed as of some men I might   (74)
> Think this of maidens also . . .

– meditates Dipsychus. Sexuality ('the young exuberance')
nags at him, but he hankers for higher things, and might settle
for sex if it would free men and women for those higher things.
The spirit's retort is a curt one:

> Stuff!
> The women like it; that's enough.   (77)

Later, when Dipsychus has to say, all to himself, that

> But for perfection attaining is only one method,
>   abstaining   (V.76)

– the Spirit suggests only that Dipsychus's 'sage' remarks,
'worthy of Malebranche or Berkeley', are drivelling as verse
(V.103). The Mephistopheles-figure no longer leads the hero
towards even an *ignis fatuus* of truth. It nudges him contemp-
tuously away:

> Better it were, thou sayest, to consent,   (V.89)
> Feast while we may . . .

It was a stroke of genius to drop the names 'Faustulus' and
'Mephistopheles', and to use 'Dipsychus' for his Everyman.

Once the dichotomy between Everyman and the 'call' that he hears is internalized as thoroughly as this, it is easy to adopt a pattern the reverse of the traditional one, to identify the higher Self with ordinariness, with the Everyman side of man's nature, and to identify the call from the Other as the path downhill into cynical self-indulgence. It could almost be said that by comparison with this, Don Juan was still a pilgrim and a hero.

III 'The Holy Grail'

According to legend, the Holy Grail is the vessel which Christ drank from at the Last Supper; and it was brought to Britain by Joseph of Arimathea, the first Christian to land here. Tennyson's chief source for this section of his *Idylls of the King* was Malory's *Morte d'Arthur*, Book 13 to 17, in Caxton's version; but he does not tell how Arthur's Knights left Camelot and the society of the Round Table, in order to go in quest of the Holy Grail, the same way as Caxton did. The differences are mainly two: but together they produce a wholly new result, and make the poem something of a freak in its time for narrative technique and a precursor of much in the twentieth century. Tennyson also proved to depart radically, though unostentatiously, from the story as Malory understood it – not merely as he told it.

Malory's narrative is slow-moving and digressive, and there are certain minor confusions or transpositions in Caxton's version, though they are not important. But in essence the tale is told simply, and it is told directly: the 'author' narrates throughout. Tennyson's version stands quite alone among his *Idylls of the King*. The others are direct narration, sometimes even a little baldly so, not altogether unlike folktales; much could be said about this, but I shall not pursue the point. 'The Holy Grail' is an intricate weave of what could almost be called *Conradian* reported and multiple narrative and reported speech. The idyll opens with the retreat and death of Perceval. Immediately, it retrogresses to say that some time before the old Monk Ambrosius died, he was talking with Perceval and asked him why he left Arthur's Court. ' . . . was it earthly passion crost?' (29). The remainder of the idyll, save for a question and a brief but important speech by Ambrosius, is spoken by Perceval in reply. He it is who recounts the story of the Grail-quest as answer to Ambrosius's enquiry about his possible 'earthly passion'.

Yet, complex as it is, the account which I have just given is in its turn a simplification. Within his own narration, Perceval narrates the speeches of others, and within these speeches are often others again. The poem is a labyrinth of narrative recession. Moreover, there is something else of a rather similar kind. By line 95, Perceval is recounting a conversation between his sister and her 100-year-old confessor – that is to say, he is presenting a situation in his narrative which in large part mirrors his own situation even as he narrates to Ambrosius. Seventy lines later he in effect reports the interchange between Galahad and Merlin. This is another complexity, because a little earlier than that in his narrative, Perceval has done something to identify his own sister and Galahad:

> and this Galahad, when he heard   (139)
> My sister's vision, filled me with amaze;
> His eyes became so like her own, they seemed
> Hers, and himself her brother more than I.

By doing this, Perceval sets before us, as we read the poem, a third situation like the first two: first himself and the aged Ambrosius, next his sister and her aged confessor, now her as-if-brother Galahad and the aged Merlin. By line 290, Perceval is reporting how Galahad reported the voice he heard. Later in the poem he reports his meeting with Sir Bors, and Bors's report of his own meeting with Lancelot (l.650). Finally, Perceval reports Lancelot's report of his ordeal at Carbonek, the Grail Castle, and then Arthur's own closing words – which he says he does not understand.

This bald summary brings out the elaboration but conceals the flow of the poem. To an attentive reader, it is never confusing. Yet the 'flow' of 'The Holy Grail' is not the flow of 'linked sweetness' that Milton praised in (one supposes) Spenser or Ariosto. It is a verbal texture sustained by deliberate, unhurried rhythm and simple but dignified language, within which events are arranged in complex multiple recessions, depth within depth, and an elaborate order of recollection. Re-arrangement and contemplation quite dominate the original sequence of the quest. In fact, this sequence is something which the reader cannot even determine from the poem if he tries. Movement is multiple and many-directioned. What we are left with is a sense of mosaic: the mosaic of many people talking and listening, of a quest that is always being suspended, distanced, recessed into something else. This is something new. It is radically different from Malory in its literary effect. *Wuthering Heights* is a more relevant comparison (though that is a narrative freak for its time); and the effect is rather similar. In the poem as in the novel, the moment of the narrat*ing* acquires prominence; and because of the brevity of the whole work, this prominence becomes a real dominance. The narrative not only recedes, but also becomes 'placed' and subordinate as that of *Wuthering Heights* does not.

But while the Grail-quest as a whole may be thus transposed (as, seeking to point out the poetic quality of the whole, one might perhaps put it) into unresolving harmonies in a remote key, the *places* in which the quest occurs – the places through which it takes the seekers – are not remote but brilliantly vivid and immediate. In most cases the descriptive passages have no counterpart in Malory: or at the most, a brief hint is developed almost out of recognition. Among examples of this are Perceval's sister's vision of the Grail in her cell (114 . . .); the Grail seen in the hall at Camelot (182 . . .); Camelot itself (338 . . .); the plowman, the milkmaid, and the golden knight (401 . . .); the extraordinary landscape of the hill, the great swamp and the self-igniting sea-bridges (489 . . . I think this is an account of Sarris as pre-medieval Glastonbury); the beautiful intermission when Ambrosius describes the abode of himself and Perceval (540 . . .); the place where the stone-circle people live – those who captured Sir Bors (655 . . .); Camelot partly in ruins when the knights return (712–30); and Lancelot's views of Carbonek and his approach to it:

the naked shore, (790)
Wide flats, where nothing but coarse grasses grew;
But such a blast, my King, began to blow,
So loud a blast along the shore and sea,
Ye could not hear the waters from the blast,

Though heapt in mounds and ridges all the sea
Drove like a cataract, and all the sand
Swept like a river, and the clouded heavens
Were shaken with the motion and the sound.
And blackening in the sea-foam sway'd a boat,
Half-swallow'd in it, anchor'd with a chain;
And in my madness to myself I said,
'I will embark . . .'

The abandoned half-derelict boat, it will be recalled, is a familiar
'property' of the quest; but Tennyson's picture of it is sharply
idiosyncratic, and so is every detail of these passages. Edged
always with a piercing, even disturbing individuality they are
what make the poem. Malory is out of sight.

One may enquire as to the way in which these brilliant
pictures contribute to the total effect of the poem. They seem
to do so in two opposite ways. Because they have the startling
vividness of dreams, it is easy, as one's mind revolves about
them, to think of the poem itself as being like a dream. At the
same time, they are not simply vivid, but detailed, coherent and
realistic. They seem like real places. Constantly, the remote,
unreal events of the Grail-quest occur between *locals* which are
solid and immediate. The world's reality, here, there, every-
where, as one reads of it in the poem, is intense and convincing.

Everything said so far goes along with a certain remarkable
fact: that Tennyson's accounts of the visions are far from
demanding, but always invite, a naturalistic explanation. What
Perceval's sister saw could be like (and surely has as its literary
source, moreover) the colours that were the result of the
moonlight as it shone through the stained-glass windows of
Madeline's cell in Keats's 'Eve of St Agnes'. Here are the
two passages side by side, first Keats:

A casement high and triple-arched there was   (XXIV.1)
. . . And diamonded with panes of quaint device . . .

Full on this casement shone the wintry moon   (XXV.1)
And threw warm gules on Madeline's fair breast,
As down she knelt for heaven's grace and boon;
Rose-bloom fell on her hands, together prest

And on her silver cross soft amethyst,
And on her hair a glory like a saint . . .

and now Tennyson's account of the vision of the 'pale nun':

' . . . and then   (115)
Streamed through my cell a cold and silver beam,
And down the long beam stole the Holy Grail,
Rose-red with beatings in it, as if alive,
Till all the white walls of my cell were dyed
With rosy colours leaping on the wall . . . '

The vision in the hall at Camelot could be taken for a great
lightning-flash:

'Then on a summer night it came to pass . . .   (179)
And all at once, as there we sat, we heard   (182)
A cracking and a riving of the roofs,
And rending, and a blast, and overhead
Thunder, and in the thunder was a cry.
And in the blast there smote along the hall
A beam of light seven times more clear than day:
And down the long beam stole the Holy Grail
All over covered with a luminous cloud,
And none might see who bare it, and it past.'

What Perceval sees over Galahad's head could be St Elmo's
fire:

. . . I saw him far on the great Sea,   (510)
In silver-shining armour starry-clear;
And o'er his head the Holy Vessel hung
Clothed in white samite or a luminous cloud.
And with exceeding swiftness ran the boat,
If boat it were – I saw not whence it came.

Galahad's vision could be a comet (a legendary blood-red one):

. . . never yet   (468)
Hath what thy sister taught me first to see,
This Holy Thing, failed from my side, nor come
Covered, but moving with me night and day,
Fainter by day, but always in the night

Blood-red, and sliding down the blackened marsh
Blood-red, and on the naked mountain top
Blood-red, and in the sleeping mere below
Blood-red.

Sir Bors's vision could be a meteor that he sees, perhaps,
crossing the stars of the Great Bear:*

> . . . Across the seven clear stars – O grace to me –   (689)
> In colour like the fingers of a hand
> Before a burning taper, the sweet Grail
> Glided and past, and close upon it pealed
> A sharp quick thunder . . .

Lancelot's vision might be an altar in a castle chapel:

> Behold, the enchanted towers of Carbonek   (810)
> A castle like a rock upon a rock . . .
> . . . up into the sounding hall I past;   (824)
> But nothing in the sounding hall I saw,
> . . . up I climbed a thousand steps   (832)
> With pain: as in a dream I seemed to climb
> For ever: at the last I reached a door,
> A light was in the crannies, and I heard
> 'Glory and joy and honour to our Lord
> And to the Holy Vessel of the Grail.'
> Then in my madness I essayed the door;
> It gave; and through a stormy glare, a heat
> As from a seventimes-heated furnace, I,
> Blasted and burnt, and blinded as I was,
> With such a fierceness that I swooned away –
> O, yet methought I saw the Holy Grail,
> All palled in crimson samite, and around
> Great angels, awful shapes, and wings and eyes . . .

---

* Lines 680–4 of the poem suggest that the 'seven stars' are the constellation
of the Great Bear (or possibly the Little Bear) and not, say, the Pleiades:

> . . . through the gap
> The seven clear stars of Arthur's Table Round –
> For, brother, so one night, because they roll
> Thro' such a round in heaven, we named the stars,
> Rejoicing in ourselves and in our King –

(this is not, of course, to imply that some stars have a rotatory motion and others
not).

None of these interpretations is inescapable; but certainly they fit Tennyson's closing lines. Here, King Arthur himself is left to say that true vision comes to him who stays at home and does his work, while the rest is likely to be nothing but 'wandering fires':

> 'And spake I not too truly, O my knights?   (884)
> Was I too dark a prophet when I said
> To those who went upon the Holy Quest,
> That most of them would follow wandering fires,
> Lost in the *quagmire*? . . . '

Tennyson's statement about 'The Holy Grail', 'I have expressed there my strong feelings as to the Reality of the Unseen' (quoted by Ricks, p. 1661), certainly does not require us to suppose that he presents the Grail visions as veridical throughout.

In short, therefore, 'The Holy Grail' may indeed be linked with other quest-poems like *Alastor* or 'Childe Roland' (see p. 220 below); but it has one level of meaning at which it relegates or even repudiates the idea of the quest. Not that Tennyson's unobtrusively ambiguous renderings of the Grail visions are the main reason why this is so. Chief weight must attach to the complex narrative recessions in which the sequence of the quest is in fact dissolved; until the spatial reality of a place and a landscape, rather than the temporal reality of a quest, is what stands out. It seems that a detailed analysis of the construction of this poem reveals how intimately and intricately its construction is one with its point of view. The ostensible, because traditional, *subject* of the poem makes claims that the supreme value of human life is in a certain quest: that for the Grail. The real and detailed construction is such as to say the opposite: it causes the poem to leave an impression that *places*, those which I noted a few moments ago, are 'brilliantly vivid and immediate'; but any sequence and concatenation of places such as, taken all in all, could make up a Quest, are left fragmented, discontinuous, dreamlike and unreal. This seems to be the resultant, as it were, of the poem; as King Arthur's closing lines make clear. Disunity and discontinuity of surface lines and ostensible narration are vehicles whereby the poem achieves and expresses a unity of conception. That unity of conception sets something against the 'wandering fires': King Arthur's belief that one who does not quest, but toils in his due and allotted place, sees visions which are more than visions and which relegate visions to their proper place. Here is the true 'Reality of the Unseen':

> ' . . . the King must guard (901)
> That which he rules, and is but as the hind
> To whom a space of land is given to plow.
> Who may not wander from the allotted field
> Before his work be done; but, being done,
> Let visions of the night or of the day
> Come, as they will; and many a time they come,
> Until this earth he walks on seems not earth,
> This light that strikes his eyeball is not light,
> This air that smites his forehead is not air
> But vision – yea, his very hand and foot –
> In moments when he feels he cannot die,
> And knows himself no vision, nor that One
> Who rose again: ye have seen what ye have seen.'

That is the end of Arthur's elucidation. The recessions of the poem return to us in its one further and closing line; and with it, Perceval establishes himself once again as a knight drawn into an action which is beyond him and which he cannot understand:

> 'So spake the King; *I knew not all he meant.*' (916)

VII

The Self
and Its Regeneration

I

This chapter will begin by briefly studying three poems which are preliminary to its main concern. The poems are Donne's 'A nocturnall upon S. Lucies day', Cowper's 'The Castaway', and Arnold's 'To Marguerite – Continued'.

In Donne's 'Nocturnall', the grave yet informal rhythms catch the speaking voice, and counterpoint with an intricate formality of metrical structure. The many turns of thought which bring the poem realistically close to the experience of love ending in disaster, combine within a texture of witty yet altogether unfrivolous hyperbole and distancing. The experience of love ending disastrously seems at once close and immediate, yet new in its presentation, and wholly shaped and controlled by the formalities of the poem. The resolution in the final stanza is felicitous yet unexpected and un-banal. Donne here confirms the link established earlier between himself and the other lovers; dismissing them as (being irrelevant to his own predicament) they must be dismissed, with a skilful inflection of remote but kindly tolerance. At the same time, 'enjoy your summer all' expresses a good reason why they will be content to depart from him, and introduces precisely such a sameness-in-difference (the lovers may prepare for summer, he will prepare for heaven) as leaves us sensing a justness in his analogy and so an order in the poem.

I must admit to feeling a certain disquiet about all poems of this kind, even about such a dazzling example of the kind as the 'Nocturnall'. That disquiet arises simply because I find that, as I get to know superbly, intricately witty poems better and better, there comes a point where they turn out to have been not quite witty enough. Their glittering maze of analogies and implications, all stated and vigorously argued out, proves to have a weak link somewhere: in fact, I hardly see how a brief poem of this particular kind could insure itself against erosion somewhere, as a result of endless re-reading and contemplation. Thus, when Donne writes:

> Study me then, all ye who lovers bee,
> For I am every dead thing
> In whom love wrought new Alchimie

there seems to be a difficulty as to why the lovers should study him: whether because they will learn about their present state of having been 'alchemized' from base metal into the gold of being lovers, or because they will learn about the later consequences of love – its ultimate transformation of the lover, through bereavement, into a nothing of nothings, a lower than death. Whichever of these senses one chooses, further difficulties seem to arise. With the first sense, the difficulty is that Donne is not, any longer, like other lovers at all, quite the reverse. In this context he is not 'every dead thing', but the one that contrasts with all the others. With the second sense, there is indeed a '*new* Alchimie' at work, and we are reminded that the 'next spring' of stanza 2, and the 'next worlde', are not alike but wholly unlike (Donne cannot say 'At the next worlde, that is at the next spring', the 'that is' disintegrates); and 'enjoy your summer all' can only become ironical.

I raise these difficulties, without pursuing them, to do no more than raise the possibility that the kind of poetry which invites us to a delighted participation in brilliantly witty verse may in the end begin to reach, as it were, a natural limit. Beyond a certain point, it cannot hope altogether to satisfy the interests which it encourages readers to cultivate and sharpen.

It is a poetry where explicit statement and an impression of argument are prominent: perhaps, to notice its limits of action may pre-dispose us to take renewed interest in a poetry where statement and argument are not so prominent. This will have its application at a later stage.

If we approach the poem from another point of view, we notice that the substance of the 'Nocturnall' is made up of two different substances. First, there is an intense personal experience of loss and so of loneliness. Second, there is much by way of ideas about this world and the next; about death and immortality; about the transience of human life; about the differences between men, animals, plants and inanimate things; and about the nature and processes of being and not-being. These ideas are dazzlingly interwoven into the contemplation of the personal experience. They become its unique embodiment, but they are by no means merely parts of that personal experience. In themselves, they are constituents of a common cultural heritage; and it is this, not any personal response or discovery, which provides the poet with what enables him to see his disastrous experience as temporary, and so to resolve and terminate his poem. What makes this resolution possible, the poet recalls from the common stock.

That the case of Cowper's 'Castaway' is (like that of the speaker in the 'Nocturnall') unique, proves to be written into the very metaphor of the poem: if a man is a castaway from a ship that speeds on, he is lost while the others are saved. The speaker's tragic isolation is an isolated tragedy. One peculiar word in the poem underlines this uniqueness. It is the word 'snatch'd' in the lines:

> When, *snatch'd* from all effectual aid,   (63)
>   We perish'd, each alone.

These lines are themselves especially prominent. Only a single couplet from the end of the poem, they are what confirm the analogy between the literal castaway, and the poet; and since 'effectual aid' is a synonym for the religious term 'effective grace', they indicate exactly how the two cases can be agonizingly alike. 'Snatch'd' is so expressive, because it almost self-evidently refers not to the working of the system of providence, but to a special and abnormal dispensation. Snatching *means* uniqueness.

So far, the poet of the 'Nocturnall', and of 'The Castaway' are alike. Each is creating a poem of the special case. The distinction between them is twofold. Put baldly, it is first that in respect of the tragic situation which it deals with, Cowper's poem impresses one as being less in earnest; and second, that Cowper's poem can put nothing forward by way of remedy for that situation.

What makes 'The Castaway' less in earnest is really its whole structure. It is written to a pattern which is frequent in poetry, and which almost always has the same effect. This pattern comprises the detailed description in literal terms of an incident or situation; and then the brief and dogmatic application of that to some wholly other incident or situation. Cowper's application is apt and ingenious. In the first stanza, the line 'When *such* a destin'd wretch as I' (3) affords the reader, at the beginning, a hint that in due course there will be an application: though not necessarily that it will be the eschatalogical one it turns out to be. In the last stanza, the detail of the application is terse and close. Sea, storm, darkness, light, and 'voice divine' which might speak over a stormy sea, all prove to be familiar ideas in either the vehicle-situation, or the tenor-situation – the literal, or the figurative. In spite of this, the standing conditions in which any 'application-poem' has to be read do not fail to have their effect. A poet who can express his conviction that he is eternally damned, through the elaborate description of an event in the life of an unknown mariner, has set that conviction at a distance. 'Application' entails remoteness. This is what I meant by saying that Cowper's poem seemed relatively less in earnest than Donne's.

It is clear also that Cowper's poem lacks the affirmative movement which gave Donne's poem its resolution:

> Since she enjoys her long night's festival,
> Let me prepare towards her . . .

This sudden and unheralded new idea was available to Donne from the common cultural heritage, and one could almost say that the poem was possible only by virtue of a dramatic temporary forgetting of what that heritage had to say. Cowper's poem, on the other hand, offers no hint of any such thing. No remedy for the speaker's plight can be foreseen.

One cannot say that this amounts to an unorthodoxy in the strict sense, because Christianity has a certain place for it. Yet, it is a little as if the poet of 'The Castaway' were trying to deal not with a traditional and long-standing but with some new spiritual ailment; something which he does not quite identify, which he lacks the terms to describe rightly, and which it is beyond him to deal with. If he really had a straightforward religious conviction that he was spiritually damned, he ought to feel more agonized than to write so neat a poem; and perhaps also, he ought to find more hope in the traditional reassurances which the religious cultural heritage could offer him.

Was Cowper on the brink of a new experience, and a new concern and perplexity, such as lies so plainly before the reader of Arnold's poem? –

Yes! in the sea of life enisled . . .   (1)
We mortal millions live *alone*.

Arnold himself italicizes the word 'alone'. Whether or not we like that particular device, it says clearly that the word needs to be pondered because its idea is startling and probably new. In any literal, obvious sense, what the poem says is false. If there are millions, they are not alone. The poem calls upon its readers to identify the novel sense in which they can indeed be so.

The first word gives an almost unique emphasis to the fact that the poem is not an ordering of experience by some traditional understanding, but is about an experience newly arrived at and newly comprehended. '*Yes!*' What, one may ask, makes Arnold burst out with this exclamation of surprised conviction and discovery? It seems there has come to him just the very metaphor which expresses, all in one, both the nature of the unfamiliar experience *and its universality*. 'Enisled'. Here is the predicament that the poem concerns itself with. It seems like a newly identified predicament. Its universality is as integral to the metaphor that conveys it, as singularity was integral to the metaphor of the castaway.

In this poem (though not in others, which will concern the main part of this chapter) Arnold has nothing to say about a remedy for the predicament his poem defines: and the last stanza builds that lack of remedy deep into the scheme of things. It is 'a God' who 'ordered' it: made it part of the order of things. He did so when he 'bade' the waters to cover the earth. The tragic divisiveness of life belongs to Creation.

A sequence therefore seems to establish itself as between Donne's poem, Cowper's, and Arnold's. All three are concerned with somewhat similar states of mind: a quintessence of 'privation' and 'emptiness'; 'wretchedness'; 'longing like despair'. For the first, the experience is private and remediable. For the second, it is private and remediless. For the third, it is universal and remediless. The second and third poems could not say these things with greater decisiveness and finality. Take either idea away, and the whole train of thought – and more than that, the whole generative metaphor of each poem – would have to be abandoned.

Historically, these three poems taken by themselves provide an impression only. All the same, it is helpful to think of them together, if they bring to a focus what we have all probably encountered in many contexts. All three are poems of the flagging and failing of the spirit. In one way or in another, all three link failure of the spirit and man's isolation from others. The second adds the idea that the spirit can undergo a disaster for which there is no remedy; and in it we also see the idea that this disastrous spiritual state is not a merely traditional ill. The third poem decisively adds the idea of the newness and as yet uncomprehendedness of this condition of spiritual failure and flagging. It adds also, equally decisively, the thought that it is no personal and distinctive crisis, and that spiritual decline and collapse which go with isolation from one's fellows are part of the human lot.

The link which these poems advance between despair and isolation is full of meaning. Many poems of the eighteenth and nineteenth centuries are poems of grief or melancholy. But if the Romantic consciousness valued the isolation of the individual, it also feared that isolation, knew it for a dispiriting power, and sought to escape it. Edward Young, as early as

1759, may have written the strangely disturbing and modern words, 'dive deep into thy bosom, cultivate full intimacy with the stranger within thee'. Rousseau may have written that he was 'Tiré je ne sais comment de l'ordre des choses' (35), that therefore 'Tout ce qui m'est extérieur m'est étranger désormais . . . Je suis sur la terre comme dans une planète étrangère' (39), and 'je m'accoutumais . . . à nourrir mon coeur de sa propre substance, et à chercher toute sa pâture au dedans de moi . . .' But that is one movement, one moment only, of Rousseau's mind. He knew perfectly well also that communion with others restored life and elasticity to the spirit. An incident in the seventh of the *Rêveries d'un Promeneur Solitaire* is illustration of this fact. Rousseau is high in the Swiss mountains, collecting plants. He thinks it a wild and lonely place, with only the original grandeur of Nature around him, and he sits down to muse and meditate. Then he hears a little noise which he cannot identify. He peers through the bushes about him, and only twenty yards away he finds a little stocking-works, one more sign of the Swiss mountaineers' ubiquitous industry and independence. One half expects him – he half expected himself – to be repulsed and alienated by the intrusion. The reverse is what happened. 'Mon premier mouvement fût un sentiment de joie de me retrouver parmi les humains' (135). Isolation may bring self-revelation ('les trésors que je portais en moi-même' (2)), but it turns out to be a poignant, precarious, probably over-demanding second-best.

II

The main part of this chapter will discuss (not in chronological order) several nineteenth-century poems: Arnold's 'Thyrsis'; Coleridge's 'Dejection: A Letter'; Wordsworth's 'Ode: Intimations of Immortality'; Shelley's 'Adonais'; Coleridge's 'Ancient Mariner' (briefly); and Tennyson's *Maud*. These are all poems which centre upon the matter (I shall not say 'idea' for a particular reason) of failure of the psychic powers and of a regeneration that restores them. Since two of these poems, however, are written in the convention of the pastoral elegy, it may be helpful to look first at the 'November Eclogue' in Spenser's *Shephearde's Calendar*, the earliest celebrated example of the *genre* in English. Doing so will help in the end to make clear how 'Thyrsis' and 'Adonais' were written by poets putting the elegy form to a new use.

The 'November Eclogue' seems to me a splendid success, though perhaps of a once not particularly difficult kind. It is also poetry of a now unfamiliar kind. It does not penetrate and explore an experience, working intimately into its nuances, evoking and suggesting; nor even seek to do these things. What it displays is a simplified comprehension, *but a mastered one*: a comprehension which is limited but perfect, and which therefore makes possible an epigrammatic brevity and shapeliness. It does not attempt to re-create thinking and speaking; the thinking had all been done, in final form, long before. So, it is free to create an impression of singing:

> But thing on earth that is of most availe,   (87)
> > As vertues braunch and beauties budde,
> Reliuen not for any good.
> > O heauie herse,
> *The braunch once dead, the budde eke needes must quaile.*
> > O carefull verse.

That virtue stands to beauty as branch to bud is an idea we have lost: but Spenser handles it as an idea perfectly understood. Because this is so, he can exploit its contradictory ('if the life, which was virtuous, has terminated, does it not follow that the beauty, mere consequence of virtue, must disappear?') in a single incisive and effortless line: 'The braunch once dead, the budde eke needes must quaile.' Here is a somewhat similar passage:

> The sonne of all the world is dimme and darke: (67)
> > The earth now lacks her wonted light,
> And all we dwell in deadly night,
> > O heauie herse.
> Break we our pypes, that *shrild as lowde as Larke* . . .

It would be easy to condemn these lines for idling pleonastically with the words *dimme, darke, deadly, night*. More significant is how the poet puts to use a plain contrast perfectly comprehended. Once he knew gaiety and exuberance directly and intimately: now he is equally familiar with lightlessness and grief. These things present themselves to him with the unforced finality of second nature. All the ease of this comprehension, all the breadth and sharpness of the contrast, show themselves in one flash in the splendid surprise of the delayed third rhyme: carke, darke . . . *Larke*. When mere rhyming and the essential nerve of the thought are as much one as this, we cannot say even which has been the means to which. For the poet who enjoys such an effortless overview of his thought, such breadth and sharpness of focus, explorativeness is jejeune. Suggestion, inter-animation and complexity would obfuscate and demean.

Such qualities of thought and creativity run through the poem:

> All Musick sleepes, where death doth leade the daunce . . .
>
> (105)

and:

> She raignes a goddesse now emong the saintes,   (175)
> That whilome was the saynt of shepheards light . . .

are two examples more. This is why it is a splendid success, though of an unfamiliar and classical kind. At the same time, Spenser's effortless limpidity of vision dominates the very hinge of his poem; even, perhaps, leaves it a little tame. The 'hinge' of a classical elegy like the 'November Eclogue' comes when the poet suddenly, dramatically calls to mind a reason why grief and dispiritedness are misplaced: a deeper comprehension of his subject tells him that the right response is not grief but joy. In the poem which served Spenser as his immediate model, and from which he derived a number at least of the more conventional turns of thought and expression in the 'November Eclogue', this turning-point is revealed with exceptional blatancy, and intimates to us the social function such verse was to serve. The poem is Marot's 1531 'Eglogue I . . . sur le Trépas de ma Dame Loyse de Savoye, Mère du Roy', and the lines in question run:

> Chantez mes vers, fresche douleur conceue.   (189)
> *Non, taisez-vous, c'est assez deploré;*

Marot's 'hinge' comes as a sudden, uncaused, arbitrary rejection of the stance which has dominated his poem for 150 lines. There is no poetic justification whatever. After 150 lines of lamentation, it is not so much a poetic as a social obligation to about turn. First there was a social obligation to celebrate grief, now comes one to celebrate that return of life-affirming-ness which, in due course, properly succeeds it. Marot's poem, one may say, is a dependent poem. It draws not merely its ideas, but its innermost structure, from what lies outside itself. One is reminded of the laboured, conventional complacencies of Claudius's suavely fake admonishment to Hamlet:

> 'Tis sweet and commendable in your nature, Hamlet.
>
> (I.ii.87)
>
> To give these mourning duties to your father;
> But you must know . . .
>   . . . to persever
> In obstinate condolement is a course
> Of *impious* stubbornness . . .
> It shows a will most *incorrect to heaven*,
> A heart unfortified . . .

The hinge in Spenser's poem, quoted below, is free from Marot's abrupt banality:

> But maugre death, and dreaded sisters deadly spight,
> And gates of hel, and fyrie furies forse:
> She hath the bonds broke of eternall night,
> Her soule vnbodied of the burdenous corpse.
> Why when weepes Lobbin so without remorse?
>   O Lobb, thy losse no longer lament,
>   Dido nis dead, but into heauen hent,
>   O happye herse,
> Cease now my Muse, now cease thy sorrowes sourse,
>   O ioyfull verse.

This poem recalls a great if covert truth which for Spenser is what ultimately, and not just socially, calls for an end to grief. The reader's thought is guided by the sequence 'gates of hel . . . bonds broke', to receive, in the next line, one of the few richly, individually charged words in the whole poem – 'vnbodied'.

The word comes disruptively, in a quite new sense. One is still entering into all it means by the time one reads the words 'burdenous corpse', which set the fact of death in so transformed a light. A mounting, chromatic progression runs through the thought: and the reader's attention is drawn to and held upon the change-in-continuity of the passage, by the complex patterns of alliteration and more particularly of assonance which run through lines 2, 3 and 4 of the stanza, and indeed to some extent through the whole of it.* We can be deluded into thinking that the passage displays only a conventional and 'poetic' vocabulary. An attentive reading will bring out how much the poet has done to release his transforming idea progressively and dramatically, to make of it an articulated and moving re-discovery.

For all that, though: 'But maugre death . . .' It is a *re-discovery* by which the poem is transformed. With the first three words of the stanza the reader knows just what that re-discovery will be. He does not know in advance the stages of re-illumination through which Spenser will mediate it to him, but he knows from the start what it is in its essence. Once again, it is something entrenched in the common cultural heritage; its availability and pre-determinedness is as assured as was the resolution of Donne's 'Nocturnall'. In fact, of course, it is the very same article of faith. One might perhaps say that there was a real voyage of discovery that ran through the *verbal* texture of the lines quoted above: but it is the voyage of discovering, stage by stage, *how* the poet is going to bring the great idea before us.

III

The nineteenth-century poems which are now to be discussed do not stand as something new in poetry simply in the sense that they brought forward some new doctrine or idea about re-generation out of the condition of psychic failure. In fact, the notion that, even in principle, one could simply have an effective new doctrine or idea about such a matter is an

---

* This transpires more clearly if the reader calls Elizabethan pronunciation to mind.

extravagance. Any *idea* for such a regenerative transformation would, if it was not part of a traditionally long-established wisdom, have to come out of a newly-identified and newly-felt *experience*. What seems most interesting in these poems is that they are not only, not even primarily, discussions or statements about psychic regeneration. Their primary concern is not to provide a detached descriptive summary of the experience of regeneration, but to re-enact it – or for all the reader can say to the contrary simply to be *the enactment itself* of that experience. The reader is not told second-hand about the experience, its possibility, importance, or anything of the kind. He finds himself really taken through the experience as if it were his own. He undergoes the state of psychic failure first-hand, and then he is taken first-hand out of it, and into regenerative release and restored life. Wordsworth's 'Immortality Ode' (also discussed below) is an exception: it draws on traditional ideas to a certain extent, and it probably ought to be seen as a more discursive poem than the others, one concerned to describe and elucidate rather than to enact.

It is the centrality of the enacting that, in several of these poems, gives such importance to the scenes and events that figure in them. The author of 'Thyrsis', for example, is meant to seem to be walking along throughout the whole length of the poem: what he *does* is what the poem *is*. 'The Ancient Mariner', and *Maud*, are both essentially narrative poems, and the subtitle of *Maud* – 'A Mono*drama*' – makes particularly clear how different this is merely from a discursive, contemplative poem. 'Dejection: a Letter' appears at first to be pure meditation, but it is a meditation on the poet's part which takes place while a storm rages outside, and Coleridge works the storm into his poem in such a way as to make this altogether other than simple description or discussion. 'Adonais' proves to have an inconspicuous but long-sustained and powerful dramatic dimension, and once again this makes the poem an action and an experience, not simply a statement and a meaning.

'Thyrsis' is a pastoral elegy lamenting the death of Arnold's friend Clough. Yet no one can read this poem and suppose that Clough – Thyrsis – is at the centre of it. In more ways than one, that subject was inconvenient or even uncongenial to

Arnold. Clough had withheld support from the poetic qualities that Arnold favoured; he had not lived, or envisaged life, much along Arnold's lines; and he had not found much inspiration in the Oxfordshire places Arnold now wanted to write about.

Arnold makes some concession, not perhaps quite enough for an adequate record, to the facts of the case. He says that it was preoccupation with 'life of men unblest' (46) which drew Clough from the pastoral Cumnor scene, and that his verse 'learnt a stormy note/ Of men contention-tossed' (223). But if these things were true, then the inconsistencies of the poem are beginning to show; Thyrsis (i.e. Clough) was far from having been 'on like quest' with the Scholar-Gipsy. The Scholar-Gipsy himself was emblem of an untiring search for the 'fugitive and gracious light' ('shy to illumine') which the poem takes its stand by. This no doubt accords with Arnold's own position and aspirations in the poem, but there is less of an affinity between Clough and the Scholar-Gipsy than of a clash. Nor could Arnold take even the place where Clough was buried as emblem of the English pastoral scene and its gracious but fugitive virtues. Clough was buried in Florence. Lines 167–190, which link him with the Great-Mother goddess and with a sanguinary elegiac pastoral of Greek tradition, digress widely and indeed disruptively from the areas of thought and feeling which make up this especially English pastoral poem as a whole.

More disruptive to the poem is something about Arnold himself: the poem seems to show him as not wholly sincere, and as if his professions diverged from his intentions.

Too rare, too rare, grow now my visits here!

The line comes twice (31, 231), and (unintentionally no doubt) Arnold throws that fact into relief by adding an exclamation mark the second time. Yet his visits are rare because he has made another choice of life. This idea indeed comes, rather in passing, in lines 38–9; but nothing is made of it, and it is lost sight of in the crucial stanzas at the close of the poem. The impression is that a mere 'whisper' (235) from what is called the voice of Thyrsis (but in fact it has to be the voice of the Scholar-Gipsy) will be enough to redeem the fevered urban context of Arnold's life, and will be enough merely in that it will 'chase fatigue and fear', not in that it will achieve anything more strenuous or illuminative. The Scholar-Gipsy (we are given to understand) never compromised, and made precisely the sacrifice which Thyrsis had no wish to make and which the poet himself is really declining to make. The result is that as soon as it is contemplated attentively, 'Thyrsis' begins to seem a little factitious, an attempted identification, by the surface texture of the poem, of attitudes and choices which really diverge. There is a sense that Arnold wanted, or perhaps only half wanted, the poem to be truer for him than it was.

Yet these points conceal some of the interest of 'Thyrsis'. Its interest is that Arnold was trying to use the pastoral elegy to perform a new and distinctive poetic task: one close as it could be to his own inner life, and meaningful for his time. We have to begin by recognizing that the poem is a far more urgently personal one than appears at first from its traditional *genre* as a pastoral elegy. It does not open with any merely general description of the Cumnor Hills west of Oxford, where Arnold had walked with Clough years before. It brings the poet himself directly before the reader, as he walks there now, and as he thinks out loud while he does so. The landscape appears only in the second place and in the second person. It is Arnold, the searcher, who is presented as at the centre of the poem; and as for Thyrsis:

> Here came I often, often, in old days –   (9)
> Thyrsis and I . . .

Thyrsis, the ostensible subject, enters as an afterthought.

The personal predicament which preoccupies Arnold is a little like that which appears in Donne's 'Nocturnall', and the two other poems already discussed along with it. The valley of the Upper Thames may be as beautiful as ever, but for all that, Arnold is assailed by a weakening and dispiriting of the psyche:

> Only, methinks, some loss of habit's power   (22)
> Befalls me wandering through this upland dim.

It is not merely the practical inconvenience that he has grown unfamiliar with the footpaths and the landmarks. The landscape is a 'country of the heart'. Its landmarks and above all its 'single elm-tree bright' articulate a lost self-fulfilment and creativity. When Arnold writes of the 'loss of habit's power', he realizes what has gone:

> Ah me! this many a year (36)
> My pipe is lost, my shepherd's holiday!

'Thyrsis' was indeed a sudden recrudescence of poetic activity after some years during which Arnold had given little sign of it. Later in the poem there comes a rather similar passage. Arnold directly identifies the fall of night in this crucial landscape with his own slowly intensifying inner predicament:

> Yes, thou art gone! and round me too the night (131)
>> In ever-nearing circle weaves her shade.
>> I see her veil draw soft across the day,
>> I feel her slowly chilling breath invade
>> The cheek grown thin, the brown hair sprent with grey;
>> I feel her finger light
> Laid pausefully upon life's headlong train;
>> The foot less prompt to meet the morning dew,
>> The heart less bounding at emotion new,
> And hope, once crushed, less quick to spring again.

All this is 'what wears out the life' of mortal men in 'The Scholar-Gipsy':

> 'Tis that repeated shocks, again, again, (144)
>> Exhaust the energy of strongest souls
>> And numb the elastic powers.

'Habit's power',/'again, again . . . the elastic powers': the word 'power' comes, in each poem, in just the same context. But the *action* of the poem is to work a way from this depletion of power into renewed power. 'Thyrsis' rehearses an experience which is to restore the depleted strength of the spirit:

> A fugitive and gracious light he seeks, (201)
>> Shy to illumine; *and I seek it* too.

But in contrast to Spenser or Donne, the poet of 'Thyrsis' found no forming idea ready to hand that might help him to create such an action. His starting-point is that the terms of life are to be sought out afresh in a self-determined, self-created effort, which can draw on no traditional framework of re-generating conceptions, but has to find the source of renewal, as if for the first time, in the poet's own first-hand and unaided experience. Where he finds it is in an almost secret place, rich with Oxfordshire local colour and its indigenous people – the boat-girl, the mowers (121–30) – and richly personal to the poet:

> I know these slopes; who knows them if not I? (111)

When the secret place is for a moment invaded by the 'troop of Oxford hunters', jovial and talkative, the poet's response is 'let me fly . . .!' to escape them. But the reward of prompt flight is to re-locate the most idiosyncratic item of all, the tree, 'bare on its lonely ridge' which Thyrsis and the poet had sought together in the past, and which was symbol to them of forces and realities which did not 'illumine' so much as 'gave . . . power' (214).

> Here was thine height of *strength*, thy golden prime! (219)
> And still the haunt beloved a *virtue* yields.

'Power', 'strength', 'virtue'. Arnold is not seeking a truth or an idea, but a regenerating experience, a regenerative force. The poem could barely do more to realize that experience in wholly distinctive, idiosyncratic terms.

·On the surface, it appears to be a lonely experience: a man past his first youth, on a solitary upland walk, as twilight fades into night. That impression may seem confirmed by the poet's flight from the jovial gregariousness of the hunters. The facts are otherwise. There is a rejection of hearty indiscriminate gregariousness; but not for the sake of self-isolation, for a chosen, elect communion, a small group. This is what the poem intimates through its whole development and in its climactic moment. It is a search for terms on which the poet may have contact once again with the unique friend and fellow-poet who has departed; and the climactic moment, when he finds the tree, does not leave him 'Sole in these fields' (192) – that by itself, says the poem, would be cause enough for 'despair'.

Arnold says that he will not despair while he still has the tree, and the reason is, the tree says to him (the words "'tis clear' (196) show it) that the Scholar-Gipsy still 'haunts' 'these slopes', endows them with his restoring spirit, and makes that available to the seeker. Arnold finds regeneration not in solitude, but in an elect if intangible company.

'Thyrsis' is thus a poem of the Self and its regeneration. It identifies an initial situation of dwindling psychic strength; and it seeks not to describe, but to enact and pass through, an experience which will restore psychic adequacy. It identifies that as something primary, personal and idiosyncratic; and it identifies recovery with a union of the poet to others. The poet ceases to be 'enisled'. He wins through that estranging severance of the 'contention-tossed' 'world and wave of men' (224, 39), and recovers the precious few who are superior to it. I argued earlier on that Arnold in fact cannot bring his own aspirations, and also Clough, and what the Scholar-Gipsy stands for, and his own actually adopted way of life, adequately into a unity in this poem. Partly, this was because he attempted to make a traditional form serve a new, more intimate and more demanding purpose.

IV

Coleridge's 'Letter to Sara Hutchinson' of 4 April 1802 (also known as 'Dejection: a Letter') was not published until 1947. It is among the handful of once-lost masterpieces of its period which have been re-discovered only in the recent past and which have provided a new and more significant picture of the Romantic age. Several critics have considered, at length, whether the 'Letter' or 'Dejection: an Ode', the abridged version of the poem which Coleridge prepared for publication in his lifetime, is the more successful. None has given a wholly satisfactory account of what the unity of the 'Letter' must be seen to consist in.

'Dejection: an Ode' may perhaps be Pindaric, but the 'Letter' is a poem that stands by itself. It is a major example of how the Romantic period broke away from traditional forms and sought to create new and unique ones. It is no verse epistle pure and simple. Much of the poem is written in a blank verse, intimate and uninsistent, which could turn it in that direction; but everywhere, it shows a tendency to break into greater animation of rhythm and greater lyricism in both diction and metre. I now quote two examples not to labour the obvious, but to add another and less obvious point that arises from them. The first consists of the whole third paragraph of the poem:

> My genial spirits fail – (44)
> And what can these avail
> To lift the smoth'ring Weight from off my Breast?
> It were a vain Endeavor,
> Tho' I should gaze for ever
> On that Green Light, which lingers in the West!
> I may not hope from outward Forms to win
> The Passion & the Life, whose Fountains are within!

This is a note quite other than what is to be found in Pope's *Epistles*, or Burns's, or for that matter Shelley's 'Letter to Maria Gisborne'.

The second passage is from later in the poem (Coleridge's italics):

> . . . There *was* a time when tho' my path was rough, (232)
> The Joy within me dallied with Distress;
> And all Misfortunes were but as the Stuff
> Whence Fancy made me Dreams of Happiness:
> For Hope grew round me, like the climbing Vine . . .
> . . . But now Ill Tidings bow me down to earth –
> Nor care I, that they rob me of my Mirth –

So far, this passage has something of the relaxed but cool and enquiring style which is characteristic of the verse epistle as a *genre*. Then, however, the poem goes on:

> But Oh! each Visitation (240)
> Suspends what Nature gave me at my Birth,
> My shaping Spirit of Imagination!

There is a recurrent to and from between epistolary and lyrical. From the standpoint of the local texture of language, this seems to be the radical principle of the poem's construction; but it will prove also to serve a purpose beyond itself.

A second look at the passages just quoted will reveal what this is. Each, in fact, is an emotional paradox. We read that the genial spirits fail; but if, out of that, Coleridge can go straight on to write:

The Passion and the Life, whose Fountains are within!

then the genial spirits have not failed. Momentarily at least, in the creation of that splendid line, all animation, all latent sensuousness, they have succeeded. Something has been made out of what is alleged in the poem to be nothing. Much the same is true of the second passage. What does 'suspend' mean here? Perhaps its primary meaning is that the shaping spirit is merely rendered null. But if the lines say no more than that, then their resonance and vividness, and their embodied sense that Imagination itself is something of an embodied daemonic visitant, belie their doleful message. The suggestion is rather that the imagination is somehow suspended, arrested, in mid-career – but in the fullness of its life.

The 'Letter to Sara Hutchinson' is one of the poems of its period which attempts to deal with a condition of psychic dispiritedness. It is not easy to be satisfied with W. J. Bate's statement (*Coleridge*, 1966, 107) even that 'the *Dejection Ode* enacts a drama of *intellectual* discovery'. The word 'intellectual' conceals the great concentration in the poem upon a richly yet delicately particularized situation, in which the poet is battling with not intellectual but psychic inadequacy. The poet's reverie, and the powerful internal movement of the poem, begin within this particularized situation: the 'dull sobbing Draft' of the night wind that 'drones and rakes' on the strings of the aeolian harp; the 'swimming phantom light' of the moon, 'rimm'd' with a silver thread; the thrush in the larch-tree

which *pushes* out in tassels green   (26)
It's *bundled* Leafits

– and the 'lazy flakes' of the thin clouds – all these turns of phrase and thought combine to create a sense of how the poet is intent upon a real situation that lies around him, impinging multifariously on his life.

But the particularity of the poem itself is not something about

description. In the first place it is the distinctive weave and turn
of the verse and language, line by line. In his best meditative
poems, Coleridge displays an almost unrivalled power to cast
his train of thought and feeling into a distinctiveness of shape
and movement. The first paragraph of the 'Letter' illustrates
this well; but it is no more than a foretaste of an idiosyncrasy
of movement that shows throughout the poem. Only in grasp-
ing what this is can one sense how Coleridge is wrestling in the
poem with the spiritual predicament in which he stands.

Even in the two early passages already quoted there was a
note of unexpectedness and idiosyncrasy: of a positive emerging
paradoxically and mysteriously out of a negative. The first
paragraph said that 'the Old Moon' was in the new moon's
'Lap' (13), and that this suggests a stormy night. There is the
plain record of what Coleridge has seen, and the simple
inference from it. But if the common musical metaphor is used,
and we call this a theme, then we must say that there is no mere
'statement' of this theme. It is not stated, in that it comes in an
elaborated, intricated form even at its first appearance. By
opening his poem with 'the grand old Ballad of Sir Patrick
Spence', Coleridge places the reader in a starting position of
seeing a great poem as something almost primaeval: an
artefact of nature, if that were possible. The line of thought
taken by the opening paragraph then is, that on the assumption
that the writer of that early folk-poem knew about weather, it
follows that the present quiet breeze will turn to storm,
because of the special fact that the old moon lies in the new
moon's arms. A plain diction for expressing a train of thought
at once involuted and lucid is characteristic of Coleridge. The
reader is drawn into a special sort of participation. He can
barely enter the poet's mind at all, unless he goes along, at
every step, with a thorough-going distinctiveness in its curve and
bias. In the first paragraph this ramifies even a stage further:

> the dull sobbing Draft, that drones & rakes　　　　(6)
> Upon the Strings of this Eolian Lute,
> *Which better far were mute.*

Why the unexpected reversal of thought in that last line? It has
a parallel at the end of the paragraph. The poet's general tone

about the coming storm has been an anxious one; and then at
the end –

> I see the Old Moon in her Lap, foretelling (13)
> The coming-on of Rain and squally Blast –
> O! Sara! that the Gust ev'n now were swelling,
> And the slant Night-shower driving loud and fast!

– another sudden reversal of thought. The anxiety over the
storm has turned to welcome. It is an opposite movement from
that over the lute. For what psychological entanglement, what
diverging of forces, is the poem preparing its reader? Why does
it say that it would be better for the breeze to mount into a
storm, yet for the lute to fall silent?

Here we see the exact grain and nerve of the distinctive
experience the poem enacts: and within which the poet is seek-
ing regeneration. What concerns him is that very core of
entanglement and involvement. Only by playing to and fro, it
seems, about the heart of it, can release and affirmation be
secured. This distinctive movement, circulatory yet centrifugal,
proceeds in what follows to shape a whole series of 'movements'
in the poem, occupying its substance before the return of the
storm in line 186.

There are four movements of thought in the poem up to that
point. First the 'grief without a pang' of the deflated and
dispirited psyche is turned to other thoughts by the song of the
thrush; and is transformed (an irregular, wavering trans-
formation) into the moment of excitement which recalls the
'Passion and the Life, whose Fountains are within'. This takes
place in lines 17–51. Second, as childhood memories, and the
thought of how he must be sharing a common experience with
the absent Sara, enter the poet's mind, he progressively breaks
from his weakness into a mood of excitement and benediction
(52–98). Third, another more recent memory of joy shared
with others undergoes a contrary kind of transformation, and
turns to regret and self-blame (99–129). Fourth, the poet
thinks of the absent Sara's present happiness with those she
loves: and grows into a realization that he would sooner con-
template this steadily, though absent from it, than have
occasional tantalizing glimpses of it in reality (130–68).

There are the four movements, each based on some sort of digression, before the return of the storm as the immediate subject:

The dark distressful Dream!   (185)
I turn from it, & *listen to the Wind*
Which long has rav'd unnotic'd . . .

Now the formation of the poem begins to transpire. What the poet says in those lines is a little simpler than the truth. The storm may have raved unmentioned, perhaps; but not 'unnotic'd'. Those who are aware of what the slow rising of a storm in the quiet and open of an exposed countryside is like, will realize that it has been present all the time in the four long paragraphs, wavering but climactic, which have just been summarized. When the storm is called a 'mighty Poet' (199), the underlying analogy between poet thinking and storm rising is more than mere similarity. The reader is asked to think once again as he did about the Sir Patrick Spence ballad. Poetic creativity is a fundamental and an ultimate; one, in the last analysis, with the simplest, most basic powers of the planet. This idea is given added depth when Coleridge once more identifies poetry and the world outside him (200–15), this time by seeing the lull and variation in the storm as if it were the variation between one poem and another, when the wind seems literally to be uttering each of them.

By accident, or design, the middle point of the poem seems to fall precisely where Coleridge writes "'Tis Midnight!' (216). Perhaps it was design: of the four trains of thought outlined above, the first and second ended (line 51, line 98) buoyantly, the third and fourth the reverse. It was at a nadir of gloom that Coleridge felt the storm break in once more. The mid-point of the night seems to come when inner life has been swept aside by all-surrounding storm.

If we regard the poem, after line 216, as entering on its second part, we soon find that this too consists of a series of movements of thought that bend back on themselves, like so much in the poem. But they do so through movement around a new idea: one that has appeared inconspicuously in the poem before, but now becomes the guiding conception. After 'midnight' there seem to be three movements in the poem, and the guiding idea which informs each is *Joy*. It is the converse of the despair which came to dominate the poem before midnight; and it accords better with that part of the night which approaches morning.

The first movement in the second half runs from line 216 to line 271. The poet recalls his power for joy in the past, but admits that his present troubles have taken away not merely gaiety, but every redeeming thing, whether the power to give meaning and dignity to localized griefs, or imagination itself. The second movement renews the thought of joy, this time in the poet's own children (272–95). But those children are too much the pledges of an inalienable deprivation, and that reassertion of joy also ends in dispiritedness. Then comes the last of the three movements in the second part: a new assertion which makes its appearance suddenly, and transforms the poem:

O Sara! we receive but what we give . . .   (296)

Joy can come neither from the past, nor from outside things in the present. It must come from within. The poem returns to the external scene it started from, but it now makes this the mere preliminary to what can really release the poet from his predicament. What was literal and external becomes internal and figurative. As against the 'phantom Light' and 'thin Clouds' of the opening paragraphs, the reader finds:

Ah! from the Soul itself must issue forth   (302)
A Light, a Glory, and a luminous Cloud
    Enveloping the Earth!

This 'Light, this Glory, this fair luminous Mist', is not weather; it is the self-affirmation of the inner world, and now it becomes an all-transforming joy from within, an exact but spectacular contrast to the deeply internalized 'Grief . . . that finds no natural Outlet' of the early part. This authentic and valid source of joy, once found, does not dissolve into dispiritedness. The poem ends on a note of triumphant jubilation expressed in imagery of the morning and the rising sun:

All Colors a Suffusion of that Light.   (323)

To thee would all Things live from Pole to Pole   (335)

O dear, as *Light* & *Impulse from above*   (339)
Thus may'st thou ever, evermore rejoice!

In concluding his poem on this note, Coleridge gives it power
and unity: the idea of internality which dominates its close
('the Life . . . within') emerges from its substance. It has been a
poem of the intensely distinctive and personalized experience,
both in its experienced *local* and setting, and in the idiosyncratic
weave which runs everywhere through the verse. Yet there has
also been much belonging to the outer world in the poem: the
poet's friends, and Sara herself and her children.

Methinks to weep with you   (256)
Were better far than to rejoice alone –

he says at one point. More than once, it has been the thought of
their oneness together, without himself, which has momentarily
restored him. If the poem ended on a note of pure internality,
it would do violence to all this part of itself that has gone before.

It does not end so. No *mere* withinness at last releases the
poem from recurrent despair into joy. Rather, it is self-release
and joy from within, which depend on an intact and triumphantly
self-affirming *social* unity, the unity of Sara and her children:

Thus, thus, should'st *thou* rejoice!   (334)

– in the closing moment of triumphant release. Sara has the
wherewithal for such an emotion immediately to hand, and
Coleridge has it (once the poem has recognized that for joy to
supervene the self must engage actively) not from any empty
internality, but from an active and delighted recollection of the
unshakeable social bond to which Sara herself belongs:

Thou being innocent & full of love,   (325)
And nested with the Darlings of thy Love,
And feeding in thy Soul, Heart, Lips, & Arms
Even what the conjugal & mother Dove,
That borrows genial Warmth from those, she warms,
Feels in the thrill'd wings, blessedly outspread –

The self is regenerated by the potent apprehension *within*, of a
matchless social order and social validity *without*.

V

Wordsworth's 'Immortality Ode' is another kind of poem, and there is no need here to discuss it in full; but to discuss it briefly throws light on Coleridge's poem, and on its poetic kind as a whole. Nothing would be easier than to suggest that the 'Immortality Ode' was the better poem. It would almost be enough to set Coleridge's:

> My genial Spirits fail –   (44)
>   And what can these avail
> To lift the smoth'ring Weight from off my Breast?
>   It were a vain Endeavour,
>   Tho' I should gaze for ever
> On that Green Light, which lingers in the West!

alongside Wordsworth's lines:

> It is not now as it hath been of yore; –   (6)
>   Turn wheresoe'er I may,
>   By night or day,
> The things which I have seen I now can see no more.

Although the 'Green Light' is memorable, Coleridge's lines confuse by over-emphasis and over-plenty. One cannot quite tell whether genial spirits of any kind, or only failing ones, would be unavailing; nor whether their failure is the same as the 'smoth'ring Weight', or the 'blank . . . eye' of a few lines earlier. This tone makes the whole passage seem a little composed and *voulu*.

By comparison, the Wordsworth lines have a modesty of tone and reticence of content exactly right for the opening of the poem. The one great fact of an all-embracing but elusive change in the poet's experience transpires without anything to complicate or distract; and the single act of specification ('by night or day') is just enough to make plain that the poem will deal not with the multifarious intricacies of experience but with what is simplest and most basic in it.

The next section of the 'Immortality Ode' confirms that impression:

> The Rainbow comes and goes,   (10)
>   And lovely is the Rose,

The Moon doth with delight
Look round her when the heavens are bare;
Waters on a starry night
Are beautiful and fair;
The sunshine is a glorious birth;
But yet I know, where'er I go,
That there hath past away a glory from the earth.

The achievement also of these lines lies in reticence. They make not a tenuous, but a sparse and chosen contact with reality. The major landmarks of a whole environment and a whole order of objects are touched out, once for all, with grave economy: leaving a sense that what is most striking is still to be said. True enough, there is more in the lines than at once meets the eye. The gazing, delighted moon, and the sun being born, convey a delicate but immense hint: that the world is somehow alive, somehow one with the speaker. The rainbow as simple play of colour, and also as a somehow magical visitation, is drawn out through the whole stanza by the three primary hues of rose, moon, and dark blue water, set in their order in the spectrum. Nor are the 'waters' quite simply dark blue. As it comes in its sequence, the very phrase which a hasty reading might pick on as empty repetition – 'beautiful *and fair*', gives just the right hint of glimmering pallor on what at first seems mere picturesque darkness.

The kind of criticism which has much to say, but selectively, about use of language, and inclines to see structure as something which can be identified through that alone, could leave an impression that Wordsworth's poem was far better than Coleridge's. Once the whole poem is read with attention, however, the stylistic shortcomings of the 'Immortality Ode' begin to transpire:

Thou, whose exterior semblance dost belie   (109)
    Thy Soul's immensity . . .

speaks quite another language from the passages quoted above. Most of the middle part of the poem (sections 5 to 9), memorable as the language is here and there, strike a high-sounding note in which the limpidity of the opening is lost. We know that the middle section was written much later than the earlier. This need not have been enough to bring about the discrepancy; but in resuming his poem, Wordsworth did not resume the situation out of which he began it. The third section opens:

> Now, while the birds *thus* sing a joyous sound . . .   (19)

But the 'thus' means little or nothing. The singing birds and bounding lambs are present only nominally. They have nothing to do with the rainbow, the moon, the dark waters; and the 'Fountains, Meadows, Hills, and Groves' of the final section are given no real, experienced unity with either. Again, in section 7 we read, of 'the Child' himself:

> See, at his feet, *some* little plan or chart,   (91)
> *Some* fragment from his dream of human life . . .

The feeble indefiniteness is very apparent: and this also shows in other ways. The opening lines of section 10:

> Then sing, ye Birds, sing, sing a joyous song!   (169)
> And let the young Lambs bound
> As to the tabor's sound!
> We in thought will join your throng . . .

What does that opening 'then' mean? Wordsworth has just said that even in the midst of sensuous experience with all its limitations and constrictions, human souls 'have sight' of preternatural reality. 'Then' cannot be a causal 'then', meaning that this fact *enables* the world of natural reality to rejoice. Perhaps Wordsworth is inviting us to see a kind of vigorous acquiescence, on his part, in the fact that the natural world rejoices: he acquiesces because, given that other and deeper fact about human insight, this as it were surface rejoicing is something he can accommodate and allot a place to. Alternatively, we can think that the birds and lambs have a knowledge of man's spiritual intimations which is somehow to be their reason for rejoicing. In either case, the slightness of the connection, and the remoteness from the beatified union with experience of the opening sections, are only too clear. There is certainly a dimension of the experienced world in the poem; but it is present erratically, even half-heartedly. The poet *makes room* for it within his scheme of things. Compare the last line above:

We *in thought* will join your throng . . .

Doubtless the literal meaning is simply that the poet will be a spectator of the lambs' dancing and will not dance himself. But the words seem revealingly non-engaged, and the 'We' is also revealing, the poet is turning editor.

In fact, the structure of this poem may be traced through its pronouns: though I am unsure whether to say that these reveal the structure, or create it. In the first four sections, the poet speaks as 'I', and in large part the other living creatures in the poem, whether the 'happy Shepherd-boy' or the animals, appear in the second person. There is a direct speaking between the poet and them, a living communion. The long middle part of the poem (sections 5 to 9) strikes another note from its very first line:

Our birth is but a sleep and a forgetting: (58)

Wordsworth, the seer, reflects on mankind. After this point, the first person singular makes its appearance fitfully and infrequently. Instead, we find the plural: 'Though inland far we be'; 'We will grieve not'; 'the human heart by which we live'. Correspondingly, the 'Child of Joy' of section 3 becomes in the middle, ruminative part of the poem no longer 'Thou', but 'him'. In the closing sections, singular and plural pronouns alternate so as to give us a thinker reflecting upon the experience of others, rather than his own experience:

The thought of *our* past years in *me* doth breed   (134)
Perpetual benediction . . .

Thanks to the human heart by which *we* live . . .   (201)
To *me* the meanest flower that blows can give
Thoughts that do often lie too deep for tears.

Something else also displays the ambivalency of the poem's action. A key passage in section 9 runs:

The thought of our past years in me doth breed
Perpetual benediction: not indeed

For that which is most worthy to be blest;
Delight and liberty . . .
    Not for these I raise
    The song of thanks and praise;
    But for those obstinate questionings
Of sense and outward things,
Fallings from us, vanishings;
    Blank misgivings of a Creature
Moving about in worlds not realized,
High instincts before which our mortal Nature
Did tremble like a guilty Thing surprised . . .

The ambiguities in these lines run on to the end of the section. Again the pronouns, and tenses also, give much away. The plural is used in two senses, neither of them the same as what the singular means. 'Our past years' must mean the generality of mankind, all those typified by the 'Child' of the middle sections. Wordsworth is reflecting, like a philosopher, on the human lot. But the change from 'doth' to 'did' in the last line is a tell-tale change. 'Our mortal Nature' cannot have a general sense if it takes a past tense. It must mean (more at least than it means anything else) Wordsworth's own 'mortal Nature' in the past; and it has been attracted to the plural partly because the general-human-lot plural was used just before, and partly because the whole dimension of first-hand personal experience, though still present in the poem, is now erratically and tenuously present. Wordsworth's first-hand experience seems to come back to him, amid all this meditating and speculating, as if *pluralized* into second-handness.

There is also an ambivalency in the very things which the poem is saying are at issue. 'Obstinate questionings/Of sense and outward things' has just the insistent and limiting quality of the middle sections of the poem. But the lines which follow ('Fallings from us', etc.) are different. It is hard to decide whether they refer plainly to the 'visionary gleam' itself, or to the equally shifting and uncertain sense that somehow it has gone ('Fallings from us, vanishings . . . misgivings' all fit this well). Either or both could be present in the sense. The lines speak much the same shadowy, exploring, visionary quality as those quoted at the beginning of this discussion. For a moment the poem seems to bring Wordsworth close to a shaping experience which is supremely important precisely because elusive. Yet the poem is sufficiently disordered for this precious strand in it to be obscured as soon as it appears. So, in a formal if not a moral sense, the 'Immortality Ode' lacks integrity. There is none of the sustained depth and distinctiveness of experience, generating the detail of the poem, present in 'Dejection: a Letter'. The 'Ode' *assembles* its items: items of sensuous life, passages of thinking, affirmation and mental response. But a major reason why they remain an assemblage is, that the poem is not even intended to make them into an integrated and unique experience. The guiding principle of the poem is not experience but exegesis: the principle of construction of the 'Immortality Ode' is an argument not an action.

VI

Shelley's 'Adonais' may be easier to understand fully if it is considered in the context of Coleridge's 'Letter' on one hand, and the 'Immortality Ode' on the other. 'Adonais' is both a statement of certain ideas, and a dramatic action or ritual embodying a distinctive experience; and the question at issue for the moment is, What is effected by the dimension of statement, and what by the dimension of embodied action? The usual answers to these questions, I believe, fail to reveal the major interest of the poem.

'Adonais' is naturally thought of, often enough, as an eloquent statement (in its later stanzas, that is) of certain philosophical ideas, those often loosely called Platonism, and on the other hand, it is easily recognized as a ritual-poem on the classical model of the pastoral elegy: the procession of mourners, the phase of total despair, the reception of the dead by Nature, the moment of reversal. Along with these, Shelley's own presence is recognized particularly in stanza 31 and thereafter; but has come to be seen chiefly as an embarrassing personal intrusion. The poem is more continuously, urgently and substantially a personal one than has been allowed; and the experience which as a whole it forms and embodies makes it a poem of poetic regeneration like others now being discussed. It is not a personal poem temporarily and by a lapse, but throughout, and through and through.

As with the 'Immortality Ode', something of the structure of the poem may be identified through attention to one inconspicuous detail: the pronouns. Shelley himself, the 'Power/Girt round with weakness' of stanza 32, appears in the poem as 'I' only in the first stanza and in the last; but for all that, he is present not merely as the speaking voice of the poem, but also as deeply engaged and involved within its situation: and it will in fact prove to be the case that he is so involved (though implicitly or indirectly so) throughout. The imperatives, and the second-person pronouns of the first seven stanzas emphasize how a kind of dialogue is going on between the poet and Urania. In stanza 18, the words 'Ah, woe is me!' bring him forward again. 'Whence are we, and why are we?' he exclaims in stanza 21. By this time there is a clear sense of him not as mourner for Adonais only, but as grieving for mankind: and in particular for himself. (What sort of a world is it for poets, the poem asks all the time, if Keats can meet such a death in youth?) The poet's own participation in the drama of the poem continues to show, not only in his veiled picture of himself as the 'Power/Girt round with weakness' (272–3) but by the stanzas which follow, in which phrases like 'Let *me* not vex . . . with inharmonious sighs,/The silence', '*Our* Adonais has drunk poison', 'fear no heavier chastisement from *me*', and 'Nor let *us* weep that our delight is fled', all sustain the impression of poet not as mere narrator but as actively participating in the whole. To put the matter, for a moment, in a terminology which in due course must be abandoned, 'Adonais' is not 'about' Keats's early death, but Shelley's own struggle and task in coming to terms with it.

In any pastoral elegy there should come a moment of transition from negative to positive. In 'Adonais' this seems to arrive abruptly, with the opening lines of stanza 39:

> Peace, peace! He is not dead, he doth not sleep – (343)
> He hath awaked from the dream of life –

But in fact, the transition to this new turn of thought is a gradual one, and as we understand its contours we see it as part of the writer's own struggle. The movement is not that of a formality and pageant, but of something more urgent, personal and striven-for. Perhaps the point may be put by saying that the stress in line 343 falls on the word 'not': 'He is *not* dead, he doth *not* sleep'. A first and merely approximate thought in the preceding stanza is being corrected. In just the same way, that stanza in its turn corrected what seemed like the implication of the ones before it. In stanzas 36 and 37, Shelley had lamented that 'Adonais' was poisoned (i.e., Keats had been struck down by vicious reviewers). In stanza 38, he qualified this to the extent of saying that that ostensible ground for sorrow was no true ground: Adonais was dead, but that meant that he had returned from the mortal world to eternity. Stanza 39 corrects once again: if he has done that, then he is now not dead at all. Rather, he has entered real life from out of 'the dream of life' (344). Then comes the last stage in the transition. If Adonais has gone not into death but into life, what he has left behind is death. That is what a sustained concentration comes to reveal as the truth of our present condition. The reversal is complete.

So, what the reader witnesses as the poem goes on is a sort of *work* of finding the answer to the cruel puzzle created by Keats's death; and, more and more prominently and explicitly, the experience of doing that work of thought embodies Shelley's own recovering of creative confidence and power. What happens in the later stanzas is that Shelley moves through the experience of mourning for Keats and celebrating Keats's death, to a release and regeneration obtained precisely through achieving a dependence upon communion with, even a kind of identification with, the dead Adonais. Moreover, like Arnold, like Coleridge, Shelley restores his own psyche in the restoration of a social bond, though again in a particular sense. The poem creates a situation in which, more and more, the reader is not told – he *finds*, that Shelley's grief has progressively modulated into joyous affirmation, his dispiritedness into self-realization: and he finds this, in that step by step the poem's action brings him to a very distinctive position: that *Keats–Adonais, and Shelley, can be one.*

In stanzas 41 to 46, there is a sequence of imagined transformations of reality, consequences of the transformation of idea ("'tis Death is dead, not he') which the poem has advanced: the poem calls upon all individual things of Nature to enjoy a new life (stanzas 41, 42); and this new life becomes the universal power, operating everywhere, of 'the one Spirit' and its transforming 'plastic stress'. But all the time, the poem is coming inconspicuously closer to Shelley's own need and predicament – and to a resolution of it. The re-energized cosmos is particularized in the earlier poets who suffered like Keats (the 'inheritors of unfulfilled renown': 397) but whom deeper understanding now shows, in the light of the "'tis Death is dead' intuition, to have had their full deserts in the end. The next stanza (47) seems at first to turn from these, in a formal, ritualistic way, back to the general idea of the mourner:

> Who mourns for Adonais? Oh, come forth,   (415)
> Fond wretch! and know thyself and him aright.

We should read those lines, though, with the opening words of the poem in mind. '*I* weep for Adonais'. What Keats is in truth, has by now been established. Appropriately therefore Shelley now begins to bring forward the matter of what in truth he is himself: and the words 'know *thyself and him*' register an implicit identification as between the two poets, which the rest of the poem is in fact to establish and confirm. First the 'fond' mourner is to make a great effort of thought, and strive to see his mistake. What he must do is something strange. He must fix his attention at one extreme upon the earth, and then, at the other extreme:

> As from a centre, dart thy spirit's light   (418)
> Beyond all worlds . . .

Finally he must 'shrink to a point within our day and night'. It is not easy to follow what is being called for; in fact, the poem must be asking the mourner somehow to identify himself, at one and the same time, with the Earth and with a star. Then he will see how ill-judged it was to mourn. Why? – Because Adonais himself has just been identified as a star. The Immortals have just said to him:

> 'Assume thy winged throne, thou *Vesper* of our throng!' (414)

The 'fond wretch' will then see the truth. His grief will cease as he himself becomes, even though for a moment only, what Adonais has become. But the nerve of this poetic movement is that it is not statement, but experience. The fond mourner does not merely understand what has happened to Keats: he is himself transformed for a moment, it happens also to him.

'Or go to Rome . . .' the next stanza begins. This may seem like a new start, but that is not so, and in reality it takes the experience of regenerative identification a step further. Rome was not only the city to which Keats–Adonais had himself gone shortly before his death. It was, one might almost say, the inevitable site in which to envisage and locate the regenerative event: a holy city, half-dead and half-derelict, but half-invaded by Nature in all its beauty and luxuriance. Heavenly, yet ruined, yet regeneratively overgrown, Rome embodied how the highest reality, death and the grave, and the whole world of natural abundance, were all ultimately one.

> Go thou to Rome, – at once the Paradise, (433)
> The grave, the city, and the wilderness;

It is because Rome is all it is, that two stanzas later the question:

> What Adonais is, why fear *we* to become? (459)

is a rhetorical question which can be put with confidence. Destruction and ruin are, here, unparalleled splendour.

That pronoun 'we' carries a special sense. Shelley's poem works out an identification with Keats not for its own sake but as part of a wider idea. It could not easily have been written in a language which (like classical Greek, say) had a dual 'we' as well as a plural one.

Over the obscure lines which precede line 459, it is beginning to become clear that for a moment the 'I' of the poem is speaking to himself:

> if the seal is set (453)
> Here, on one fountain of a mourning mind,
> Break it not thou!

The reference is to Shelley's own son William, who was buried in the Protestant cemetery at Rome in June 1819, about

eighteen months before Keats. Shelley is telling himself not to
allow his grief for his son to be re-awakened: the 'thou' (the
'fond wretch' of stanza 47) and the 'I' of the poem are nearer
now to becoming one. This is what a dual plural, a dual 'we',
would have made precipitately prominent. But all the time, the
conviction that Shelley's regeneration is to come somehow along
the lines of doing what Adonais has done moves more and more
into the forefront.

The line which immediately follows is a celebrated one:

> The One remains, the many change and pass . . . (459)

But only half of its meaning, in the strangely fluid and ever-
regrouping texture of Shelleyan verse at its most animated, has
been recognized. It does not only point forward to the antithesis
between life and eternity which occupies most of the rest of the
stanza. Also it looks backward, and one can almost say that it
justifies the obvious answer to that rhetorical question in the
preceding line:

> What Adonais is, why fear we to become? –
> *The One remains, the many change and pass*;

To be the same as Adonais, one with him, is to be incorporated
into the One, and so is permanence and release.

With the next stanza, what has been moving forward half-
submerged in the sense seems at last almost to become overt:

> Why linger, why turn back, why shrink, my Heart? (469)
> Thy hopes are gone before . . .

The 'heart' and its 'hopes' of lines 422–3 have re-appeared and
we have a new 'Thou', closer still to the poet; until in the
penultimate stanza, the resolution is transparent at last:

> That Light whose smile kindles the Universe, (478)
> That Beauty in which all things work and move,
> That Benediction . . .
>   . . . now beams *on me*
> Consuming the last clouds of cold mortality.

Nothing in the closing section can be said to put forward the
idea of suicide: there is only awareness that death approaches,

and a readiness for or even willing acquiesence in that fact, because it can complete the process of identification which the poem has long been carrying forward: and indeed, can do more than that, can bring out its meaning more fully than ever. Insofar as Shelley is one with Adonais, he is one with more than Adonais:

> The breath whose might I have invoked in song   (487)
> Descends on me; my spirit's bark is driven,
> Far from the shore . . .
> I am borne darkly, fearfully, afar;
> Whilst burning through the inmost veil of Heaven,
> The soul of Adonais, like a star,
> Beacons from the abode *where the Eternal are*.

In the dimension of assertion, statement and description, Shelley's poem meets the formal requirements of the elegy, and expresses a certain point of view about the relation between sensible and eternal reality; but more implicitly, more in its whole depth and in how the experience of reading progressively blocks itself out, it takes on the contour of the other poems discussed in this chapter. The 'power girt round with weakness', the creative spirit that at first cannot but 'linger', 'turn back' and 'shrink' (469), regenerates in an experience that re-establishes an elect communion ('far from the trembling throng' though this may be) with others.

With what others? The 'breath' of line 487 is, to begin with, the general *animus* of poetic inspiration (twin, one might say, with that of the 'Ode to the West Wind'). But it is more than that. The mighty breath that descends on the poet from the 'fire for which all thirst', is no ordinary wind, blowing simply behind Shelley and his 'spirit's bark'. It lies in front and works from in front. It is drawing him *towards* itself, towards the star Keats–Adonais, which is burning and beaconing from 'the abode *where the Eternal are*'. That plural verb, the last word of the poem, adds something quite decisive. The 'abode' is the home of *all* those 'sons of light' (36) in whom the creative and fulfilled spirit became finally and triumphantly regenerate. By the end of the poem, Shelley has moved to a position where restoration of the psyche lies in a journey, death-journey though it may well prove to be, towards communion with the company of great creative spirits of the past. Shelley *meets* Adonais in this poem, and the meeting is a restorative one like Wordsworth's meeting with his Leech-Gatherer on the lonely moor.

VII

The following brief note on Coleridge's 'Rime of the Ancient Mariner' is for the purpose of bringing out a single fact about it. One can see, without lengthy discussion, that this poem enacts something like the pattern of psychic collapse and regeneration which has now been discussed at length. The Mariner shoots the albatross (82) and the sequel is a terrible and destructive *doldrum*:

> And every tongue, through utter drought   (135)
> Was withered at the root

– a 'weary time' (143) of 'Life-in-Death' (193). The Mariner finds himself

> Alone, alone, all, all alone   (232)
> Alone on a wide wide sea!

The moment of regeneration came when the Mariner saw the water-snakes and 'blessed them unaware' (285). It was a moment of re-established affinity with other living creatures (if not other human beings), and is followed by the partial return from death of the other sailors (330 . . .), or rather, the moment of their bodies' being re-animated by the 'troop of spirits blest' (348).

It seems plain that Coleridge, here too, is dealing with the flagging and recovery of the psyche; but doing so now in the form of an objective narrative not a subjective experience. The narrative form is especially interesting, however, because at the end of the poem the Mariner puts the strongest stress on how the psychic crisis and its resolution is met, in this sort of poem, not by an argument reaching a discursive conclusion, but through creating, by means of the poem, a ritual through which the protagonist takes himself in order to be released from his psychic predicament.

It is this which is the point of the Mariner's closing words:

> . . . this frame of mine was wrenched (578)
> With a woful agony,
> Which forced me to begin my tale;
> And then it left me free.

Release lies not in knowing the meaning of the tale, but in the abreactive experience of reciting it through:

> Since then, at an uncertain hour, (581)
> The agony returns:
> And till my ghastly tale is told,
> This heart within me burns . . .

In other words, the poem has the status of a purgative ritual experience: release lies not in its message but its performance, from beginning duly through to end. Nothing could make this aspect of the poem of regeneration clearer.

VIII

Maud is a 'Monodrama' in which the whole movement of the narrative is the protagonist's attempted movement out of an empty and into a fulfilled condition of life. 'My pulses closed their gates', he says at the beginning, recounting the suicide of his father and the effect it had on himself (I.i.iv). 'My pulses closed their gates' is almost a Blakeian phrase:

> Till a morbid hate* and horror have grown
> Of a world in which I have hardly mixt,
> And a morbid eating lichen fixt
> On a heart half-turn'd to stone. (I.vi.viii)

The analogy also with the condition of mind of the 'Ancient Mariner', or Coleridge's own condition in the 'Letter', is unmistakable. So also is the link the poem has between this negative condition on the one hand, and an isolation from the nexus of any real society on the other. The connection between the two is made again elsewhere:

---

* Corrected thus in Errata Sheet 2 for Ricks's edition.

. . . I well could weep for a time so sordid and mean
And myself so languid and base.   (I.v.ii)

But then, immediately after the speaker has said that his heart
is turned to stone, comes the beginning of the characteristic
movement:

O heart of stone, are you flesh . . . ?   (I.vi.ix)

Those who recall the earlier poems will sense, from that one
line, how the kind of experience that those poems dramatize is
going in essence to be presented once again.

In certain respects the experience is not the same; and the
differences are characteristic of the time of the poem, and
significant in themselves. To begin with, something dis-
tinguishes *Maud* both from the earlier poems and from the
present day. *Maud*, we may say, is a dynastic poem. It takes for
granted certain ideas about the ways a man's own life is related
to the situation of his family, his 'House'. These are not to be
found in the poems of Coleridge or Keats discussed above, and
are unfamiliar today; so also is the poem's conception of what a
deep and passionate relation between a man and a woman is
like. The first of these two matters, the elaborate involvement
of the lovers in the financial, dynastic and territorial circum-
stances of their respective families, is what mainly enables
Tennyson to give his fiction some analogy with Greek tragic
myth:

. . . the feud,
The household Fury sprinkled with blood
By which our houses are torn: (I.xix.iv)

This dimension of the story proves to be no mere literary
convention arbitrarily or pointlessly imposed on the fiction.

Partly, the poem is difficult for the modern reader because of
the character of Maud herself. In her extreme youth ('Maud
is just sixteen'), and in the fact that she takes a man much older
than herself as lover, Maud reflects customs and assumptions
about sexual love to which readers today are not necessarily
sympathetic. But it would be an error to think of Maud as like
an irresponsible child-wife, a Dora Spenlow in *David Copperfield*.
True, the enraptured lover thinks of her 'little head, sunning

over with curls' (I.xxii.ix). But the main thing that line does is to illustrate our insoluble difficulty, in English, with affectionate diminutives. Turgenev had no such problem when he wrote of his heroine's 'little head' in *Fathers and Sons*. The little head sunning over with curls must be set alongside the earlier references to Maud's pride and dignity, to her 'cold and clear-cut face', her beauty which at first sight seems 'faultily faultless, icily regular, splendidly null', superbly remote from childish-ness, and with an underlip 'you may call it a little too ripe, too full', making clear enough, in the reticent convention of the time, not only Maud's maturity into full womanhood, but also her strong if still latent passional nature. The sexual and marital conventions of the poem may be remote from ours, but they are not to be discredited by any idea of the limited under-standing in these matters of 'Victorianism'.

Maud is Tennyson's great mid-Victorian novel. The works to which it related most nearly are the novels of the time which are panoramic pictures of mid-nineteenth-century provincial life, with its family or dynastic intricacies, its financial involve-ments, its intense if covert struggles between passionate sexual feeling and social responsibility and respectability. In reading *Maud*, one should think of George Eliot's *Felix Holt* or *The Mill on the Floss*, Charlotte Brontë's *Jane Eyre* or Emily's *Wuthering Heights*, all novels almost exactly contemporaneous with it. In the briefer, more incisive and synoptic mode of verse, *Maud* is a panorama of its time comparable with any of these.

To say that is not merely to call to mind the ironical passages of the opening section, passages in which the speaker openly attacks

. . . the days of advance, the works of the men of mind (I.i.vii)

nor to call to mind the references in the final part of the poem to what is evidently the Crimean War. The story of Maud and her lover runs in intimate and accumulative detail right through the heart of provincial nineteenth-century England. The germ of the tale lies in the 'scheme', the 'vast speculation' that the two families joined together in. When that failed, one family was left isolated and ruined, the other 'gorg'd' with vulgar wealth. We see what that vulgar wealth looked like, in the contours of the time:

There are workmen up at the Hall! – They are coming back
from abroad . . .   (I.i.xvii)

As the poem proceeds, the detail accumulates: the Hall with its
cedar tree, rose-garden, panelled rooms and King Charles
spaniel; the village street with its 'blossom'd gable-ends' and
gentry strolling about; the men drinking together and planning
the kind of territorial, dynastic marriage that kept Victorian
genteel society in being in the provinces (I.vii); the mediaeval
church with its eighteenth-century family monuments (invoked
with astonishing succinctness in I.viii) and its

> . . . snowy-banded, dilettante,
> Delicate-handed priest

redolent of the Oxford Movement and the Cambridge
Ecclesiologists; the wealthy riders across the moor, one of
them the 'new-made lord' whose father made his money in coal-
mines and whose 'gew-gaw' castle, new as his title, is set (like
Sir Walter Scott's house at Abbotsford) amid the newly
planted conifers of the *arriviste*. There is also the radical
Little-Englander in his broad-brimm'd hat and 'ear . . .
crammed with his cotton' (I.x.iii); and on the other side, the
'grand political dinner' in the Tory interest (I.xx.iii), occasion
of the crucial meeting between the protagonist, Maud and her
brother, and so of the duel and the tragedy.

The tale of *Maud* is thus no tale told in isolation or abstrac-
tion from society: as is the case with Wordsworth's 'Guilt and
Sorrow' or 'The Ancient Mariner' or Keats's 'The Eve of St
Agnes'. It is a study of contemporary society and its tendencies
and stresses; the poem's enmeshment in contemporary life is
intrinsic to it. No doubt Tennyson told the tale of a despondent
and withdrawn man in part because that found an echo in one
side of his own nature. Yet *Maud*, as a poem, makes use of such
a nature but arises out of an ampler and stronger one. In this
work Tennyson must be said to set out to review whether – in
Lukàcs's terms* – man is something no more than 'cast aside'
into the world, or a 'ζόον πολίτικον', a social and political being

---

* See 'The ideology of modernism', p. 19 and *passim*, in *The Meaning of Contem-
porary Realism*, trans. J. and N. Mander, 1963.

whose nature is fulfilled in integration with others and with his environment. His answer appears to be that it is indeed, and inescapably, the latter; but that in the age depicted by the poem, to live the life of a ζόον πολίτικον is fraught not just with great but with insuperable difficulty.

'Insuperable' is a strong word. It negates what is positive in Tennyson's answer: and that is what he does himself. Involvement in the social and environmental texture does not make release and self-fulfilment easier for Tennyson's lovers; nor, in particular, for his protagonist. What we find is something not unlike what we find in the later novels of Dickens: a conviction that such release is a vital ingredient of man's being, without which life is simply not a living thing; and at the same time an over-mastering, ever-returning conviction that release, when achieved, will collapse, or be a fraud, or at the very best be some kind of local and over-indulgent accident on the part of the course of events. Tennyson said himself that the closing, war-section of *Maud* was no more than an 'incident'; and that the essence of the poem was to show what the power of love had to offer to men. That that closing section constitutes no release into self-fulfilment for the protagonist is generally agreed; though the wrong reason seems to be accepted for thinking so. It cannot be, that the solution offered there is no solution because partaking in war is in itself no adequate integration with one's fellow men. When Achilles, in the *Iliad*, ceases to sulk in his tent and returns to lead the Achaians, Homer offers (XVIII, 98–103; 128–9) this to his readers as a life restored and vindicated in social togetherness, and no one could see that as a radical error in the strategy of his poem.

The flaw in *Maud* at this point is a most inward one. It arises because the poem is so much a reflective and analytical poem socially: section I of the work makes this explicit, and the structured social background throughout Part II does as much implicitly. If social analyses are to be offered, however, they need to be adequate. But the references in Part II to the reasons *why* the war can solve the protagonist's crisis of personality are empty and unpersuasive:

An *iron tyranny* now should bend or cease . . .   (III.vi.ii)

Yet God's just wrath shall be wreaked on a *giant liar*

(III.vi.iv)

Tennyson would have had to do very little to change his poem at this point, in an unexpected direction, and have made the whole idea of fulfilment in the war a self-deflating piece of dramatic irony. Indeed, it is almost possible to read the poem, as it stands, in just that way.

It is not easy to see the last section as a trivial, not particularly successful coda to the poem, written by Tennyson in response to the time and from the slighter side of his nature. Yet if the central fiction of the work, the tale of Maud and her lover and their disaster, be considered by itself, one is left with a deeply ambiguous sense of how release and fulfilment are at once imperatively needful and hopelessly over-ambitious. Like Dickens, Tennyson depicts a society which threatens to make men's life a task that is beyond them.

In one respect, this ambivalence of impression lies at the heart of the imagery of the work. The ambivalence is easy to see, if one begins to consider what picture the poem gives of how social *milieu* opens out into the *milieu* of nature: the whole environment and topography in which the action is set. The action, after all, is like the story of Pip in *Great Expectations* or Lady Dedlock in *Bleak House*, or of characters in George Eliot's work like Tito Melema or Lydgate; or like Trollope's *The Way we Live Now* or *The Last Chronicle of Barset*. It is the story of life destroyed or nearly destroyed by the power of money. If there is a wild and almost desperate note about parts of *Maud* (or, indeed, about almost the whole of it), that note is present because Tennyson, or perhaps one should say the protagonist, cannot quite bring himself to assert that any part of the human environment, or any force in nature, is wholly free from what he ironically calls in the poem 'the print/of the *golden* age' (I.i.viii):

A million emeralds break from the *ruby*-budded lime   (I.iv.i)

or:

The silent *sapphire*-spangled marriage ring of the land (I.iv.i)

or:

A livelier *emerald* twinkles in the grass,
A purer *sapphire* melts into the sea. (I.xviii.vi)

How are such lines to be read? One must see them not only as
more than vivid description, but also as more than a merely
academic 'keeping' of the money-decorum of the poem. One
must remember the lines in the first section:

. . . out he walked when the wind like a broken worlding
wailed,
And the flying gold of the ruined woodlands drove through
the air. (I.i.iii)

The poem is asking us to consider whether the very environ-
ment itself is not in some obscure way infected by a rapacious
and all-consuming greed.

. . . nature is one with rapine, a harm no preacher can heal;
The Mayfly is torn by the swallow, the sparrow speared by
the shrike,
And the whole little wood where I sit is a world of plunder
and prey. (I.iv.iv)

(I shall come to what else the 'little wood' means.) Because of
this, the sense of things in the poem is more comprehensive and
integrated than it would otherwise be; the sweep and inte-
gration of its mood weave deep into the imagery.

This ambivalence is not a matter of Tennyson's having used
the money-world of the story as part of what was available to
him for the description of nature. The two characters who
polarize its values are each of them explicitly identified, and
contrastingly identified, with the jewels that make up that
picture:

. . . that dandy-despot, he,
That *jewelled* mass of millinery, (I.vi.vi)

. . . his essences turned the live air sick,
And barbarous opulence *jewel*-thick
Sunned itself on his breast and his hands. (I.xiii.i)

This is no less a parallel to the jewelled splendour of nature
than:

What, has he found *my jewel* out? (I.x.ii)

or

>. . . I saw the *treasured* splendour, her hand,
>Come sliding out of her sacred glove
>And the sunlight broke from her lip? (I.vi.ix)

Maud, who will 'wear her jewels' (I.xx.ii) at the 'grand political dinner', seems as much one with the money-cosmos, as she does with the rose-garden she comes out into at night to be queen of 'In gloss of satin and glimmer of pearls' (I.xxii.ix).

Thus the many ways in which the idea and image of the jewel enters the poem call in question any easy contrast between a naturalness which is good and a sociability which is evil. Poem invites reader to contemplate the possibility that nature itself suffers from an evil similar to what is rampant in society. Moreover, the invitation to consider this for nature is an invitation to consider it for Maud. There is nothing in the poem which directly asks us to see Maud as wanting; but indirectly, the poem opens up the possibility that for all her personal goodness she represents, in her capacity of the force of love in the poem, something which, in the world as we have it, is doomed to realize its destructive potential and to be thwarted over its creative potential.

Here one must begin to consider certain of the less conspicuous aspects of the poem. Whether Tennyson fully intended them, or even clearly saw them, I do not know. But what matters is the definitive reality of the poem as we have it, as it stands once for all. As Part II proceeds, it mirrors the progressive disintegration of what is normal and coherently affirmative. Alone among all Tennysons's poems, *Maud* increasingly adopts a kind of nightmare *collage* technique. The closing sections of Part II represent the delirious dream of the protagonist when, near to madness, he sees himself buried at the cross-roads with a stake through his heart, the traditional fate of the *felo-de-se*. McLuhan, in a brilliant early essay,* has argued that in this poem, and especially this part of it, Tennyson

---

* 'Tennyson and picturesque poetry', *Essays in Criticism*, 1951, reprinted in J. Kilham, ed., *Critical Essays on the Poetry of Tennyson*, 1960.

really broke through to reach the fundamental technique of
Modernist verse – the technique of *The Waste Land,* of the
Cantos – and drew back, because he rejected the role of the
highbrow minority poet, or the poet of total isolation, which he
would have committed himself to had he gone on. However
that may be, the structure of the poem at this decisive point is
indeed a structure of what might be called meaningful dis-
integration; and the fact that this is so at so important a
juncture in the work, entitles us to open questions and possi-
bilities about the poem's total sense as one would hesitate to do
in the case of a poem organized on more conventional,
traditional lines.

If we let the whole tissue of the poem speak to us without
reserve, what it seems to express is much other than what we
should expect from a mid-Victorian poet laureate. One part of
this may be put by saying that while everything at the level of
explicit statement tells the reader that Maud remains 'maiden
Maud', everything at the level of symbol and suggestion says
the opposite.

> Maud has a garden of roses
> And lilies fair on a lawn;
> There she walks in her state
> And tends upon bed and bower,
> And thither I climbed at dawn
> And stood by her garden-gate;
> A lion ramps at the top,
> He is claspt by a passion-flower.   (I.xiv.i)

> Go not, happy day,
>   From the shining fields,
> Go not, happy day,
>   Till the maiden yields . . .   (I.xvii)

> I have led her home, my love, my only friend.
> There is none like her, none.
> And never yet so warmly ran my blood
> And sweetly, on and on
> Calming itself to the long-wished-for end,
> Full to the banks, close on the promised good.   (I.xviii.i)

Does that slightly unidiomatic 'close on', mean simply 'near to', or does 'close' also suggest itself as an imperative form of the verb? Here, the reader surely encounters a deeper, more disruptive layer of meaning in the poem. To assert that Maud becomes the protagonist's lover in the full physical sense would be a crude way of dealing with the evidence. There is no need to crave this kind of explicitness. The poem intimates that there is no need to labour the details: the lovers were 'as if' they had had each other in the fullest sense. The poem demands that we see how this and nothing short of it is what is at issue. In those terms, the rose-garden of the crucial meeting at night, the rivulet that runs down to link Maud's rose-garden with the protagonist's 'own dark wood', and most of all perhaps the fact that the lover's secret meetings are in the wood that belongs to the speaker (the full point of this will transpire in a moment), contribute to make clear that the poem uncompromisingly takes in the total physical realities of love.

If one asks why it is fair to say that the meetings in the dark wood express this 'most of all', the answer lies in the extraordinary account of that wood which comes in the opening stanzas of the poem. One asks oneself incredulously, how the wild and almost hysterical *doubles entendres* of this passage could have been overlooked; or how, in the face of them, we could have come to think that the Victorians were unaware of the monstrous images of the unconscious life, or their power for destructive inroad into daylight and normality. The poem opens:

> I hate *the dreadful hollow behind the little wood*,
> Its lips in the field above are dabbled with blood-red heath,
> The red-ribbed ledges drip with a silent horror of blood.
> And Echo there, whatever is asked her, answers 'Death'.
>
> For there in the ghastly pit long since a body was found,
> His who had given me life – O father! O God! was it well? –

This is the 'red-ribb'd hollow behind the wood' where the lovers met, and where the protagonist and Maud's brother fought the duel. The poem calls it, there, the 'joyous wood'. No reader can miss the overtones and suggestiveness of these passages all taken together. For the speaker, there is an ambivalence about physical love, and the physical birth which it leads to (and which, of course, has also led to it), rather like the ambivalence about the natural environment which was mentioned above. What the protagonist is revealing in the opening stanzas is something like a horror of the fact of birth itself; and more particularly of the place of birth, in all its intimacy, and of the events his father figured in which led to the speaker's own birth. Against the force of the opening stanza, the later lines:

Villainy somewhere! whose? One says, we are villains all.
Not he: his honest fame should at least by me be maintained
(I.i.v)

look more like half-admission of the father's questionable conduct than out-and-out assertion of his innocence. What the opening stanzas seem implicitly to say, is what is said in stanza x of the section:

. . . the spirit of murder works in the very means of life.

Once it becomes clear that this is so over the events of a generation ago, it is clear that the same must be said of the imagery of the duel-scene (II.i). Then, it becomes unmistakable that the 'red-ribb'd hollow behind the wood' of II.i symbolizes, in the loose and open way of the whole mode of presentation of this poem and especially of this part of it, the place central to the physical realities of the passionate relation between Maud and the speaker. What therefore, in the same loosely suggestive fashion, the poem implicitly states when it sets the destructive duel, the duel which embodies the murderous rivalry of two males of the second generation, in that little red hollow, is that there is no separating the wonderful life-fulfilling and life-restoring powers of such love from its power for destruction, chaos and death. The rosy sunset (I.xvii), the red rose, and the red, dark rose-garden of love, are all one with the red hollow of a destructive force which, sex-like, fulfils itself, generation after generation, in bloody death not life.

Maud therefore represents two substantial departures from the pattern of the major regeneration-poems of the Romantic period. Doubtless under the influence of the novel or at least of the predominance of the novel in its period, it traces the regenerative process for the individual not simply internally, and not simply in the small social group of the family or the pair of lovers. *Maud* sets its fiction, solidly and in detail, within the whole landscape of provincial England, and at the end it claims (though ineffectively), to re-integrate the speaker into the whole united social fabric. But besides this, *Maud* differs from the earlier poems of the regeneration kind in another respect: what it depicts is not regeneration at all, but effort to re-generate, and then failure. The love-phase of the process fails directly, and the narrative ends in disaster and loneliness. The war-phase does so indirectly, through its emptiness and its quality of gesture. This is not to say that love and the power of love prove in this poem to be cheats. They do not. But they prove to be something like the striking, iridescent part of what in the end is only a chaos of iridescences, a brilliant but frag-mentary nightmare world where creation and destruction, good and evil, peace and violence tumble over each other to no purpose:

> . . . Strike dead the whole weak race of venomous worms,
> That sting each other here in the dust;
> We are not worthy to live.   (II.i.ii)

Those words are the speaker's at almost the height of his despair and distraction; but nothing in the poem can claim to be remote from, or unimpaired by, what they say.

Nothing, that is, in the fiction transacted or the ideas and attitudes directly expressed. Yet if one asks what impression the poem leaves in the mind after one has become familiar with it, there is something beside all these things. For *Maud*, and especially for the essential *Maud* (by which I mean the first two parts of the poem), does not remain in the mind as a testament of seeking, but of failure to find, release and fulfilment for a 'heart half turn'd to stone'. In its astonishing intricacy and fluidity of organization, its reverberant richness of meaning and suggestion that every re-reading amplifies further, its almost matchless metrical variety and vitality, and its meticulously sharp, broadly sweeping, yet unobtrusive marshalling of the detail of story and milieu of a major novel, *Maud* is surely one of the two or three most original and ambitious English poems of the century and (despite its flaws) one of the two or three greatest as well. The 'I' of the poem may be regenerated only in what fails to maintain itself; and again, in the war section, through an empty-gesture kind of resolution for the speaker's predicament. The poem itself remains as something more positive and achieved.

Here, at last, it is right to take notice of the fact that to speak of the 'protagonist' and 'the speaker' of the poem, as has been done throughout so far, is in accordance with the poet's invitation not to see him as the speaker of the poem, '*Maud, a monodrama*'. Yet that defers to a difference within which lies an identity. This is no ordinary dramatic poem, where the distinction between speaker and poet is like that between Coleridge and the Ancient Mariner, or Browning and his characters, or Tennyson and Ulysses, or St Simeon Stylites. Insofar as the speaker is 'morbid' (as Tennyson called him), self-preoccupied, weak, isolated, maybe he and the poet himself ask to be kept apart. Insofar as he is the speaker, in his own voice, of such a lyrical series as this, memorable in their variety, their virtuosity, and above all in their sustained resonance and self-assertive energy, he is Tennyson. Despite the disaster of the tale, the poem does indeed find regeneration, release and fulfilment for the individual. It finds these things in the achievement of art. One may compare the fourth Book of the *Dunciad*; and one may suggest that Tennyson, though like Dickens he senses how the society of his time made fulfilment in love difficult or more than difficult, could assert and display fulfilment in the achievement of poetry. Looking backward one may find a parallel in *Prometheus Unbound*, and forward, in 'Sailing to Byzantium', Valéry's 'Le Cimetière Marin', Stevens's 'The Idea of Order at Key West', or Pound's 'Hugh Selwyn Mauberley'. *Maud* was moving towards the idea that what can be achieved in a society hostile to achievement and fulfilment is achievement and fulfilment within the triumphant poem.

VIII

The Zero Life

The group of poems now to be discussed have something in common which is easily seen if they are compared, say, with Pope's 'Eloisa to Abelard'. It is easy enough to characterize the type to which Pope's poem belongs: the designation of it as belonging to the genre of the heroic epistle is enough by itself to indicate that the poem's task is to narrate an exceptional occurrence and to find interest in the things that made it exceptional. Few lovers, the poem indicates by its very *genre*, have experienced such elevated and intense emotions as Abelard and Eloisa. The sighs of few of them have wafted 'from Indus to the Pole'. 'Devotion's self shall steal a thought from heav'n' (357) for such a case. Eloisa imagines the future death of Abelard as the end of the world:

> Bright clouds descend, and Angels watch thee round, (340)
> From op'ning skies may streaming glories shine,
> And Saints embrace thee with a love like mine.

The last line of the quotation expresses the loftiness and intensity of Eloisa's emotions as forcefully as she could, now, possibly express them. For Abelard she would scorn (or at least, would have scorned) 'the world's great master':

> Not Cæsar's empress would I deign to prove; (87)
> No, make me mistress to the man I love . . .

In the end, the case is exceptional in disaster as in intensity: What Eloisa knows is only 'a sad variety of woe' (36).

To narrate some spectacularly exceptional case of this kind seems to constitute one of the fundamental literary forms; and perhaps most major literary works are of this kind. To say that such works narrate the exceptional case is a useful preliminary, but in the end it is far from adequate. Everything, no doubt, becomes exceptional if described in sufficient detail. Works such as 'Eloisa to Abelard' (or *Macbeth*, or *Phèdre*, or *Hedda Gabler*) depict exceptional cases in that they concentrate attention upon aspects of behaviour (passionate love, ambition, self-love, destructiveness) which are commonly taken to be interesting and remarkable, and narrate a case in which there is shown to be more than usual of what is interesting and remarkable. As the power and intensity of the case become clear, it seems to rise parabola-like from the norms of human life.

Such fictions have perennially interested human beings; but it seems to have been assumed a little too easily that this is because of their instructiveness, in a straightforward sense, about life. Happily, for most men the highly exceptional case is not instructive in this way. Coleridge thought he had something of the Hamlet in him, and possibly that was so; but for most men, the interest of such works seems to be greatly in excess of the degree to which they come home directly to life and show men *what life is like*. Such works are not straightforwardly 'about life' or 'true'. They do not show the 'what inevitably happens' in life; and at least when we are not engaging in literary criticism, we know that the appalling disasters in which they culminate are not what usually follow from the failings or even vices they depict. *Anna Karenina*, *Antony and Cleopatra*, do not show 'laws' of experience. If anything, one may venture the guess that the penalties of concupiscence are usually too subtle and inconspicuous to be observed at all by those who have practised the failings which incur them.

In the later eighteenth century and after, it continues to be easy to find poems written on the plan of 'Eloisa to Abelard'. The biographies recorded in Johnson's *Vanity of Human Wishes* conform to this pattern; they are extreme and spectacular cases

of a kind of folly which is familiar to all, at least in idea. Nor are
Crabbe's poems other than this, in spite of a first impression
that there will be something new about them:

> I paint the Cot.   (*The Village*, I.53)
> As Truth will paint it, and as Bards will not.

Admittedly, Crabbe has individual scenes that seem to belong to
another awareness of life or conception of literary interest:

> . . . yon house that holds the parish poor,   (I.228)
> Whose walls of mud scarce bear the broken door;
> There, where the putrid vapours, flagging, play,
> And the dull wheel hums doleful through the day –

This is the poorhouse in *The Village*. *The Borough* opens with
an intimation that we are to turn from what is spectacular to
something very different:

> Could he, who sang so well the Grecian fleet,   (Letter I, 9)
> So well have sung of alley, lane, or street?

After a brief account of the work of a fisherman and his wife,
the poem continues:

> Can scenes like these withdraw thee from thy wood,   (25)
> Thy upland forest or thy valley's flood?
> Seek then thy garden's shrubby bound, and look,
> As it steals by, upon the bordering brook . . .

The sense that interest will be found in the drab not the
picturesque or striking is sustained:

> Then the broad bosom of the ocean keeps   (179)
> An equal motion, swelling as it sleeps,
> Then slowly sinking; curling to the strand,
> Faint, lazy waves o'ercreep the ridgy sand.
> Or tap the tarry boat with gentle blow,
> And back return in silence, smooth and slow.

But there is one level at which Crabbe's approach is original,
and another at which it is not. Certainly he chooses (in his early
works especially) the poor not the rich for his matter, and
certainly he sees how poetic life may be drawn from the drab

scene as much as from the colourful one. Yet as soon as the
fiction gets under way, the reader encounters what is exceptional
and spectacular once again. The lines quoted above are from
Letter I of *The Borough*, the 'General Description'. Some lines
from Letter XXII, 'Peter Grimes', are reminiscent of them:

> Thus by himself compell'd to live each day,   (171)
> To wait for certain hours the tide's delay;
> At the same time the same dull views to see,
> The bounding marsh-bank and the blighted tree;
> The water only, when the tides were high,
> When low, the mud half-cover'd and half-dry . . .

Here the context is enough to show how little Crabbe does in
his fictions what he found congenial in his descriptions. The drab
monotony of the mud-bank is part of the 'sere and yellow leaf'
phase of life of a village Richard Crookback. Similarly – there
is no need to elaborate the point – with most of the later *Tales*.
'Edward Shore' recounts the life of a reckless worshipper of
reason who ends up as an idiot. 'Sir Owen Dale' is the story of
two illicit lovers whose brief ecstasies are followed (Crabbe
informs us with distasteful relish) by long and fearful distress.
Again, we have the parabolic curve from height to depth.
Crabbe's originality was greater as an observer than as a
narrator.

Many of the dramatic monologues of the nineteenth century in
effect narrate, or at least intimate, the whole biography of the
monologist: and in doing so, conform to this same narrative
pattern. The tale is worth telling because the speaker is
special and his situation is striking. Tennyson's 'St Simeon
Stylites' is an example. Simeon is one among all the saints – but
is an especially saintly one:

> Although I be the basest of mankind,   (1)
> From scalp to sole one slough and crust of sin . . .
> I will not cease to grasp the hope I hold
> Of saintdom . . .

> O Jesus, if thou wilt not save my soul,   (45)
> Who may be saved? who is it may be saved?
> Who may be made a saint, if I fail here? . . .

God only through his bounty hath thought fit,   (182)
Among the powers and princes of this world,
To make me an example to mankind
Which few can reach to.

Simeon's closing thoughts in the poem are of approaching
sainthood; but the situation is more complex than he supposes.
He is right in seeing himself as exceptional in his mode of
living and degree of suffering, but he turns out to be exceptional
also in colossal and revolting self-absorption and pride. At the
end, he thinks he has a vision of an angel coming to him with a
heavenly crown, but the reader reserves judgment. In the case
of so peculiarly odious a man, it is more likely to be a deceiving
devil. That Simeon is an extreme and altogether special case,
'which few can reach to', remains true in more respects than
one.

In one way, Simeon is a Browningesque figure, all complexity
and ignorance of self. Tennyson's monologue-characters are less
consistently like this than Browning's, but it is worth noting
that here he was drawn in Browning's direction. Perhaps one
significant distinction between poetic character-study in this
period, and earlier, lies in this very matter. Earlier portraits of
lack of self-knowledge, like what we find in *Paradise Lost*, or in
The Vanity of Human Wishes, centre upon some single, all-
powerful failure of insight. This is the pattern one should
expect to see when the basis of literary creativity is a categorical
moral order of good and evil, and a sense of personality which
is polarized in the way that morality must necessarily be
polarized. In the nineteenth century, character came to be seen
less exclusively like this. It was seen as lying in many smaller
facets of personality, operating and inter-operating over a long
period. But from another and fuller point of view, what is at
first seen as 'aspects of personality' may be recognized as having
a social dimension: they are the manifold points at which the
individual's life touches the texture of the society he lives in.
In the course of the earlier nineteenth century, and to some
extent before, history and the social sciences came to have a
dominant place in consciousness, and to fill men's minds with a
sense of how slowly and inconspicuously, but irresistibly and

comprehensively, the individual's life was moulded by forces of history and forces of society. Mill's account of the 'logic of the moral sciences' – the mere existence of this whole section in his *System of Logic* is by itself eloquent – will make the point by itself:

> It is necessary to consider what is a state of society:
> (it is) the simultaneous state of all the greater social facts
> . . . when we say that (this can be) the subject of a science,
> we imply that there exists natural correlations among the
> different elements; that not every variety of combination
> of these general social facts is possible, but only certain
> combinations . . . such is indeed a necessary consequence
> of the influence exercised by every one of these phenomena
> on every other. (1843 ed., VI.x)

Writers like Wordsworth, Dickens, Charlotte Brontë and George Eliot, for whom freewill, conscience and self-regeneration were ultimates of all-consuming importance and interest, still saw those moral forces as operating in a new way, because they operated in a new context of social determinants.

In 'The Old Cumberland Beggar', Wordsworth did what Crabbe seems almost never to have done. The poem is a meditation rather than a narrative; but its effect is to establish a man, and a life, just as much as Pope's epistle or Tennyson's monologue, yet along a radically different line: what we may call not the spectacular but the anti-spectacular. What Crabbe could see as the interest of a tidal estuary, Wordsworth could see as the interest of a life.

Clearly Wordsworth regarded the Old Cumberland Beggar as a deeply significant and rewarding figure, one that called for pondering and contemplation. A sort of *Gestalt* of the beggar as object of contemplation is sustained throughout the poem. 'I *saw* an aged beggar in my walk', runs the opening line. The 'Sauntering Horseman', even as he rides on after giving the beggar alms, '*watches* him . . . with a look/Sidelong, and half-reverted'. All the villagers, whatever they are like, '*behold* in him' (ll.89–90, and 122) a 'silent monitor' who fills their minds with thought and who, finally, both lives and dies '*in the eye* of Nature' (ll.195–6). All this is integral to the poem. The

old man is presented throughout as *something to be long looked at*.
The 'vast solitude' (163: cf.44), both social and topographical,
through which the old man wanders, seems to be something
which reinforces this. It isolates him out, as an object of
contemplation, from all others.

What sort of interest does the old beggar invite? At first he
may seem to be an extreme case, an extreme development like
Eloisa, Simeon and others. After all, he is poorer than anyone
else in the poem: he is as poor as can be. But if the beggar is
an extreme case, it is one of quite a new kind. With him, there
is no sense of a spectacular, aberrant development. On the
contrary, he has the qualities of existence not more than others,
but less. He is the limiting case of something that applies to
all. All his fellows are poor, but he is poor absolutely. Not the
parabola rising to a great aberrant maximum, but the hyper-
bola, approaching its limit asymptotically, might be taken as
representing his situation.

Significantly, also, in a further respect, the Old Cumberland
Beggar's life may indeed be said to approach *Zero*. This not so
much in respect of his poverty, as of a kind of subdued eventless-
ness. It was of course a great point to Wordsworth that such
lives were fit subjects for poetry. As he tells the reader in 'Simon
Lee', one may find a tale in everything upon the one condition
of just such 'silent thought' as he was so persistently 'inviting'
for the Old Cumberland Beggar. The dull actualities of exist-
ence have more interest than its spectacular aberrancies – that
is exactly his point.

But featurelessness in life seems in this poem to be the
result of something distinctive. Simeon Stylites's life must have
been very featureless, but as a result of a grandiose choice
through a great and sustained act of the will, or perhaps, rather
than that, arrogance and obstinacy. The beggar's life is
featureless through an extreme degree of something which,
more or less, applies universally. He is 'helpless' (l.24), 'weary'
(l.53), 'so still (i.e. silent . . .) in look and motion' (l.61); and
what keeps him alive in these circumstances is even more
significant. It is the 'mild *necessity* of use' (i.e. of custom) which
prompts the villagers to give to him now as they have given
often enough in the past. The 'necessity' of use is the operation

of social causality, of the nexus of society. The beggar's life is
what it is because of how life works for all and all the time.
Causal influences operate *on* him to make him aged and poor
and yet taken care of by others all the same; and they operate
from him, back again, in reticulations of kindly feeling, affec-
tionate recollection, and sense of goodness modestly achieved,
among the villagers. 'The Old Cumberland Beggar' shows a
man subdued to the mutual web, as George Eliot called it, of that
long-sustained though inconspicuous causal influence. It is this
mutual web that subdues the lives of men, as Arnold says in
'A Summer Night', to a passive pattern of 'unmeaning taskwork'
and helplessness. It is the old beggar's very passivity, his total
subjection to these causal forces, which enabled them to operate
on beyond him, back upon the other villagers. The poem
concerns itself not with life's spectacular potentialities, but its
drab actualities: a diametrically opposite task.

Browning does not take aged and destitute English country-
men as his subjects. Yet in certain of his dramatic monologues,
he seems to carry out with his people something quite like
what Wordsworth did with those.

Andrea del Sarto, as he soliloquizes to his indifferent wife
at evening-time on the balcony, is a man whose life has also
settled into a passive pattern:

A common grayness silvers everything, –   (35)
 All in a twilight, you and I alike . . .

Those last tactless words perhaps show why Andrea has been
unsuccessful with his wife. They are far from true. He and she
are not alike. But for him, it is not quite the passivity of inaction;
rather of toil, but toil without creative urge or self-pride –
Arnold's 'unmeaning taskwork', without significant result save
money to give his wife for her to give to her lover.

While hand and eye and something of a heart   (225)
Are left me, work's my ware, and what it's worth?
I'll pay my fancy. Only let me sit
The gray remainder of the evening out . . .

Andrea's father and mother died of poverty, and he in his turn
has 'laboured' and not been paid overmuch for it. Now he

submits to the necessities of his environment. His 'low-puls'd
. . . craftsman's hand' (82) accepts its subordinate rôle:

I feel he laid the fetter: let it lie! (52)

And exactly, the 'fetter' brings something inescapably to mind,
something of the sense that Browning's own age had of social
integration that creates a new, submitting rôle for the self:

Eh? the whole seems to fall into a shape (46)
As if I saw alike my work and self
And all that I was born to be and do,
A twilight-peace. Love, we are in God's hand.
How strange now, looks the life he makes us lead;
So free we seem, so fettered fast we are!

It is a remarkable passage, full of the nineteenth-century sense
of the integratedness of the social whole, and the heavy shadow
that it seems so often to spread all across the individual's moral
life. For a moment Andrea, the 'sorry little scrub' who yet has
a great gift, imagines how he might have risen, parabola-like,
to the dizzy heights of the great painter. In what one may
perhaps call the placidly restless movement of the poem, an
impotence not quite quieted, the thought recurs:

If really there was such a chance, so lost, – (201)

He sees the two life-lines clearly enough: but he has already
recognized that his is the line which approaches zero, and he
turns away from the spectacular life to his present one:

I might have done it for you. So it seems: (132)
Perhaps not. All is as God over-rules.

The 'common grayness' has been 'all toned down' in the rhythms
and the diction of the poem also. There is nothing of Browning's
gift for the abrupt and abrasive, no flashes and rasps, kinetic
hypertrophy, no dazzling vagaries of lexicon. What is left for
Andrea is the 'melancholy little house' and to 'sit/The gray
remainder of the evening out'. Of course, the milieu of the poem,
even expressed in the most general terms, is quite other than
that in the Wordsworth poem: the faultless painter's point of

reference are the great artists and the great painters of his time. Of course also, his personality, in its details, is wholly other than that of the Old Cumberland Beggar (insofar, indeed, as the latter may be said to have had a personality at all). At another and more basic level, there is a firm similarity. It is in the fundamental rôle of the protagonist, and so in the function of the poem.

'The Bishop Orders his Tomb at St Praxted's Church': this Bishop is filled, even at the moment of death, with eager, restless ambition for a splendid tomb adorned with lapis lazuli and choice Latinity, with spiteful animosity towards his predecessor, with distrustful attachment and affection for his so-called 'nephews' (especially the youngest one) and with nostalgic recollection of the woman whom, as the poem proceeds, he forgets not to call their mother. On one side, he is a mass of busy and conflicting emotions. The poem's total structure is more than that, and includes what puts it in an unexpected perspective:

Vanity, saith the preacher, vanity!   (1)

That is how the poem begins; and it is what we see. The ambitious and energy-filled Bishop is old and dying. His sons listen in silence to his pleas for a tomb of stony grandeur. His mistress is long gone and may not have had any love for him even in life. He can do nothing but threaten, probably to no effect, about his legacies. Against the genuine if perhaps confused religious feeling of:

. . . then how shall I lie through centuries   (80)
And hear the blessed mutter of the mass
And see God made and eaten all day long . . .

– against that must be set the fact that at some time in the past, he stole from his own church, as it burnt out in a fire, so as to put treasures aside for his future tomb.

Evil and brief hath been my pilgrimage.   (101)

Yet it is not his evil, but its insignificance now, which deserves to be stressed:

H   [217]

As here I lie (10)
In this state-chamber, dying by degrees,
Hours and long hours in the dead night, I ask
'Do I live, am I dead?' Peace, peace seems all.

The Bishop's energies of mind are only too much like Andrea's talents. They too have come to nothing. He too has become a powerless figure, acted upon (largely from within, though that sounds paradoxical) but unable save negatively to act in response. The 'common grayness' of Andrea's life does not characterize the externals of the Bishop's life, but does indeed characterize its inwardness and essence: a helpless, muddled, bad old man whom no one wants any more. To go behind the distinctive aspects of characterization, to the more general aspect, is once again to reach something like the Old Cumberland Beggar. Each poem depicts a man who, whatever his distinctive qualities, has as general quality to be among those who can only see their lives out passively because they are approaching towards Zero Lives.

'Dis Aliter Visum' is spoken by a woman who, ten years ago, was young. She was in love with a distinguished poet and, as the poem opens, she has just discovered from him that he came very near to asking to marry her. But it seemed to him to be too chancy, too unconventional, and too much of a sacrifice merely for 'two cheeks freshened by youth and sea' (95). Both dropped the unspoken though near-spoken idea. Not completely: the last stanza reveals that the poet later married a famous dancer, who seems to have been younger than he was (but she has since gone to pieces and lost her talent), while the girl, also true to the pattern of the happiness she so nearly achieved with the poet, has since married a husband who sounds older than herself ('here comes my husband from his whist)'. Clearly enough, their life together is a humdrum one.

Perhaps one may say that this poem analyses and articulates the situation of people who reject the offer of parabola-lives, and chose hyperbola-lives asymptotically approaching zero instead. If middle-aged poet and young slip of a thing had set up together, she might have had a few years of exceptional happiness and a long and lonely widowhood – one of major grief, or perhaps of great residual joy – the exceptional life, the spectacular and extreme case. The poem does not consider these possibilities. What we know is that the four people chose the other course. They did not

> . . . make time break (117)
> And let us pent-up creatures through
> Into eternity, our due . . .

There was

> No forcing earth teach heaven's employ . . . (120)

They chose, by and large, to be the creatures of circumstance, to be like everyone else.

Here is the key idea. The new poetic task which Wordsworth undertook was to create figures who were epitomes of the general condition of human life. They represented man, either within the detail of society or sometimes upon the periphery of that, enmeshed in a causal necessity which in the last analysis allots him a rôle that is passive. 'In the last analysis' may be much to the point. The Leech-Gatherer has his resolution and independence; Andrea, his cultivation of mind and artistic talent; the Bishop, all his spectrum of energies and desires; and the famous poet in 'Dis Aliter Visum' his success and his many-sided life. But the resolution, as Wordsworth saw it, was a resolution (more or less conscious) to find dignity in subjection. Part of the originality of Browning's achievement was to show how men's subjection to the slow-moving but inevitable causality of life can hold good, quite regardless of all their show and brilliance. Characters such as had served hitherto only for fictions of the great and aberrant, could serve for this new, Wordsworthian purpose almost as well as Wordsworth's ancient countrymen.

I now wish, for a particular reason, to digress to a poem of another kind, Tennyson's *Ulysses*. One cannot see this as epitomizing man's subjection to the causal web. Rather, Ulysses is one who does indeed propose to 'make time break'. He is representative of the inexpugnable potentiality in mankind to strike out for parabola- not asymptote-biographies. Possibly, Ulysses himself will seem to some as almost the *archetype* of a certain human response, a certain human potentiality.

Archetype – what features of the structure of this poem induce one to speak in this way? It did not strike one as the right word in respect of Andrea or the Bishop, though it might have suited the Leech-Gatherer or the Old Cumberland Beggar. In part, at least, the answer is surely what transpired in chapter IV above: the withdrawal of all three from the social ocean of *milieu*, of multifarious everyday detail. Representation of this kind is remote from the *milieu*-creation of the nineteenth century. It turns its back on that, striving to be fundamentally another mode of presentation of reality; a mode that could exist, and indeed did exist, long before man had the literary, social or indeed technical conditions for *milieu*-literature. When we use words like 'archetypal' or 'mythopoeic' about a literary work, one part of what we are trying to give recognition to is exactly this tendency towards the fictive form from which *milieu* and the social ocean were remote.

Browning, needless to say, is for the most part a social-ocean writer. His Victorian zest for objects, his marvellous powers of multifarious historical re-creation, his nineteenth-century novelist's insight into eddy and diversity of character, all turn him powerfully this way. But there is one poem, exceptional among his works, which can indeed be seen as a mythopoeic rendering of the idea of the life-determined man.

This is 'Childe Roland to the Dark Tower Came'. Characteristically for the period, the energies of this poem go much into a vividly, detailedly realistic creation of scene and landscape. It is not detail of quite the common kind, though. The poem represents not so much the appearances of things as their great, but suspended, causal powers. The scene is one transfused with a ferocious potential energy of destructive causation. This is the world through which the knight passes, and which at the end of the poem is somehow to engulf him. But while the last nightmarish phase of the journey takes place, destructive causality holds off. As he journeys on through a space which is discontinuous (see stanza 9) with the space of the landscape, the rider is somehow all the time held in isolation: a figure apart, the apartness conducive to the myth.

Yet the true situation, though suspended in this way, is by no means concealed. Childe Roland, right from the moment he meets the 'hoary cripple' who is going to delude and entrap him as he has entrapped everyone else before him, is the pre-destined victim of his environment. If we begin by thinking that the quest to which his life has been devoted is a mark of activity, of man imposing his will upon what surrounds him, we are soon enough disabused. Determination from outside is altogether preponderant, in a quest where there is no choosing either to go back, or what road to take forward. What we have here is the *harsh* necessity of use (i.e., custom), not the Old Cumberland Beggar's 'mild necessity'. At the culmination of the poem, the knight seems more quarry than hunter. He is caught in the waiting ring of hills, and before a very peculiar audience. What transpires at the end is that all those who have tried the quest before him, and who seem from the earlier part of the poem to have failed, have in fact succeeded precisely as much as or little as he has. They are all waiting there, waiting to watch his arrival. What seemed to be turning into a unique achievement, is transformed in the very moment of occurrence. It proves to be the universal achievement – or non-achievement: which is, in some elusive sense to be the passive victim of what occurs in the world. One is its victim even in the moment of seeming to be its master.

Browning sensed the fact that the structure of society could be more complex than Wordsworth had seen or perhaps than he had needed to see. It could be such that a man might stand at the periphery of society and undergo a kind of zero life with respect to it from one point of view, although from another point of view he could be well established within society. The zero life was not confined to helpless destitution. Two poems of T. S. Eliot embody this conception and perhaps extend it. They are 'The Love Song of J. Alfred Prufrock' and 'Portrait of a Lady'. Like 'Andrea del Sarto', these are both poems of the 'gray remainder of the evening'. In the former:*

Let us go then, you and I,　　　　　　　　　　　　　　(11)
When the evening is spread out against the sky . . .

---

* References in the quotations which follow are to *page*, not line numbers.

And the afternoon, the evening, sleeps so peacefully!   (13)

and in 'Portrait of a Lady':

Among the smoke and fog of a December afternoon . . .   (16)

Well! and what if she should die some afternoon,   (20)
Afternoon grey and smoky, evening yellow and rose . . .

By now, the *persona* of the zero life is familiar, and there is no
need to confirm and illustrate in detail how much these poems
illustrate it. Prufrock realizes that he lacks the power to 'force
the moment to its crisis'; and as he comes to realize that, he
decides also that it would not 'have been worth it' even if he
could have done so.

No! I am not Prince Hamlet, nor was meant to be;   (15)
Am an attendant lord . . .

From the lines that follow, it becomes clear that the 'attendant
lord' is a reminder of Polonius: 'I grow old' . . . 'almost, at
times, the Fool'.

In 'Portrait of a Lady', the Lady's life is 'composed so much,
so much of odds and ends' (16), the man smiles, listens, goes on
drinking tea, takes his hat and leaves, sits every morning in
the park reading the least meaningful pages of the newspaper,
and at the end of the poem is perhaps going to sit

Not knowing what to feel or if I understood   (20)
Or whether wise or foolish . . .

'We are really in the dark' (19).

The substantial conformity of these two poems to the type
with which this chapter is concerned must be clear enough.
What is perhaps less so is that they seem to represent a further
and indeed disquieting extension of that kind of poem. Why this
is so will perhaps transpire from a consideration of two poems,
one by Wordsworth and one by Browning, which could well
have been introduced at an earlier stage.

'Resolution and Independence' has been universally recog-
nized as one of its author's most memorable poems. It is surely
also one of its strangest. Everyone recalls the stanzas in which

the Leech-Gatherer first appears on the scene, like a stone, like a sea-beast, like a cloud, as if he emanates from earth, from water, from air, the three elements that make the whole of the abiding and ordered edifice of Nature. This is Wordsworth at the height of his extraordinary and visionary power. When he so writes, one hardly knows what other poet in our literature to set beside him. Clearly, there is one sense in which the Leech-Gatherer is at the nadir of existence. His words come feebly, he seems weighed down by a 'more than human weight' of 'dire constraint', he is in 'extreme old age', his penurious existence depends upon haunting the loneliest places in search of the lowliest creatures. These are the leeches, that have 'dwindled long by slow decay' until it seems they must reach a zero, and him a zero with them. But in the main, that memorable image is conveyed to the reader in a few stanzas in the middle of the poem.

Before them, and emerging out of them also towards the end of the poem, is a quite elaborate setting of something very different. The stone-like longevity of the Leech-Gatherer makes its appearance within a setting, created by the earlier part of the poem, of a characteristic eighteenth-century idea, the idea of vicissitude: his elemental permanence emerges from a scene of night-time storm followed by morning gaiety, and alongside that, gaiety in the poet's mind followed by sudden, unpredictable gloom. The structure of the poem is more inclusive and more significant than transpires at first, and it is a typically Wordsworthian structure. We may recall *The Prelude*:

Tumult and peace, the darkness and the light –   (VI.635)
Were all like workings of one mind . . .
The types and symbols of Eternity
Of First, and last, and midst, and without end.

The Leech-Gatherer is a type and symbol of eternity. In contrast to the changefulness of Nature's outward face, there is the speaking eventlessness of his own life.

That it is indeed a speaking life means much to the plan of the poem. The vicissitude of the opening stanzas is a thinking vicissitude. The poet says that his whole life has been a life of 'pleasant thought' (36). Now, in a sudden mood of fear and dejection, his mind fills with ideas of the unhappy poets of the past, and more generally with a 'dim sadness' of 'blind thoughts' that he can hardly identify. It is upon this busy texture of thought and feeling that the image of the Leech-Gatherer supervenes; and at this point there comes what is perhaps the most unexpected feature of the poem. The Leech-Gatherer translates his *image* into his *story*. 'He told . . . '. But not once only. It seems as if, just in the way that God spoke to the young Samuel when he was with the aged Eli (I Samuel 3, 4–14), the poet receives the Leech-Gatherer's message three times over. The first time is in response to his opening enquiry, and comes in stanza 15. The second comes in stanza 18, after the poet's disquiet of mind has made him ask his question over again:

> Perplexed, and longing to be comforted . . .   (117)
> My question eagerly I did renew . . .

Finally, it seems that at the end of stanza 19 the Leech-Gatherer delivers his message, in the face of the poet's continuing 'trouble' of mind, a third time. The folk-tale quality of the exchange cannot be overlooked. The old man's message is the crucial feature of the experience, the passing of it on must be re-enacted a second and a third time, then its full potency will be assured. That message, one should notice, supervenes upon a continuing tissue of thought on the poet's part. After the first explanation, and in spite of it:

> My former thoughts returned: the fear that kills;   (st. 17)
> And hope that is unwilling to be fed;
> Cold, pain, and labour, and all fleshly ills;
> And mighty poets in their misery dead . . .

During the Leech-Gatherer's second explanation, the same movement of relapse on the poet's part occurs for a second time:

> While he was talking thus, the lonely place,   (st.19)
> The old Man's shape, and speech – all troubled me . . .

It is as this trouble of mind develops:

> While I these thoughts within myself pursued   (132)

that the third and seemingly effective explanation on the Leech-Gatherer's part takes place. Nor must one overlook the distinctive mental situation within which the triad of explanation occurs. It is a situation of which phrases like 'My question eagerly I did renew', 'My former thoughts returned', and 'I these thoughts within myself pursued' are the distinguishing marks: a situation of intense and sustained meditation and questioning. 'I'll think of the Leech-Gatherer on the lonely moor' is the poem's closing line; and that thought is to be 'my help and stay *secure*', the poet says. The Old Man is a source of vision and insight, the intense meditative and cognitive effort of the poet himself is rewarded with a secure issue because it is a lucid and distinct one. Profound as the distinctions of course are, the lineaments of the solitary Cartesian search for enlightenment are distinguishable in the poem.

Most of Browning's dramatic monologues are spoken by the person in the poem who invites the reader's primary interest; but 'How it Strikes a Contemporary' is not. The speaker is the contemporary, and he deserves that designation simply because he is contemporary with the enigmatical Poet who is the prime centre of interest. Browning's Poet also would appear to be an insatiable learner:

Scenting the world, looking it full in face (11)

he goes through his city with his 'scrutinizing hat', watching, glancing – but the glance is an all-penetrating one – taking cognizance, making notes. Certainly from one point of view, his life is a kind of zero life. He goes 'up and down Valladolid' a little as the Old Cumberland Beggar goes up and down the English village. His biography is eventless, and he lives as poorly and simply as may be. He has no conventional place within his own society, no routine niche. If he has an allotted and meaningful rôle, it is operative outside that society and in respect of another social relation. People thought that this poet was perhaps the King's private magistrate, acting as personal observer and messenger. 'St . . . the Corregidor!' said the speaker's father to him when a boy (90). But the Poet was not a magistrate, even in disguise: 'that was not the man' (98). Neither the speaker nor his father understand the matter at all.

'This, or something like it', his poem begins, with unconscious irony. The true poet may indeed have an unobtrusive mien and with it an all-observing eye, but he is not the 'recording chief-inquisitor' (39) for the reigning monarch.

Not, that is, unless one asks a little further who that monarch may be: then it is that the 'something like it' reveals its fuller meaning, and the underlying precision of thought of the poem begins to emerge. There is indeed a King to whom the true poet could venture without effrontery to report; a King who would care, also, for the version of reality that is what the true poet supplies us with. This would be a King who, when his long-trusted reporter correspondent came at last to die, could indeed send bedside ministers:

With the heavenly manner of relieving guard . . .   (103)

It would be God himself. To be his messenger and representative, says Browning, is the true poet's rôle: not the 'corregidor', the magistrate-representative of an earthly monarch, but the unrecognized though in the end all-influential corregidor of the King of Kings. 'Poets are the unacknowledged legislators of the world': it is that Shelleyan idea which Browning, confident both that it will not be missed and also that it is true, has secreted at the heart of his poem.

Two questions may be asked about this whole group of poems; and the distinctive answers which Eliot's poems suggest in this matter are thrown into prominence by having added 'Resolution and Independence' and 'How it Strikes a Contemporary' to the group. First, one may enquire as to the relation which holds, in each case, between the protagonist of the poem and the society in which he lives. The protagonists of Wordsworth's 'Old Cumberland Beggar' and 'Resolution and Independence' have particularly clear places within their societies. True enough, the rôle they fulfil is a distinctive one, and belongs to the zero life. But the rôle of each is quite specific. 'The Old Cumberland Beggar' is a poem the very purpose of which is to show that one who seems to have no social rôle in fact has a very real one: 'deem not this man useless!' The Leech-Gatherer has a minimal but for all that quite distinctive and definite productive rôle. Beyond that, his function is not altogether unlike that of the Old Cumberland Beggar. To understand him, to contemplate him, is regenerative for at least one other member of his society.

Browning's protagonists, in the poems that have been discussed, also have determinate places within their societies. Childe Roland's seemingly isolated, solitary, unique quest proves to be entirely typical and representative: all have undergone it, all have doubtless supposed themselves to be isolated and unique in the process, all have discovered their error. Andrea and the Bishop of St Praxted's have descended into ineffectiveness and passivity, but in both cases this is firmly within the contexts of their house, their wife, their work, or their church and status – and sons. The people in 'Dis Aliter Visum' have their careers, marriages and 'circle'. Browning's Poet is exceptional in that he has no positive function within the little world of Valladolid itself: but that is precisely because his function in the larger society (whether that of the state and its ruling monarch within the apparent and ironical structure, or of God, eternal truth and the verdict of history in the covert structure) is definite and significant.

Not so with Prufrock, or with the speaker and the Lady in 'Portrait of a Lady'. Prufrock does not belong to the society of the women who talk of Michelangelo. He is no more one with that world than Lazarus 'come from the dead'. Rather than that he should have lived (he says) as some faceless, anonymous creature at the bottom of the sea. Should he speak to others, their inevitable retort would be to say he had misunderstood them. The Lady, in the other poem, says she is sure that her friend reaches out his hand; but the irony is clear, and she herself admits that the reaching is 'across the gulf'. She is to sit 'serving tea to friends': but the chance for her of a real social bond – a last chance – was with the man who is going away abroad from it all. 'Perhaps you can write': the meaningless gesture, only too much an acknowledgment that there is no bond to sustain by writing, is what restores the man's '*self-possession*' (the irony is inescapable) because his own significance is for there to be no bond.

The second question concerns the self-knowledge and comprehension shown by the people in these poems, or by the writers of

them. Wordsworth's Old Cumberland Beggar is uncomprehend-
ing; but his Leech-Gatherer is very different, a man of wisdom:

> Choice word and measured phrase, above the reach   (95)
> Of ordinary men; a stately speech . . .

Wisdom and insight proceed from him. It is not the spectacle of
his life only, but also it is what he has to say, that rewards the
poet's own intent search for enlightenment. Both poems
conclude by presenting themselves to the reader as reaching a
considered and definitive lucidity. The enquiring imagination
has in the end been fully vindicated.

Browning's protagonists, on the other hand, seem to compre-
hend intermittently or successively rather than with the assured
wisdom of the Leech-Gatherer. About Browning's 'Poet', we
are not told. Andrea knows, but not for sure:

> Still, all I care for, if he spoke the truth . . .   (198)
>
> If really there was such a chance . . .

Certainly he strives on, all the way through his monologue, to
grasp the truth of his case. The Bishop of St Praxted's sees by
glimpses:

> Life, how and what is it? As here I lie   (10)
> In this state-chamber, dying by degrees,
> Hours and hours long hours in the dead night, I ask
> 'Do I live, am I dead?' Peace, peace seems all.

Only occasionally can he come out with:

> Evil and brief hath been my pilgrimage   (101)

– and immediately is back with his lapis lazuli. Childe Roland,
at the beginning of his poem, is wholly innocent of the truth
about his situation. But his achievement is to discover that
truth in the course of the poem; not to fail to see it when it lies
before him; and not to give way to despair when he sees what
in his own case the 'mutual web' actually means. The young
woman, finally, who is speaking in 'Dis Aliter Visum' opens
the poem with the dramatic words:

Stop, *let me have the truth* of that!
Is that all true? . . .

After ten years, the realities of her situation in the past, and the man's, have come out at last; and as she takes stock of that situation, she masters it:

Now I may speak: you fool, for all   (111)
   Your lore!

It is she who sees what a 'wise beginning' for the two of them would have been like. The truth she learns makes her scorn his orderly wisdom of middle-age. Her youthful passionate involvement, Childe Roland's steadfast effort, Andrea's patient attempts to comprehend, suggest how the dramatic poet has transferred, to his characters, the striving towards insight and enlightenment that Wordsworth has expressed as his own.

I suggested earlier on that the protagonists in Eliot's 'Prufrock' and 'Portrait of a Lady' do not come near to understanding their situation, as on the whole those in the Browning poems do. This calls for a little reflection. Browning's own credentials for understanding the situations of his characters are simply that he shows them understanding on their own account. But what must a dramatic writer do to show that he himself has an understanding of his characters' situation, when he wants to depict them as lacking it themselves? Of course, there must be a dimension of irony in his work. But there must be more than what could be called a negative irony: the creation of a double strand of meaning such that the second calls in question the first. If there is no more than that, we shall have a text where the irony establishes that the characters are at a loss over their situation, and that the author knows that that is the case. This does not establish that the author comprehends. It is not comprehension, to have insight enough to see that another's sense of a situation is no sense of it. The irony carried by the second strand of meaning must somehow integrate into a second and alternative interpretation, one which will establish itself as the writer's own sustained if implicit meaning.

'How it Strikes a Contemporary' does exactly this. The amiable but shallow and somewhat worldly speaker of the lines

('Let's to the Prado and make the most of time') thinks, as we saw, that the Poet writes for the ruler of the state, the King. Browning's irony conveys his own opinion, that the 'precious life-blood of a master-spirit' is authorship worthy of the Author of Nature, by a second meaning sustained throughout his poem. Unfailingly, the poem uses a capital for 'King': which usually, in fact, reads, 'our Lord the King'. The first reference to the Poet in this context refers to him as 'recording chief inquisitor'. He is 'doing the King's work'. He gets 'never word or sign' of the approval of his Master. At the end, there is the 'heavenly' watch-guard that will be round his bed, and the underlying point is surely clinched in the closing lines: the Poet dies, and we read:

> And, now the day was won, relieved *at once*! (109)

Immediately, the shallow-minded speaker goes on to think of how he and his listener are wearing fine clothes, not old and worn ones like the poet. But for them too death will come, and then:

> *A second*, and the angels alter that. (113)

Those two lines are separated in the text by only three others; and together, they make Browning's second meaning absolutely clear. What definitely establishes it as his own considered reading of the case, however, is the way in which it is sustained and integrated throughout the poem. It is this integration which establishes that the poet wishes his irony not merely to challenge and reject the interpretation set on the facts by the dramatis personae, but to substitute for it an authoritative interpretation of his own.

There is much irony in Eliot's two poems, but it does not function in this way.

> In the room the women come and go (11)
> Talking of Michelangelo.

The pat rhyme, the rhythmic collapse in the second line of the couplet, create an irony that is enough to discredit such conversation. The beautifully unobtrusive pun (it is less unobtrusive in an American voice) in the lines:

And I have known the eyes already, known them all – (13)
The eyes that fix you in a *formulated** phrase,
And when I am formulated, sprawling on a pin . . .

is (whether we think that Prufrock means it, or utters it by
accident, makes little difference to the present point) enough to
send an ironical discrediting to flicker to and fro between
speaker and subject. Again,

I should have been a pair of ragged claws (13)
Scuttling across the floors of *silent* seas

ironically invites the reader to reflect that there is a sense in
which Prufrock's meditation, that touches so probingly on the
vapidity of others, might itself just as well have been left
unsaid. The last line of the poem:

Till human voices wake us, and we drown (15)

is as much as to say, ironically, that true humanity is something
none of the persons making up the 'we' of the poem could either
make contact with, or even withstand. At all these points in the
text, there are negative ironies poignantly conveying how
Eliot sees he has indeed not created a Prince Hamlet. But they
do not come together to delineate any interpretation that has
authority because it proves to be the poet's own. Rather, they
remain in discreteness and isolation.

Is not the same true of 'Portrait of a Lady'?

She has a bowl of lilacs in her room (17)
And twists one in her fingers while she talks.
'Ah, my friend, you do not know, you do not know
What life is, you who hold it in your hands';
(Slowly twisting the lilac stalks) . . .

The Lady, it is clear, does not know where life is to be found,
nor perhaps what a friend is. If that is so:

I shall sit here serving tea to friends (18)

also carries its irony. Then, this being so, her offer of

---

* 'Formulated' must be pronounced American-wise to bring out the pun on
'formalin'.

> Only the friendship and the sympathy
> Of one about to reach her journey's end

has something ironical to say about the quality of what sympathy she has to offer. These 'regrets', like those earlier in the poem, are somewhat 'carefully caught'.

> You do not know . . .   (16)
> . . . how rare and strange it is . . .
> To find a friend who has *these* qualities,
> Who has, and gives
> *Those* qualities upon which friendship lives.

The empty repetition, and suave change in the demonstrative, indeed makes it rare and strange, despair begotten upon impossibility. The Lady can ring changes upon her words because her innermost being is no better than to be an idle kaleidoscope of unrealities. But her interlocutor is much the same:

> My self-possession flares up for a second . . .   (19)

Already, an ear awakened by the other ironies of the poem detects a false note; when the self-possession, a few lines later, is said to 'gutter', the point is made. It is the last flicker of (and the symbol has its own and further meaning) an expiring candle. The young man is 'really in the dark'. Observations like these could be continued; but the further they are taken, the more clearly do they transpire as a sequence of ironies that are unrelated and in that sense negative. What Eliot, in these poems, knows, and knows with (to revert to 'Eloisa to Abelard') 'all the sad variety of woe', is first that his characters do not know. They are in a darkness so great that it numbs to behold. Then, more than that. The writer of these poems is as ignorant as they.

IX

'No Answerer I'

I

We are still coming to terms with all that is meant by Hardy's having been a major novelist, and in addition to that, a major poet.

By the time of his death in 1928, poets were beginning to see the value of his work, and to take him as a poet who had a great deal to teach them. His influence on poets of the 1930s like Auden and especially C. Day Lewis was undoubtedly great, and everyone knows that he and Gerard Manley Hopkins were the two nineteenth-century poets who most influenced English verse once the impact of T. S. Eliot had been felt. Yet all the same, Hardy's true position is still not often seen; his poetry is regarded narrowly, with the novels temporarily forgotten. To be sure, Hardy has a special position even from that point of view. In matters of style, most Victorian poets followed chiefly Keats, or Wordsworth's blank verse, or Shakespeare. This gave them a varied diction, but one that tended towards the ambitious or aspiring.

Hardy offers something else. In his work we find not an ambitious and aspiring style, but the informal and unassuming. Even in his unhappy poems he often writes with a strange kind of unlaboured jauntiness. He knew the earlier English poets, but other traditions of verse had entered his mind and become second nature to him. What touched him most deeply were the folksongs, ballads, popular songs and rhymes of the people which he knew from his West Country childhood and youth.

Sing, Ballad-singer, raise a hearty tune . . .
Rhyme, Ballad-rhymer, start a country song . . .
Sing, Ballad-singer, from your little book . . .

– these are the first lines of the three stanzas of 'At Casterbridge Fair'. Probably, it is this background, and Hardy's interest also (it has been little studied) in popular Victorian song, which brought it about that so many of Hardy's poems are in the three-time rhythms which have for the most part not been successful in serious English verse. When they succeed in Hardy, their background in the music and song of the people is often very evident, as in 'A Merrymaking in Question' (p. 436):

'I will get a new string for my fiddle,
    And call to the neighbours to come,
And partners shall dance down the middle
    Until the old pewter-ware hum:
    And we'll sip the mead, cider, and rum!'

That is one example, but there are many.

This strong link with popular music and singing is important, for it is what distinguishes Hardy's rhythms from those of Wordsworth, the other great English poet of country life. Wordsworth's *Lyrical Ballads* grew out of the broadside ballads of the eighteenth century, but Wordsworth was not much of a musical man, and the music and singing of the people marked out a course he could not follow.

Today, we are familiar with lyrical poems that simply record some straightforward event of everyday life the poet purports either to have lived through or to have seen as a bystander; so familiar, in fact, that we tend to forget how this is a comparatively recent invention in poetry. Wordsworth, virtually the first English poet to write this way, did so only to a limited extent. He wrote only a couple of dozen or so such poems, and they are about ordinary life only in a special sense. True enough, they are about ordinary people, if that means poor, country-dwelling people; but they are not about people the poet thinks of as quite like himself. 'Humble and rustic life' . . . Wordsworth's characters are near the bottom of the social scale – an old Cumberland beggar, poverty-stricken peasant farmers, a wandering leech-gatherer, the children of the poor. In their simplicity and innocence, and in their standing apart from the respectable framework of society, the poet hoped to contact the deepest rhythms and meanings of life. But at the same time it is fair to say that Wordsworth makes these 'characters' his own social inferiors. In some of his short poems he is rather conspicuously conscious of how they are so. One example is 'Alice Fell', about the orphan girl whose coat catches in the wheel of the poet's coach.

Hardy never shows himself conscious of any such gap between himself and the people in his poems. So far is he from setting any distance between himself and them that often he puts his poem into the mouth of the principal character. One example is 'The Pine-Planters', a poem published in *Time's Laughing-Stocks* (1909), and given (it is a reminiscence from *The Woodlanders*) the sub-title, 'Marty South's Reverie'. Marty, in simple words and bald rhythms, sings of how she toils all day to help the man she loves as he works in the forest; but she knows that his thoughts are full of someone else.

Another example is what Hardy is said to have seen as his most successful poem: 'A Trampwoman's Tragedy': the woman, with a vagrant's defiant fecklessness, teases and provokes the man she loves, until he murders his supposed rival. His execution empties her life of meaning. From one point of view, the poem is a searching psychological study, a revelation of one kind of primitive perversity-yet-integrity. This is far from anything attempted in the ballad tradition, and it is no wonder that Hardy lapses into a diction –

> I teased my fancy-man in play   (183)
>   And wanton idleness

– which is hard to imagine any tramp-woman having at her command. Yet this makes the point all the clearer. Even when it might have been better not to, Hardy's instinct was to identify himself with his subject, rather than stand back from it and perhaps give an impression of standing above it.

Like a novelist, Hardy was interested in his verse to record the great variety of life, and all the detail, strangeness and poignancy which he found in every moment of experience, more or less wherever he looked. He did not take the whole of the social spectrum for his subject, and he had a certain 'idiosyncratic mode of regard' (his own phrase). The titles of his books – *Life's Little Ironies, Time's Laughing-Stocks, Satires of Circumstance, Winter Words* – indicate what it was. But quite apart from Hardy's 'pessimism', which is familiar ground enough (though often understood over-simply), it is as an almost encyclopaedic recorder of everyday human life, throughout the whole range of his experience of it, that he deserves recognition. He was the first English poet to achieve this: the first genuinely novelist-poet. In his verse we find the rich and multifarious picture of everyday, common, even humble life, which is so much a part of the great nineteenth-century novels but (Hardy aside) seldom a part of nineteenth-century poetry.

The staple of Hardy's verse is represented, one could almost say, in a poem like 'Seen by the Waits': the carol-singers at the manor-house, as they stand in the snow, simply happen to catch sight of the lady of the house silently dancing to herself because she has learnt that her good-for-nothing husband is dead. Another instance would be – 'At the Word "Farewell" ': the young man visiting a house simply kisses the host's daughter in the garden, as he leaves, very early in the morning.

Many indeed are the scenes and situations from daily life that work their way into Hardy's poems: an old woman thinking life over as she mechanically rakes up the dead leaves; a milk-maid, in the idyllic peace and richness of dairy-land country, her heart full of innocent vanity and thoughts of a young man; someone plodding along through a storm; two lovers at night, under the last lamp in a street; a small boy playing his fiddle on a railway platform, to while away the time for a convict travelling under guard; a woman thinking of how the outline of her son's face – someone had drawn it long ago on the wall – is still there, under the new whitewash; a young wife complacently making tea for her husband and a visitor – the woman he has secretly loved all the time; a small boy on the night train, with his ticket in the band of his hat, and the key to his box on a string round his neck. These are only a few.

There are scores, perhaps even hundreds of poems of this kind in Hardy's work as a whole: created for him, out of the daily scene of the West Country of the last century, by his novelist's eye. The conviction that romance and deep feeling and true poetry surround us everywhere in 'common life' was a recurrent theme in the literature of Hardy's time. In a way, it is no more than the application in literature of the democratic idea. Hardy was the writer who established and naturalized this concept in our poetry. That is one great measure of our debt to him. It is a measure also of the break he made with the tradition this book discusses.

II

If the entry of the world and potentialities of the novelist into poetry is one dimension of Hardy's originality, another relates to the conception of the poetic task which purports to underlie his work. I say 'purports', because what is at issue is not how Hardy really, and in his own personal life, consciously conceived the task he undertook; but how his poems enable us to construct it.

Poems as various as Shelley's *Alastor* or 'Adonais', Tennyson's *Ulysses*, Johnson's *Vanity of Human Wishes*, Pope's *Heroic Epistles*, Coleridge's 'Ancient Mariner', Keats's *Endymion*, may diverge almost as much as poems can possibly diverge; but they have two great things in common. The first of these relates to the kind of tale they tell or the portrait of a man they construct. It is something that might be called their *implicit declaration* as fictions. The poems declare that they deal with events or with characters that are outstanding and notable, that rise above the common run of life. Moreover, the justification for writing the poem – for narrating the events narrated in poetic form, and not some other or none at all – is the suggestion that poetry is a mode of expression (or more specifically, of narration) which is both the sign and the consequence of having something to tell about those who are, or whose lives are, above the general level of experience.

Browning may seem a contrast: but that is an illusion. Browning does not reject this poetic structure outright; but retains it in essence while calling it in question on the surface.

This seems to be what happens in poems like 'Cleon', 'Abt Vogler', 'Bishop Blougram', 'Fra Lippo Lippi', 'Andrea del Sarto'. In each case, the monologue figure can monologuize for a very special and significant reason: because of his talents, perception, fluency, almost limitless power to reflect on his situation or to want, to wonder, to desire or dissect. What is distinctive in the poems – what Browning does that Tennyson is far from doing – is to add a note of interrogation to all this: to introduce a questioning, which often enough is a self-questioning by the monologuist. That question is, whether, in this life of great subtlety and endless self-scrutiny, there is not also, and essentially, a note of radical inadequacy and failure. Sometimes, as in 'The Bishop Orders his Tomb', Browning emphasizes that note of inadequacy, even of fault. The bishop is far (or should I say, is probably far?) from seeing how much his life and his present state leave to be desired. Sometimes, as with Bishop Blougram, one can almost believe – not quite – that the inadequacy is a fiction. But seldom do Browning's characters, whatever their limitations and failings, turn from being significant, interesting people, into people whose interest lies in their own very dullness, unawareness.

Interest cannot lie in dullness if that word is used in its full sense. But on the other hand, Wordsworth's *Lyrical Ballads* do indeed claim something of this kind as their underlying conception. Simon Lee or the Old Cumberland Beggar, the woman in 'The Thorn', the shepherd in 'The Last of the Flock', the child in 'Anecdote for Fathers', are people of another kind from the characters in Shelley's or Tennyson's or Browning's poems. They belong to the featureless and their interest is so to belong.

I suggested that there were two things that poems like *Alastor* and the others which I mentioned had in common. The second of these things is that the poems all declare, more or less overtly, that just as their *subjects* were persons who stood out above the common run of life and the common range of experience, so were their *authors*. Both character and author alike present themselves through the poem as being in the 'master class'. Narrative poems are declarative of such facts or alleged facts. They make such declarations about their authors by how, as poems, they set about the fictive task; by their stance, as poems,

of issuing from total and authoritative knowledge and compre-
hension of what they are about. All these things add up to an
intimation of what the author claims about himself as author. It
is clear enough that Wordsworth makes such claims for himself,
by the structure that he gives his poems. Poems like 'Resolution
and Independence' or, at another level, 'Alice Fell' make this
clear. The contrast between poet and character is comprehen-
sive. True, Wordsworth in a certain sense actually humbles
himself before his humble and rustic characters. He learns from
them. But even within this fact, the structure remains. Words-
worth is a grand and monumental learner from such a range of
experience. What lies before him may be humble and rustic
life. But the experiences the poet elicits from it are master-class
experiences after all: 'thoughts that do often lie too deep for
tears'.

This second dimension of the familiar poetic stance, Hardy
drops as well as the first. A poem like 'Mute Opinion' (115)
will clarify the point. The poet says there that in life he
'traversed a dominion' whose 'spokesmen spake out strong' in
expressing their views upon every matter: by contrast, he
'scarce had means to note' the minority who, 'large-eyed' but
'dumb', did not share the views of the noisy pontificators. But
then, after his death, the poet contemplates that range of
experience to better effect. This time he is able to see that the
'web unbroken' of human history ran in a way exactly so as to
reject the stance, the pose, of the magisterial, all-knowing self:

> Not as the loud had spoken,
> But as the mute had thought.

It is worth noticing in particular that the 'loud' include
pontificator-poets as much as others of the kind: they are those
who declared themselves

> Through pulpit, press, *and song*

. . . and the slight, almost sing-song rhythms of this poem
confirm it as a repudiation of 'poetry is a criticism of life', save
in a distinctive, unobvious, even paradoxical sense.

There is no difficulty in seeing that Hardy's *characters* belong
to 'A Commonplace Day' – one of his own titles. But the great

novelty in his verse is that *he belongs also*. In the poems, or in a large number of his poems, what the text says about the poet is: 'No answerer I'. Those words are from one of the *Wessex Poems*: 'Nature's Questioning' (58). The poet 'looks forth' at dawn, and the common features of the landscape seem to speak to him, though in a speaking silence, of how they are in one way or another (he cannot tell just what, nor can they) victims of a remoter but hidden power. This silent speech is question only, not assertion. Nature questions – 'thus things around', the poem says – but cannot answer. Even so, all the activity, such as it is, falls there. '*No answerer I . . .* '. The poet does nothing but 'look forth', and remain, with those three self-abnegating words, a passive spectator.

This passiveness, beside which even the 'chastened children sitting silent in a school' mean activity, has one curious effect, not conspicuous but in the end significant. There is little sense that the 'I' of the poem is composer of the poem. The sense left with the reader is more of a poem somehow written by accident or writing itself. Partly, this seems to come from the fact that almost half the poem, in length, consists of questions put to the poet, to the 'I' – who can find nothing to say in reply. Partly it lies in the effect, not uncommon in Hardy, of a metrical flow which – the combination sounds a strange one – is *compelling yet awkward*. Stanza 1, for example, makes an awkward, graceless start, yet at the same time it presses the reader forward in an effort to resolve the awkwardness. The swiftly moving rhythm, and light yet prominent rhymes, bring him promptly to the end of the stanza. Elsewhere in the poem, an awkwardness in the syntax again presses the reader into taking hold of the entire stanza as a unity, in an effort to resolve the as it were tangential forces which predominate if he fails to do so. Result: a sense of poetic momentum, yet a momentum that, because it is realized through the reader's efforts to resolve awkwardnesses, seems to be a momentum, an energy, detached from authorship. The sense of a creative and governing mind is at a minimum. Hence the beautiful nonce-word 'lippings' in 'Nature's Questioning' presents itself in a manner wholly opposite to that of Hopkin's coinages. Such a deviation from the standard language leaves the impression rather that the poet's control is incomplete or intermittent, than that he is indulging his pre-eminent creativity and masterfully re-enlivening the language.

This kind of negative impression is common with Hardy. It is part of the general sense that the poet (the 'I' often enough) is, by the usual standard of the 'poetic character', as Keats put it, a person of no account. This poem is as if writing itself.

'A Sign-Seeker', another outstanding early poem (43), has a remarkably similar structure of passive and active as between poet and subject. The 'I' of the poem is almost wholly a 'witness' only. He 'sees', 'marks', 'views'. Activity lies elsewhere. His fellow-men, active enough, 'surge', 'meet' and 'part'; yet even in that, they sound more like the sea than like humans. It is, in fact, inanimate nature which comes nearest to animate activity. The months in 'livery', hissing rain, lightning like a sword, leaping meteor, earthquake's 'lifting arm' – as between the conventional traditional idea of the active and creative poet, and his environment, there is something like a reversal of rôles. What the poet has seen, or what he knows (like when the eclipses will come) carries no weight. The question that he cares about is what he knows nothing about. 'That I fain would wot of shuns my sense'. Once again, all he can say is 'No answerer I'. Nothing, he has to admit, comes to 'open out his limitings'. Passivity is unrelieved. Our experience of the poem is that its haunting and felicitous nonce-words – 'unheed', 'outbreathing', 'limitings' – and its turns of ingenious paradox – 'clang negligently', 'radiant hints' –are once again at the other extreme from those of Hopkins or Donne. They leave the impression, more than anything else, of a self-creating language, not of a dialect of the tribe magisterially purified by the creator-poet.

In one way or another, this is the situation in a good many of Hardy's poems. In 'A Commonplace Day' (104), Hardy's rôle is again to be, one might say, *the poet as nobody*. He quietly rakes out the fire at dusk, and he sits in the growing darkness and thinks about how he has done 'nothing of tiniest worth' all day. Nor, so far as the poet can tell, was the day's story different anywhere else. The poem comes to rest in an idea of abundance and life – but quite in some unknown place and in the abstract. Nothing could more clearly show how a Hardy poem depersonalizes creativity. The wild glissades of diction, from 'beamless black impends' (vivid but contorted) through the abstract formality of 'diurnal unit', to the terse, quiet power, acted out in modulating vowels and consonants of 'Wanly upon the panes/The rain slides' – or 'Some intent upstole/Of . . . enkindling ardency', are thus left seemingly without relation to the unifying mind of a writer who composed. Instabilities and irregularities of decorum, of keeping, do not carry their usual sense of a lapse of creative integrity. The language of the poem also merely 'upstole' as an 'undervoicing': those words are Hardy's own.

Perhaps it is worth while to enquire where, in a Hardy poem, energy is characteristically made to reside. If not in the composing, creating poet himself, is it, one may ask, in those realities – whether people or objects – that the poem is composed about? or if not in them, is it somewhere else or nowhere at all? 'Afterwards' (521) is interesting in this respect. It begins by speaking of the time after the poet's death:

> When the Present has latched its postern behind my
>   tremulous stay . . .

The 'tremulous stay' of the poet was one merely of seeing, of 'noticing', and of striving to save small animals and such from harm –

> But he could do little for them, and now he is gone.

It is certainly not in the 'I' of the poem, 'stilled at last', that energy resides: every single stanza rings to a close with some assertion of his innocent ineffectiveness or his passivity. Equally though, by its very form the poem precludes our seeing those who speak of the poet, after his death, as the centre of activity and energy. This is for a definite reason: their position is always relegated to (in effect) the interrogative mood. 'Will the neighbours say . . . ?'; ' . . . a gazer may think'; ' . . . one may say . . . '; 'Will this thought rise . . . ?'; 'And will any say . . . ?' There are no more than five stanzas, and those are the phrases that gave each of them the form of a question merely. So far as those who *may* think of the poet after his death (will they?), all is hypothetical and contingent. By its form, the poem seems at pains to preclude our thinking of the poet's passivity as countered by activity on their part.

More than in either poet or those who may come to think of him, this poem presents the things of man's natural environment as where energy resides. The spring season ('May month') that 'flaps its glad green leaves like wings' might seem to be conceived of in the poem as if it were a single gigantic bird. There is the 'dewfall hawk' crossing to the 'wind-warped' upland thorn, the 'mothy and warm' darkness in which the hedgehog travels. Above all, the marvellous last stanza has the stroke of the bell ('bell of quittance': the language resonant from the pun on 'bill of quittance' and also the ring of the last of those words): the bell rings out at first, then spreads itself over the darkness (the 'outrollings'), then is 'cut' by the cross-breeze, and finally comes to a kind of second life which is enacted with great economy and yet evocative power in the single line (about the 'outrollings' after they have temporarily faded):

Till they rise again, as they were a new bell's boom.

Surely it is in these that the energies released within the poem may be felt to reside, rather than either the poet himself, or those who may possibly come to speak of him.

Yet one cannot be fully satisfied with this account. The rich-seeming 'mothy and warm' night is somehow distanced and relegated after all, when one takes the fuller suggestiveness of the suddenly vacuous words 'some nocturnal blackness'; and that it is 'furtively' the hedgehog travels through this blackness, is not without its point. The 'full-starred heavens' of stanza four after all do nothing: winter *sees* them, that is all that the poem says. The dewfall-hawk (stanza 2) is effortless and sound-less; in the final stanza, we have bell-note and breeze and darkness and nothing else: about the whole scene and everything in it, there is a curiously insistent insubstantiality, when one comes as it were to assemble and integrate it second time round. The 'May month', finally, is not in fact conceived of as a gigantic bird, but (' . . . wings/Delicate-filmed as new-spun silk'), as that lightest, most insubstantial-seeming of all creatures, the May-fly, or perhaps the lace-wing which Hardy of course would have been familiar with, and which has wings of extraordinary delicacy, a clear pale-green gauzy film. All these facts about the poem, uninsisted-upon in it as they are, set aside the idea that the poem finds much energy in the things of nature; or much more, indeed, than it found in those figures whose thoughts it presented only as possibilities and in questions.

A poem published late in Hardy's life, 'I am the One' (799), illustrates a remarkably similar assemblage. Once again, and as conspicuously as ever, the poem repudiates anything in the nature of a heroic stance for its author. In fact, quite the contrary: the doves say ' . . . it's only he' when he passes; the hares see him as one for whom 'nobody cares'; the mourners think how he does not 'quizz' their unhappiness (meaning, no doubt, take stock of it unfeelingly). Once again, the poem presents its creator as one whose distinguishing mark is insignificance and inactivity. Yet, the contrast which would so readily suggest itself between the inactive poet-observer, and what he observes, does not develop; the poem seems to give almost equal weight to presenting the things he observes as inactive too. The doves '*do not* rouse' when they see him, the hares 'stir' as he passes only to resume their eating, the mourners glance and then disregard. In the last stanza, what is said about the stars is very explicit: the stars tell each other that, hard as the poet stares at them, they must 'lend no fierce regard' in return – look down on him harmfully, that is ('scathe him'). The reason lies in the stars' closing words, which in the light of the poem as a whole, take on a sense that is not obvious at first:

> . . . scathe him not. He is one with us
>   Beginning and end.

Stars, animals, birds and indeed humans also when they are about such tasks as are part of their natural place in the scheme of things, present themselves in the same mild, un-selfassertive light as the poet; and they do so for the most basic of reasons. That un-selfassertive quality is the poet's for no other reason than that he is one with nature and it is nature's proper and peculiar quality. Maybe the stars can exert, as men have thought, a malign influence. That may be among their exceptional potentialities. But their characteristic, as a part of nature, is rather to be devoid of active harm: to pursue their own paths in quietness like the rest of creation.

This balance of mildness and passivity, struck almost equally between poet, and what else enters his piece, is the foundation of this poem for the reason that it is seen as integral to the scheme of things as a whole.

'The Wind's Prophecy' (464), a poem published in 1917 after having been 'rewritten from an old copy', invites a rather different interpretation. The poem doubtless embellishes (or for that matter invents) an incident of about 1870, when Hardy would have been travelling westward into Cornwall, his mind full of Tryphena Sparks, only to meet Emma Gifford when he got there and fall in love with her instead. Once again, the position of the poet in the poem is characteristically unheroic. We see that the opening words, 'I travel on . . . ', govern the poem's whole length: and over the length of this travelling, the noise of the wind seems constantly to reply to the poet's thoughts as he pursues his journey, and constantly to contradict and correct those thoughts.

This is the single, almost naive dialogue-structure of the poem. Within such a structure is generated the impression of a great deal of energy, little of it the steadily journeying poet's, and much of it emanating from the riotous and vital landscape he goes through. As is very characteristic of our language, movement and force come to be expressed (generated rather) in the adverbial particles: the 'gulls glint *out*', a cloud bellies *down*, light blinks *up*, the sun *ups* it (adverb coined into verb), the wind outshrieks (meaning simply 'shriek *out*', not shriek louder than something else). Yet more than this, energy seems to break out everywhere in this rocky exposed seaboard place where the tides smite and slam, and the wind comes from 'hoarse skies', from 'points and peaks' and every 'dip and rise', and is like 'bursting bonds'; and where there is a continual vivid chiaroscuro, first of silver-glinting gulls against black-bellied cloud, then of white foam *clots* (vivid, robust word) against the sea's dull and 'muddy monochrome', and finally, as night falls, of rocky coombes and inlets that 'blacken' where the headland lighthouses shine out one by one between them.

Here indeed is energy: is there not, though, something else

which is part of the experience of reading this poem? One thing about it has gone unmentioned: it is five stanzas long, and so far as the main idea of the stanzas as against their detail is concerned, they are strikingly similar and repetitive. Each time, the journeying poet thinks warmly of the girl who has been his beloved hitherto, and who lives somewhere behind him to the eastward. Each time, over and over, the wind corrects that thought by mention of the beloved-to-be: un-met, unknown, and somewhere before him to westward. What results from this, unless it is a mere dissipation of the poem's interest, because of the monotony of its repetitions?

At this stage in the discussion one must refer to certain things in the poem almost mechanical in their nature but not at all mechanical in their contribution. The key to the metrical scheme of the poem is the seventh line of the stanza, with its internal rhyme: 'The wind replies from dip and rise', 'Like bursting bonds the wind responds', and so on. The effect of this is curious: each stanza comprises a pair of what, virtually, are internally rhymed quatrains, and the two virtual quatrains may be seen as lines 1 to 4, and lines 6 to 8, in each case: but since lines 6 to 8 are of course only three lines not four, as they are printed, the impression also persists that lines 5 to 8, the second half of each stanza, count as the quatrain; and therefore that the two quatrains are bonded together by the rhymes ('alarms/ arms', etc.) which occur each time between lines 5 and 4. One must notice also how the rhymes run in each of the quatrains (whether lines 1–4, or lines 6–8). Their *abba* pattern means that the closing rhyme comes back as a sort of answer and completion. In other words, the quatrains all act out the basic pattern in the logic, as it were, of the dialogue between the poet and the wind. The simple but ingenious rhyming means that the metrics of the poem constantly impose and re-impose the poem's dialogue-pattern upon our whole experience of it.

There is something else in the structure of the stanzas which ought to be considered at this point; the inconspicuous, but in fact quite extreme, formality of the pattern of dialogue-and-description. In the first three stanzas, the traveller-poet's thought is introduced by the first two words of line 5 ('I say', 'I sigh', 'Say I') and occupies lines 5 and 6. In the last two

stanzas, the 'I cry' and 'Say I' open line 6 instead of line 5, and
this is the sole element of variation. Otherwise, lines 1–4
invariably describe the journey and the scene, and line 7 the
wind; while lines 5 and 6 consist of the poet's thought, and line
8, the wind's correcting reply.

In my own experience of reading the poem, this formality of
pattern seems to interact with the ingenious formalities of the
rhyme-scheme so as to produce a distinctive result. It may be
thought that in pursuing the analysis of a single one of Hardy's
poems, the larger contours of the present enquiry are being
forgotten. Such is not the case. The formalities of rhythm,
stanza, rhyme and dialogue- or description-pattern have the
result, first of all, that the reader is continuously, without inter-
mission, conscious of the movement and progress of the *poem as
such* as the primary and most prominent reality of the experience
of reading. Thoughtful reading, re-reading, and study of any
good poem of course makes one conscious of just such movement
and progress: to think about these matters is something like
the essence of writing and revising a poem, and must therefore
transpire as such, sooner or later, for the good reader. But it is
one kind of poetic experience when they do so from the first,
and quite another when they do so at last. Hardy – in this
particular respect like Yeats, Tennyson, Herbert, or most
writers of lyrics – produces poems that are emphatically of the
former kind. What we are initially and primarily conscious of,
as we read, is that in reading, we are watching and registering
the progress and resolution of a *poem*, an artefact in poetry. But
the natural and usual corollary of this, Hardy avoids. This
corollary is that as one reads the poem, the presence in it of the
poet establishes itself with a special prominence and authority:
the effortful, all-experiencing, all-organizing poet – much the
rôle, that is, of the aspiring Self discussed in the first chapter of
this book. Repeatedly, Hardy's more memorable poems achieve
the effect that the poem, as an artefact, organizes and dominates
the experience it describes, while the poet is present in his
poem conspicuously as one who is nothing of an organizer and
dominator, and indeed quite the contrary.

'The Last Signal' (444), a short but beautifully successful
'Memory of William Barnes', perhaps elucidates the point. It is

evening-time, and the poet is walking eastward, on the way to Barnes's funeral. He arrives just as the coffin is being carried out from Barnes's house on to the road, and – it is one of those slight but bizarre experiences that Hardy makes a number of his better poems from – suddenly he sees a flash of light before him. Then comes the line:

Looking hard and harder I knew what it meant –

As we read, we are reminded of the efforts and comprehendings of the enquiring self as poet. No such matter, though. This poet is no seer. 'Silently I footed by an uphill road', he character-istically, self-effacing begins the poem. The 'looking hard and harder' is no vatic intent regard, but just an attempt to grasp the simple surface reality: which in fact is just a momentary reflection, flashing from the coffin, of the setting sun. The poet is altogether a modest, unassuming figure in this poem. The dead man seems to establish a kind of ascendancy over him, with what is presented as his brief, almost lordly gesture (the flash) which the poet is at first hard put to it to understand at all:

Thus a farewell to me he signalled on his grave-way,
    As with a wave of his hand.

When one re-reads the poem, it more and more asserts *itself* over the experience it records. Its intricate internal rhyming and complex sound patterns, and its exact but economical descrip-tion of the event, arranged so as first to mystify the reader about just what has happened and then, with beautiful economy, to elucidate it for him, are a *tour de force* that yet leaves the impres-sion of total ease. Above all, the comparison saved up for the last line draws the situation together, gives it, one might say, a shape, in a manner which seems wholly right, but in reality is quite *imposed on the experience* of the poem. It is, surely, the leisured and informal rhythms of the lines, as they fall into their effortlessly shapely stanzas, which make that 'wave' of the hand irresistibly convincing. The poem itself is indeed masterly, even masterful: only, it creates at the same time as we see this, the sense that it will not have been written by the gentle, even retiring 'I' who figures in it.

Two poems from the well-known 1912–13 series written

about the memory of Hardy's first wife are in place here. Each, in its own characteristic way, offers confirmation of how often in Hardy's work it is the poem itself which establishes a kind of ascendancy, not only over the presence of the author as he appears within his poem, but also over the whole experience that the poem deals with. 'The Voice' (325) immediately sub-ordinates the author's presence to that of the dead woman: 'Woman much missed, how you call to me, call to me' . . . 'Can it be you that I hear? Let me view you, then . . . ' Then there is a modulation. The present reality of the dead woman is doubted:

> Or is it only the breeze, in its listlessness
> . . . You being ever dissolved to wan wistlessness . . . ?

– and these lines reflect a new significance back on to the 'original air-blue gown' of the woman who is now being dissolved into air. Her reality, though doubted, is not rejected: the last line of the poem is 'And the woman calling'. The closing stanza seems movingly to establish the faltering man, the wan woman, and the winter scene around them, in something like an equality of etiolated existence and common tragedy and wretchedness:

> Thus I; faltering forward,
> Leaves around me falling,
> Wind oozing thin through the thorn from norward,
> And the woman calling.

It is with these lines, though, and their suddenly quite new rhythms, that the decisive organization and force of the poem emerges. Here, indeed, are rhythms that seem to 'falter' for-ward, to stumble indeed to a halt. The rhythms throughout the first three stanzas, by contrast, have a swift, airy, to a certain degree assured movement. 'To a certain degree', because we find, at the same time as the fleetness and run of these lines, a great uncertainty as quite how their rhythms are to be under-stood. 'Counting by taps and knocks' (as I called this kind of scanning, a long time ago, in another work) will give, mechani-cally, four-stress lines that rattle along altogether at the expense of the meaning. Trying to do justice to the meaning proves to require that the reader recognize most of the lines can be scanned in any of several rhythms, and in particular that there is much ambiguity about the number of stresses in each line – most of them run, if anything, better with five stresses than with four. Result of all this: the ambiguous, elusive rhythms, swiftly yet uncertainly running, seem like the woman's own spirit as it speaks to the man; and the heavier, 'faltering' lines at the end, the man's reply. The essential encounter between them seems to take place, not in the winter landscape – then merely to be *described* in the poem – but throughout the totality and essence of the verbal structure. Once again, the poem itself, as a distinctive and powerful verbal artefact is what transpires as the manifestation of energy and integrating, constructing power: but it does so, seeming to have little or nothing to do with the 'faltering forward' of the 'I' who strictly, prosaically speaking, is its creator.

The other 1912–13 poem, 'After a Journey' (328), begins:

> Hereto I come to view a voiceless ghost;
> Whither, O whither will its whim now draw me?
> Up the cliff, down, till I'm lonely, lost,
> And the unseen waters' ejaculations awe me . . .

The strange rhythmic quality which runs throughout this famous poem, and which these opening lines establish, seems to be key to the whole. This quality – strange only because this poem establishes it from the start, authoritatively yet not by any obvious means – is simply the *isochrony* of the lines. The poem has to be heard in the mind's ear, or to be spoken aloud, with those constant minute departures from the timing of ordinary speech which would also result from its being set to music of a traditional kind. Trying, for example, to speak 'everywhere' (1.6), 'coming and going' (1.8) or 'leading me on' (1.17) strictly with the durations of ordinary speech, will make the lines they occur in grotesque and broken-backed; it is this isochrony, in fact, that which makes a line like

> Up the cliff, down, till I'm lonely, lost,

possible at all. Of course, the isochrony of the lines is one with their loose-limbed fluctuating patterns of stress and unstress, patterns that run throughout.

'After a Journey' begins as an encounter between a real, living man and a 'voiceless ghost': but the phrase, 'When we *haunted* here together' (ostensibly about the time of their youthful past), and also the words, 'the thin ghost that I now *frailly* follow', carry another suggestion ('frail' doubtless points in the first instance to the elderly poet's age). It is, that the man and the woman are *both* ghost figures, re-united in a timeless, ageless moment in which they are at once disembodied spirits (the woman who has died, the man's spirit haunting the past), and at the same time people restored to the time of youth and love ('your . . . rose-flush coming and going', 'I am just the same as when/Our days were a joy . . . '). With remarkable economy of means, the poem seems to have dismantled the scene and situation as it might be known to a realistic experience, and to have constructed another reality in which past and present, youth and age, are at once integrated and superseded.

In view of this, the insistent rhythms of the poem, its faltering but isochronous quality, does not come, in the reading, merely as a clever exercise in sing-song versification: and the key line for affording a recognition of its real contribution seems to be:

The waked birds preen and the seals *flop lazily*:

The poet has been wandering all night, 'up the cliff, down'. From first to last, it is a poem of to-and-fro wandering by the sea-coast; and the rhythms combine with the up-and-down of the cliff and the lazy flop of the seals to evoke, for the attentive reader, the movements, varying yet with an underlying regularity, of the poet on the one hand, and the steadily breaking sea on the other. It is these things which those rhythms cause to echo, as it were, throughout the poem; and with them also, perhaps, a certain tick-tocking sense of time itself which 'What you have *now* found to say of our *past*?' is at once (like the experience which the poem seems on reflection not so much to record as to construct) past time, and present. Hardy has again found means to have his poem create an experience beyond, and indeed counter to, experience as we know it, while maintaining all the while his characteristic *persona*.

That suggestion about the surreptitious presence of Time in the poem is perhaps rendered more plausible by 'The Musical Box' (453), the last of Hardy's poems which I shall discuss. The incident the poem describes is a characteristic one – a moment of common, everyday experience that suddenly seems both poignant and bizarre, as the 'white-muslined' girl stands at the house-door in the dusk while bats are flying about the house and a small musical-box is playing indoors. Once again, Hardy's poem quickly establishes certain unexpected but powerful connections between the ideas that enter the poem. The bats' wings whirr (Hardy is using the word for the visual effect only, and with great aptness) 'Like the wheels of ancient clocks': but the rhyming 'tuneful box' that is 'intoning' the greeting the girl laughs out as the 'swart bats' surround her, then comes by the help of something else in the poem to be both musical-box and register of time as well.

The 'something else' is what comes in the opening lines; and waits, almost throughout the poem, to be explained.

> Lifelong to be
> Seemed the fair colour of the time;
> That there was standing shadowed near
> A spirit who sang to the gentle chime
> Of the self-struck notes, I did not hear . . .

By the end, the poem has teased out for us that the chime is also clock-chime, the dead chime of time. The 'shadowed' figure surrounds the girl's youthful life much as the 'swart bats' do: and it warns the caller (stanza 2) to be heedful of the joy of the present that 'shines about' his welcoming much as the gay music makes a setting of sound for it. Yet the uncertainty and ambiguity of the moment find other reflections: the 'dusky house' surrounds – like the bats – the girl who is herself 'white-muslined' and like a ghost; and the evening scene as a whole (in stanza 3 which it is easy to take as casual description only) proves at a deeper level to reflect the lovers' future: a mere 'sense' of warmth where real warmth has gone (because evening has come), and a spectacle (the mill-pool waterlilies) of flowers that cannot be reached. At every turn, the poem interprets and complicates the present; sees its unhappy ambiguities; sees the unhappiness of the future reflected in its moment of joy; and yet, what its creator says *of himself* is:

I did not hear in my dull soul-swoon –
I did not see.

Poet and poem are at opposite poles. The one is all energy, organization, a power by no means interpretative of experience only, because (we see in the end) nothing short of masterfully reconstructive of it. That is the poem. It seems to have nothing to do with the other, the poet. He is made to seem all modesty, unawareness and self-effacement.

Hardy made a great discovery, of a strictly poetic kind, penetrate throughout the whole fabric of his verse. There is a sense in which he rediscovered a tremendous additional dimension within which to communicate. When Donne, Hopkins or Yeats write of their despair, the thoughtful reader is likely to sense an area of experience where he cannot quite believe what the poet tells him. Such poets, for all their grief, still have a marvellous reserve of creative energy, of power to master language in the making of art-works. They never seem to have despaired so far as to lack heart for this: and that means that they retain, in spite of all, a reason for jubilant self-recovery. Hence, their poems have to be read within a structure of creative convention. Hardy got away from that. He got away from 'art-work'. His finest lyrics are the heroic achievements of a poet whose rôle was that of anti-hero. I do not know whether Hardy was himself aware of the originality, or anyhow the magnitude of what he did, and incline to think he was not.

X

Postscript

I said, at the end of chapter I, that the 'theme of the soaring mind' and the 'proud knowledge' had probably been one of the greatest over the past five centuries, but that it might now be drawing to a close. There is no need to withdraw that suggestion, merely in order to take stock of how the last two chapters, those on 'The Zero Life' and on Hardy, may seem to over-stress this idea and to give the history of the 'proud knowledge' a rise and fall, a drama and symmetry, much clearer than in all probability it has. It must be nearly self-evident that in regard to major twentieth-century poets like (for example) Yeats, Pound, Eliot and Wallace Stevens, the preoccupations of this book have as it were taken on a new lease of life.

In the second section of 'The Tower', Yeats writes:

> *I pace upon the battlements*, and stare   (p. 219)
> On the foundations of a house . . .
> And *send imagination forth*
> Under the day's declining beam, and *call*
> *Images and memories* . . .
> *For I would ask a question of them all.*

This stance of the seer-poet is familiarly recurrent in Yeats. Of the great creative artist ('Michael Angelo') it may be said that 'his mind moves upon silence' like the long-legged fly on the stream; and then, whole generations apprehend essential truth because of him. As Yeats says of himself, the poet has 'a

marvellous thing to say'. 'All Souls' Night', from which those
words come, was in fact his epilogue to *A Vision.* Pound
entitles chapter 5 of his *Guide to Kulchur* 'Zweck or the Aim',
and almost his opening words in it are '. . . I occasionally cause
the reader "suddenly to see" . . . That being the point of
writing . . . the writer's aim, at least this writer's aim, being
revelation' (p. 51). The *Cantos* open with a solemn *pastiche* of
the Homeric Odysseus setting sail for his voyage to the farthest
limits of human experience and beyond, a voyage both to seek
knowledge and to bring men to their home; the burden of the
Cantos is to identify and thus to possess *cheng ming*: a lucid
precision of language which is almost of necessity insight,
virtue and social health at once. 'Where shall the word be
found . . .?', asks the speaking voice in the first section of *Ash-
Wednesday.* '*Da*' the Thunder seems to reply, introducing the
climactic words of *The Waste Land.* The 'simple soul' of 'Ani-
mula' that is 'unable to fare forward or retreat' seems to receive
its answer in 'The Dry Salvages' ('Fare forward, travellers!')
or still more in the quest-odyssey words of 'Little Gidding':

> We shall not cease from exploration (p. 43)
> And the end of all our exploring
> Will be to arrive where we started
> And know the place for the first time.

In all these examples we glimpse the ambitions, and indeed the
very images, familiar from the present book as a whole.

There is also another side to the matter. It is as if the poets
of the twentieth century indeed sensed great potentialities (or,
it may be, a great necessity simply) in respect of the proud
knowledge, but at the same time approached it with a degree of
misgiving, or alternatively of indirectness, greater than ever
before. It is this remarkable and rich two-sidedness in their
work that has made me decide to attempt only the briefest
preliminary sketch here: to do more would lengthen the present
book unacceptably, and would also forestall the writing of a
wider-ranging book on the poetry of the twentieth century that
I have in mind, if time remains, for the future.

The rich ambiguity and dubiety of these poets' position is
not in doubt. Yeats's recurrent revulsion against the life of

enquiry and intellect goes far deeper than the old man's momentary genial preoccupation with a pretty girl in 'Politics'. The response in:

> I would be – for no knowledge is worth a straw – (p. 164)
> Ignorant and wanton as the dawn

recurs in lines like:

> Have I, that put it into words,
> *Spoilt* what old loins have sent?

and in how Yeats sees his Japanese sword ('my symbol of life': *Letters*, p. 729) that lies on his table

> That it may moralize   (227)
> My days out of their aimlessness.

The perfected, self-contained aesthetic and sensuous reality of the sword outweighs and relegates the intellect.

Largely, this negative side of Yeats's work in respect of the proud knowledge shows not in his explicit professions at all, but in the fundamental organization of many of the poems: their masses of detail, tangential fresh starts, dissolution into imagery, arcane elusiveness. Such matters, spoken of thus briefly, can do no more than indicate some of the lines along which a full discussion of Yeats's poetry in this context would have to proceed. With Pound, it seems to me that the situation, not altogether dissimilar, is in fact much more accentuated and extreme. In 'E.P. Ode pour l'Élection de son Sepulchre' we may sense that the Hugh Selwyn Mauberley *persona* is almost wholly transparent, and then:

> . . . out of key with his time
> He strove to resuscitate the dead art
> Of poetry; to maintain 'the sublime'
> In the old sense. Wrong from the start –
>
> No, hardly, but . . .
>   . . . out of date

could be set beside Yeats's desire (in his 'fool-driven land': 'All Things Can Tempt me', 109) to set aside the 'airs' of the traditional poet and be

Colder and dumber and deafer than a fish . . .

But more, in Pound, than such instances as this, is the sig-
nificance of the poet's fundamental method in the *Cantos*: the
immense, proliferating, in the end open-ended and 'sufficient
phalanx of particulars' (Canto LXXIV: 469) out of which
insight of the 'generalities' is ultimately to transpire. 'What we
know we know by ripples and spirals eddying out from us and
from our own time', Pound wrote in the *Guide to Kulchur* (60).
The most ambitious poetic *summa* of the twentieth century was
to grow out of an unparalleled indirectness and miscellaneity.
Pound's ripples and spiralling eddies, in which masterful inter-
pretations have – allegedly – no place, is in one direction the
very humility of knowledge.

Eliot's enquiring *dramatis personae* – Prufrock, the Lady (and
with them one might include Gerontion) – were discussed
earlier. In Eliot's earlier work also, something like the
'ideogrammic method' of Pound is plain enough. Most
interesting, perhaps, in this context, is Eliot's reliance in his
later work on the 'auditory imagination'

> . . . the feeling for syllable and rhythm, penetrating far
> below the conscious level of thought and feeling . . .
> sinking to the most primitive and forgotten, returning to
> the origin and bringing something back, seeking the
> beginning and the end . . . it works through meanings,
> certainly, or not without meanings. (*The Use of Poetry*,
> pp.118–19)

'What we call the beginning is often the end': 'Taking the
route you would be likely to take/From the place you would be
likely to come from'; 'Not known . . . But heard, half-heard, in
the stillness' – those clear verbal echoes are meaningful indeed.
The Beethovenian intricacies, half-recapitulations, and always
self-renewing rhythmic flow of 'Little Gidding' seems the
clearest embodiment of what Eliot meant by 'auditory imagina-
tion'. From the standpoint of the present discussion, it is the
words

> Not known, because not looked for,
> But heard, half-heard, in the stillness

that most eloquently reveal the extent of the submission that Eliot the seer-poet makes to the difficulties and disabilities of the task. Even in so dedicated and determined a case, and even when (it seems) he sensed that his work was completed and laid aside his pen, it is to this glimpsed and elusive final wisdom, this hinted poignant instant of 'Quick, now, here, now, always' (like the 'Quick quick quick, quick' of the birds singing in the very early 'Cape Ann') that the Proud Knowledge has come.

Books Quoted

The list which follows briefly records works or editions from which quotations appear in the text, or which are cited extensively. Translations appear under the names of original authors. Place of publication is London unless stated otherwise.

Adams, George, *Microcosmographia Illustra: or the Microscope Explained*, 1771.
Arnold, Matthew, *Poems*, ed. K. Allott, 1965.
Bacon, Francis, *The Advancement of Learning*, Book 1, ed. W. A. Armstrong, 1975.
Blake, William, *Complete Writings*, ed. G. Keynes, 1966.
Browning, Robert, *Poetical Works 1833–1864*, ed. Ian Jack, 1970.
Bunyan, John, *The Pilgrim's Progress from this World to That which is to Come*, ed. James Blanton Wharey, 2nd ed., revised by Roger Sharrock, 1960.
——, *Works*, 3 vols, 1853, ed. G. Offor (for the *Exposition of the First Ten Chapters of Genesis*).
Byron, George Gordon, *Poetical Works*, ed. F. Page, revised by J. Jump, Oxford, 1970.
Cassirer, E., and others, eds, *The Renaissance Philosophy of Man*, Chicago, 1948.
Clare, John, *Selected Poems*, ed. G. Grigson, 1950.
Clough, Arthur Hugh, *Poems*, ed. F. L. Mulhauser, 2nd ed., 1974.
Cockeram, Henry, *The English Dictionarie*, 1623; 2nd ed., 1626.
Coleridge, Samuel Taylor, *Poems*, ed. J. Beer, 1974.
Cowper, William, *Poetical Works*, ed. H. S. Milford, 1934; 1950 printing.
Crabbe, George, *Poems*, ed. A. W. Ward, 3 vols, 1905.
Dante Alighieri, *La Divina Commedia*, ed. L. Magugliani, 3 vols, Milan, 1949.
——, *The Vision: or Hell, Purgatory and Paradise of Dante Alighieri*, trans. H. F. Cary, 3 vols, 1814.
Defoe, Daniel, *The Life and Strange Surprizing Adventures of Robinson Crusoe of York, Mariner*, ed. Donald Cowley, 1972.

Descartes, René, *Discours de la Méthode*, ed. L. Liard, Paris, Garnier, 1960.

Donne, John, *Poems*, ed. H. J. C. Grierson, Oxford, 1912; 1958 printing.

Dryden, John, *Poems*, ed. James Kinsley, vol. 1, 1958.

——, *Of Dramatic Poesy and other Critical Essays*, ed. G. Watson, 2 vols, 1962.

Eliot, Thomas Stearns, *Collected Poems, 1909–1935*, 1936.

——, *Four Quartets*, 1944.

——, *The Use of Poetry and the Use of Criticism*, 1933; 1946 printing.

Goethe, A. W. von, *Werke* (Hamburg, 1961 ed.): vol. IX, *Dichtung und Wahrheit*; (or see Goethe, *Autobiography*, trans. J. Oxenford, 2 vols, 1971).

Gray, Thomas, see *The Poems of Gray, Collins and Goldsmith*, ed. R. Lonsdale, 1969.

Hardy, Thomas, *Collected Poems*, 4th ed., 1930; 1952 printing.

Hume, David, *The Treatise of Human Nature*, ed. L. A. Selby-Bigge, 1886; 1967 printing.

Johnson, Samuel, *Lives of the English Poets*, ed. G. B. Hill, 3 vols, 1905.

Keats, John, *Poems*, ed. Miriam Allott, 1970.

——, *Letters*, ed. M. Buxton Forman, 4th ed., 1952.

Kirkconnell, Watson, *The Celestial Cycle and the Theme of 'Paradise Lost' in world literature with translations of the major analogues*, Toronto, 1952.

Langhorne, John, *Poetical Works*, Cooke's pocket edition, 1798.

Marlowe, Christopher, *Complete Works*, ed. Fredson Bowers, Cambridge, 1973.

Marot, Clément, *Oeuvres Lyriques*, ed. C. A. Mayer, 1964.

Mill, John Stuart, *A System of Logic*, 2 vols, 1843.

Milton, John, *Works*, ed. F. A. Patterson and others, Columbia University Press, 1931: vol. I, part I, *Minor Poems*; vol. II, parts I and II, *Paradise Lost*.

——, *Private Correspondence and Academic Exercises*, ed. P. B. and E. M. W. Tillyard, Cambridge, 1932.

Pluche, Abbé le, *Spectacle de la Nature: or, Nature Delineated*, trans. John Kelly, D. D. Bellamy and J. Sparrow, 3rd ed., 1743.

Pope, Alexander, *Poetical Works*, ed. H. Davies, 1966.

Pound, Ezra, *The Cantos*, 1954.

——, *Guide to Kulchur*, 1938; 1968 printing.

Ray, John, *The Wisdom of God Manifested in the Works of the Creation*, 1691.

Rochester, Earl of, (John Wilmot), *Complete Poems*, ed. David M. Vieth, 1968.

Rousseau, J.-J., *Emile ou de l' Education*, ed. F. and P. Richard, Paris, Garnier, n.d.

——, *Rêveries d'un Promeneur Solitaire*, Paris, Garnier-Flammarion, 1964.

Shakespeare, William, *Complete Works*, ed. P. Alexander: vol. 3, Tragedies; vol. 4, Tragedies and Poems, 1958.

Shelley, Percy Bysshe, *Complete Works*, ed. Roger Ingpen and Walter E. Peck, New York, 1965 (*Poems*, vols I–IV).

Southey, Robert, *Poems*, ed. M. H. Fitzgerald, 1909.

——, *Common-Place Book*, ed. J. W. Warter, Series 1–4, 1849–51.

Spenser, Edmund, *Minor Poems*, ed. C. G. Osgood and H. G. Lotspeich, Johns Hopkins Press: vol. I, 1943, vol. II, 1947.

Spinoza, B. de, *Correspondence*, trans. and ed. A. Wolf, 1928.

Sprat, Thomas, *History of the Royal Society*, ed. J. I. Cope and H. W. Jones, Routledge & Kegan Paul, 1959.

Swift, Jonathan, *Gulliver's Travels*, ed. Harold Williams, Oxford, Blackwell, 1941.

Tennyson, Alfred, *Poems*, ed. C. Ricks, 1969.

Thomson, James, *Poetical Works*, ed. J. Logie Robertson, Oxford, 1908; reprinted 1971.

Vaughan, Henry, *Works*, ed. L. C. Martin, 2nd ed., 1957.

Vico, Giambattista, *Autobiography*, trans. M. H. Fisch, and T. G. Bergin, Ithaca, 1944.

Wordsworth, William, *The Prelude: a Parallel Text*, ed. J. C. Maxwell, 1971.

——, *Poetical Works*, ed. E. de Selincourt and Helen Darbishire, vol. II, vol. V, 1947.

Yeats, William Butler, *Collected Poems*, 1933; 1950 printing.

Index of Works
Discussed

Brief passing reference are not included

Index